Lecture Notes in Computer Science 9477

Commenced Publication in 1973
Founding and Former Series Editors:
Gerhard Goos, Juris Hartmanis, and Jan van Leeuwen

More information about this series at http://www.springer.com/series/7407

Adrian-Horia Dediu · Luis Magdalena
Carlos Martín-Vide (Eds.)

Theory and Practice of Natural Computing

Fourth International Conference, TPNC 2015
Mieres, Spain, December 15–16, 2015
Proceedings

 Springer

Editors
Adrian-Horia Dediu
Research Group on Mathematical
  Linguistics
Universitat Rovira i Virgili
Tarragona
Spain

Carlos Martín-Vide
Research Group on Mathematical
  Linguistics
Universitat Rovira i Virgili
Tarragona
Spain

Luis Magdalena
European Centre for Soft Computing
Asturias
Spain

ISSN 0302-9743   ISSN 1611-3349 (electronic)
Lecture Notes in Computer Science
ISBN 978-3-319-26840-8   ISBN 978-3-319-26841-5   (eBook)
DOI 10.1007/978-3-319-26841-5

Library of Congress Control Number: 2015954959

LNCS Sublibrary: SL1 – Theoretical Computer Science and General Issues

Springer Cham Heidelberg New York Dordrecht London

Printed on acid-free paper

Springer International Publishing AG Switzerland is part of Springer Science+Business Media
(www.springer.com)

Preface

This volume contains the papers presented at the 4th International Conference on the Theory and Practice of Natural Computing (TPNC 2015), held in Mieres, Spain during December 15–16, 2015.

The scope of TPNC is rather broad, containing topics of theoretical, experimental, or applied interest. The topics include but are not limited to:

- Theoretical contributions to: amorphous computing; artificial chemistry; artificial immune systems; artificial life; bacterial foraging; cellular automata; chaos and dynamical systems-based computing; complex adaptive systems; computing with DNA; computing with words; developmental systems; evolutionary computing; fractal geometry; gene assembly in unicellular organisms; granular computation; intelligent systems; membrane computing; nanocomputing; neural computing; optical computing; physarum computing; quantum computing and quantum information; reaction-diffusion computing; rough/fuzzy computing in nature; self-organizing systems; swarm intelligence; synthetic biology.
- Applications of natural computing to: algorithms; bioinformatics; control; cryptography; design; economics; graphics; hardware; human–computer interaction; knowledge discovery; learning; logistics; medicine; natural language processing; optimization; pattern recognition; planning and scheduling; programming; robotics; telecommunications; Web intelligence.

There were 30 submissions. The committee decided to accept 12 papers, which represents an acceptance rate of 40 %. The program of the conference also included three invited talks.

Part of the success in the management of the submissions and reviews is due to the excellent facilities provided by the EasyChair conference management system.

We would like to thank all invited speakers and authors for their contributions, the Program Committee and the external reviewers for their cooperation, the European Centre for Soft Computing for the excellent facilities put at our disposal, and Springer for its very professional publishing work.

September 2015

Adrian-Horia Dediu
Luis Magdalena
Carlos Martín-Vide

Organization

TPNC 2015 was organized by the European Centre for Soft Computing in Mieres, Spain, and the Research Group on Mathematical Linguistics – GRLMC, from Rovira i Virgili University, Tarragona, Spain.

Program Committee

Hussein Abbass	University of New South Wales, Canberra, Australia
Andrew Adamatzky	University of the West of England, Bristol, UK
Humberto Bustince	Public University of Navarra, Pamplona, Spain
Pei-Chann Chang	Yuan Ze University, Taoyuan, Taiwan
Shyi-Ming Chen	National Taiwan University of Science and Technology, Taipei, Taiwan
Óscar Cordón	University of Granada, Spain
Swagatam Das	Indian Statistical Institute, Kolkata, India
Gianni Di Caro	Dalle Molle Institute for Artificial Intelligence, Lugano, Switzerland
Tharam Dillon	La Trobe University, Melbourne, Australia
Agoston E. Eiben	VU University Amsterdam, The Netherlands
János Fodor	Óbuda University, Budapest, Hungary
Fernando Gomide	University of Campinas, Brazil
Maoguo Gong	Xidian University, Xi'an, China
Salvatore Greco	Universiy of Catania, Italy
Jin-Kao Hao	University of Angers, France
Francisco Herrera	University of Granada, Spain
Robert John	University of Nottingham, UK
Fakhri Karray	University of Waterloo, Canada
László T. Kóczy	Budapest University of Technology and Economics, Hungary
Rudolf Kruse	University of Magdeburg, Germany
José A. Lozano	University of the Basque Country, Donostia, Spain
Jianquan Lu	Southeast University, Nanjing, China
Vittorio Maniezzo	University of Bologna, Italy
Carlos Martín-Vide (Chair)	Rovira i Virgili University, Tarragona, Spain
Ujjwal Maulik	Jadavpur University, Kolkata, India
Marjan Mernik	University of Maribor, Slovenia
Radko Mesiar	Slovak University of Technology, Bratislava, Slovakia
Risto Miikkulainen	University of Texas, Austin, USA
Tal Mor	Technion, Haifa, Israel
Vilém Novák	University of Ostrava, Czech Republic
Sankar K. Pal	Indian Statistical Institute, Kolkata, India
Günther Palm	Ulm University, Germany

Linqiang Pan	Huazhong University of Science and Technology, Wuhan, China
Lech Polkowski	Polish-Japanese Academy of Information Technology, Warsaw, Poland
Dan Ralescu	University of Cincinnati, USA
Friedrich Simmel	Technical University of Munich, Germany
Guy Theraulaz	Paul Sabatier University, Toulouse, France
Vicenç Torra	University of Skövde, Sweden
José Luis Verdegay	University of Granada, Spain
David Wolpert	Santa Fe Institute, USA
Ronald R. Yager	Iona College, New Rochelle, USA
Shengxiang Yang	De Montfort University, Leicester, UK
Xin-She Yang	Middlesex University, London, UK
Hao Ying	Wayne State University, Detroit, USA
Mingsheng Ying	University of Technology, Sydney, Australia
Mengjie Zhang	Victoria University of Wellington, New Zealand
Qingfu Zhang	City University of Hong Kong, China
William Zhu	Minnan Normal University, Zhangzhou, China
Marek Żukowski	University of Gdansk, Poland

Additional Reviewers

Christian Braune
George Leu
Lulu Li
Lvzhou Li

Organizing Committee

Adrian-Horia Dediu	Rovira i Virgili University, Tarragona, Spain
Luis Magdalena (Co-chair)	European Centre for Soft Computing, Mieres, Spain
Carlos Martín-Vide (Co-chair)	Rovira i Virgili University, Tarragona, Spain
Daniel Sánchez	European Centre for Soft Computing, Mieres, Spain
Gracián Triviño	European Centre for Soft Computing, Mieres, Spain
Florentina-Lilica Voicu	Rovira i Virgili University, Tarragona, Spain

Invited Papers

EvoSphere: The World of Robot Evolution

A.E. Eiben

VU University Amsterdam, The Netherlands
a.e.eiben@vu.nl

Abstract. In this paper I describe EvoSphere, a tangible realization of the general Evolution of Things concept. EvoSphere can be used as a research platform to study the evolution of intelligent machines for practical as well as theoretical purposes. On the one hand, it can be used to develop robots that are hard to obtain with traditional design and optimization techniques and it can deliver original solutions that are unlikely to be conceived by a human designer. On the other hand, EvoSphere forms an evolving ecosystem that enables fundamental research into evolution and embodied intelligence. The use of real hardware is a pivotal feature as it avoids the reality gap and guarantees that the evolved solutions are physically feasible. On the long term, EvoSphere technology can pave the way for robot populations that evolve 'in the wild' and can adapt to unforeseen and changing circumstances.

Theory and Practice of Quantum Computing

John A. Smolin

IBM T.J. Watson Research Center, Yorktown Heights
801 Kitchawan Road, Yorktown, NY 10598, USA

Abstract. In 1982 Richard Feynman observed that though quantum systems are extremely hard to simulate, perhaps a *quantum computer* could simulate them efficiently. Inspired by this idea, quantum computation—wherein the full computational power allowed by physics is exploited to solve hard problems— was born. This has opened fascinating foundational questions such as what is the nature of information in a quantum world, what are the ultimate limits of computing imposed by reality itself? More practically, in 1994 Peter Shor gave an algorithm for efficient factoring. I will explain how this works, and describe some of the newer quantum algorithms it has spawned.

The actual implementation of quantum computers is comparatively in its infancy, and building a working quantum computer is one of the grand technological endeavors of the twenty-first century. There are many candidate physical systems for building quantum computers each with its own set of advantages and challenges. I also give an overview of the beautiful theory of fault-tolerance which will be essential for raising any of these implementations from the exciting toys of today into the powerful new tools of tomorrow.

Contents

Formal Models

Invited Paper

EvoSphere: The World of Robot Evolution

A.E. Eiben$^{(\boxtimes)}$

VU University Amsterdam, Amsterdam, The Netherlands
a.e.eiben@vu.nl

Abstract. In this paper I describe EvoSphere, a tangible realization of the general Evolution of Things concept. EvoSphere can be used as a research platform to study the evolution of intelligent machines for practical as well as theoretical purposes. On the one hand, it can be used to develop robots that are hard to obtain with traditional design and optimization techniques and it can deliver original solutions that are unlikely to be conceived by a human designer. On the other hand, EvoSphere forms an evolving ecosystem that enables fundamental research into evolution and embodied intelligence. The use of real hardware is a pivotal feature as it avoids the reality gap and guarantees that the evolved solutions are physically feasible. On the long term, EvoSphere technology can pave the way for robot populations that evolve 'in the wild' and can adapt to unforeseen and changing circumstances.

Keywords: Evolutionary robotics · Embodied evolution · Artificial life · Evolution of things

1 Introduction

This paper corresponds to my keynote talk on the 2015 International Conference on the Theory and Practice of Natural Computing. It builds upon a number of earlier papers and presentations about the Evolution of Things, that is, artificial evolutionary systems that work in populations of physical entities.

I started to publicise these ideas with my 2011 TED talk[1] that presented the vision of such systems to a broad audience and the 2012 paper in the *Evolutionary Intelligence* journal that provided a professional discussion of the main concepts [9]. This paper also introduced the name Evolution of Things (EoT). Several talks and papers followed that addressed the subject from different angles. The most important technical papers are those on the 2013 *European Artificial Life Conference*, that outlined an appropriate algorithmic framework to build EoT systems [11], and the one on the 2014 *IEEE Conference on Evolvable Systems* that presented the first working implementation of this framework in a population of robots that 'live' and reproduce in a simulated world [27]. The use of a simulator here is ironic – after all, the vision entails evolving populations of **physical** entities. However, the current technology lacks essential components

---

[1] http://tedxtalks.ted.com/video/TEDxDanubia-2011-goston-Eiben-T.

© Springer International Publishing Switzerland 2015
A.-H. Dediu et al. (Eds.): TPNC 2015, LNCS 9477, pp. 3–19, 2015.
DOI: 10.1007/978-3-319-26841-5_1

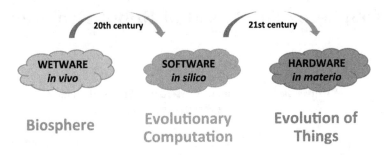

Fig. 1. The Evolution of Things concept illustrated and positioned from the perspective of the underlying substrate.

to this end, in particular the mechanisms that enable that robots reproduce, i.e., 'have children'. Nevertheless, this paper is important because it provides a proof-of-concept based on existing robots, the Roombots [23], and a high-fidelity simulator, Webots[2]. Hence, the system is in principle constructible.

A different angle is taken by another set of papers that are less concerned with implementation and actual experimentation, focussing on the conceptual aspects instead. The keynote / paper on the 2014 *Conference on Parallel Problem Solving from Nature* discussed the Why and the How of the Evolution of Things in general, and elaborated on the specific challenges and opportunities it represents for the evolutionary computing community [8]. I received many enthusiastic reactions for this – and not only compliments on the title. A sister paper aiming at the robotics community in the *Frontiers in Robotics and AI* journal described evolutionary robotics as "a test ground or experimental toolbox to study various issues arising on the road to intelligent and autonomous machines" and presented three so-called grand challenges, including Self-Reproducing Robots that Evolve in Real Time and Real Space and another one regarding Open-Ended Robot Evolution.

Last but not least, the 2015 paper in *Nature* foresees a fruitful cross-fertilization of evolutionary computing with biology in the coming decade [12]. "Artificial evolution implemented on real hardware, as in evolutionary robotics, offers a new research instrument" that can provide "new insights into fundamental issues such as the factors influencing evolvability, resilience, the rate of progress under various circumstances, or the co-evolution of mind and body". Furthermore, the paper positions the Evolution of Things on a historical scale from the perspective of the underlying substrate as illustrated in Fig. 1.

In the present paper I describe a particular realization of the general Evolution of Things concept, dubbed EvoSphere. EvoSphere is a tangible design template of a habitat for evolving robot populations. It identifies the principal components of such evolving systems, thus it provides a basis for a real-world implementation. I argue that EvoSphere can be used as a research instrument to study the evolution of intelligent machines for practical as well as theoretical

---

[2] https://www.cyberbotics.com.

purposes without the usual drawbacks of simulations [14]. Furthermore, advanced future versions of EvoSphere technology can enable robot populations that evolve 'in the wild' and can adapt to unforeseen and changing circumstances.

2   The Evolution of Things

The defining property that distinguishes the Evolution of Things from other evolutionary systems is the underlying substrate: the EoT is implemented in **physical artifacts**. The *physical* distinguishes it from evolutionary computing and the *artifact* sets it apart from natural evolution.

As explained in [8] it is useful to distinguish mindless or dumb things and animate or smart artifacts (smartifacts) Objects in the first category, e.g., sunglasses, radio antennas, and pottery, can be designed and optimized by an evolutionary process. This can take place in computer simulations as in traditional evolutionary design [3,4]. Alternatively, the evolutionary process can be conducted in hardware, but since the evolving individuals are dumb objects without agency they will undergo this process passively. The active force will be an evolutionary algorithm that drives the system by performing the principal operations, selection, variation, and evaluation, cf. Figure 2. Hence, the only significant difference between this process and the traditional evolutionary design approach is the evaluation of fitness: in an EoT framework individuals in the population are physical objects that are evaluated in the physical space, in hardware, as opposed to the traditional way of evaluating digital objects in software.[3] Whether hardware evaluations are preferable depends on the application specific details. The most important factors are the costs and the accuracy of simulations. In general, software trials are cheaper, they are often faster too, but simulations may miss crucial aspects of the real world and contain errors. A low-fidelity simulator can mislead the selection operators and drive the evolutionary process towards suboptimal designs.

In the rest of this paper I will not consider the evolution of dumb things. I will focus on smartifacts, that is, smart, animate objects with agency because they are a more interesting substrate for evolution. Artifacts of this type (called robots in the sequel) have the ability to sense, make decisions, and perform actions autonomously. Thus, in principle, they can induce the evolutionary process 'from inside' by playing an active part of the selection and/or variation operators of the evolutionary algorithm. This opens up unprecedented opportunities for more natural, autonomous evolutionary systems, that are not driven by a centralized evolution manager and can operate without human intervention, for instance in remote areas, such as other planets.

To prepare and motivate the design choices behind EvoSphere let me make a few notes first.

---

[3] There exist systems that mix the two in a certain way. The idea is that the principal method is a traditional digital EA with simulated fitness evaluations, but every now and then an individual in the population is physically constructed and evaluated in the real world.

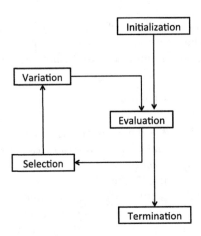

Fig. 2. The generic scheme of evolutionary algorithms

Note 1. Robots have agency because they have a control system that processes their sensory inputs and determines their actions. There are countless possible kinds of sensors, control systems and forms of actuation but with a useful abstraction we can say that a robot is made up of two major constituents: a body (morphology, hardware) and a mind (controller, software). In an EoT system with smartifacts evolution affects both constituents, the bodies as well as the minds.

Note 2. In an evolutionary system that affects the bodies as well as the minds there must be reproduction mechanisms (mutation and crossover) for both. The easy part is obviously the reproduction of the controller, the software component. Creating an offspring only requires the creation of a new piece of software code. This has been done within evolutionary computing for decades. The hard part is the reproduction of the body, because it requires the creation of a new piece of hardware. An additional challenge directly implied by reproducing both bodies and minds is the alignment between the two. Parents that survive long enough and get selected for reproduction are fit by definition, i.e., they must have a well aligned body and mind. However, in general we cannot assume that this will hold for the body and mind of the 'robot baby' that results from (randomized) crossover and/or mutation.

Note 3. Fitness in an EoT system has a natural and an artificial component. The fact that robots operate in the physical world implies that above all they must be viable. That is, they must be able to sustain their integrity, replenish their energy, avoid fatal accidents, etc. In evolutionary terms, this means that the fitness of robots is primarily based on the environment. Additionally, the fitness of robots can include artificial elements based on their utility for the user. For instance, the utility of a robot can be equated to its task performance and the system can be set up in such a way that utility influences selection mechanisms. Obviously, the laws of physics do not depend on the application or user preferences. Hence, the environmental fitness cannot be ignored and evolution will always progress towards increased levels of viability. In contrast, the details –and even the existence– of a utility-based fitness component depends on the user. A (nonconventional) biologist may just want to study open ended evolution without an explicit target, but an industrial designer would want to evolve robots optimized for a specific purpose.

The proverbial Cycle of Life revolves around birth and so does a system of self-reproducing robots. To capture the relevant components of such a robotic life cycle we need a loop that does not run from birth to death, but from conception (being conceived) to conception (conceiving one or more children). To this end we adopt the natural genotype-phenotype dichotomy. That is, we presume that the physical robots are the phenotypes encoded by their genotypes. In other words, the robots can be seen as the expression of a piece of code called the genome. As part of this assumption we postulate that reproduction takes place at the genotypic level. This means that mutation and crossover are applied to the genotypes (the code that specifies the parent robots) and not to the phenotypes (the parent robots themselves). The creation of new pieces of code by crossover and mutation must then be followed by the physical production of the robot by a birth or morphogenesis process. This is the most important feature of EoT systems that distinguishes them from digital evolution: in digital evolutionary systems genotypes and phenotypes are virtual (pieces of code), while in an EoT system genotypes are digital, but phenotypes are physical.

Figure 3 exhibits a robotic life cycle after [11]. This triangular diagram – dubbed the Triangle of Life (ToL)– can be perceived as the equivalent of one cycle of an evolutionary algorithm, cf. Figure 2. Similarly to the general EA scheme that does not specify the representation of candidate solutions, the ToL does not make assumptions regarding the physical makeup of the robots. The robots can have usual mechatronic bodies, be soft robots with nonconventional bodies and forms of control, or the combination of the two.[4] For the Evolution of Things, the Triangle of Life represents a functional decomposition of an evolutionary robot system. It captures the most important constituents, such as a component for the physical construction of new phenotypes (essential for working with *things*) and a component for aligning bodies and minds after birth (cf. Note 2 above).

To conclude this section let me note that birth should be implemented by a centralized system component, by a 'Birth Clinic'. In principle, an EoT system can employ distributed mechanisms, such as the equivalents of 'pregnancy' or 'eggs'. However, for reasons of safety such solutions must be avoided. Instead, the reproductive system should have a single point of failure that can be used by the user as a kill switch if the evolutionary process needs to be halted. The reason for this is obvious, runaway evolution in a computer can only do limited harm (memory overflow or computer crash), but consequences in the real world

---

[4] The paper [11] illustrated the components of this framework one by one using the modular robots of the Symbrion project. However, Symbrion was not aiming at physically evolving morphologies and the components of the ToL have not been integrated.

Fig. 3. Robotic life cycle captured as a triangle after [11]. The pivotal moments that span the triangle are: (1) Conception: A new genome is activated, construction of a new robot starts. (2) Delivery: Construction of the new robot is completed. (3) Fertility: The robot becomes ready to conceive offspring.

can be much more severe. I consider this an important issue and emphasize that all physically embodied evolutionary systems of the future must be designed with a shutdown guarantee, cf. Section 6.3 in [9].

3   Related Work

The Evolution of Things concept captures all artificial evolutionary systems that work in populations of physical entities. Relevant scientific insights, algorithms, and know-how can be found within different research areas, such as evolutionary computing, artificial life, robotics, multi-agent systems, machine learning, and autonomous systems. This makes the identification of related work quite challenging. For a better focus let me highlight three essential aspects and concentrate on these in this section.

1. **PHYSICAL EVOLUTION**
   Evolution takes place in physical robots.
2. **MORPHOLOGICAL EVOLUTION**
   Evolution concerns the morphologies of the robots. Implicitly, this implies controller evolution as well.
3. **ONLINE, AUTONOMOUS EVOLUTION**
   Robots evolve in an online fashion, during their operational time.[5] Furthermore, it is the robots themselves that make the decisions needed for 'having children' and not an external (centralized) evolution manager.

---

[5] The alternative is offline evolution during the design stage of the robots. See [8] and Chap. 17 in [10] for a discussion.

The earliest work on evolution in physical robots I know of is from 1999 in a population of five mobile robots [21]. The robots have collision and proximity sensors and neural network (NN) controllers, their task is to learn obstacle avoidance. Evolution is applied to obtain appropriate NN parameters as well as to learn which sensors are active. Each individual genome (NN weights) is evaluated for several minutes on the five robots and after the evaluation phase there is a breeding phase in which each robot broadcasts its genome and fitness value. The receiving robots select an incoming genome for crossover with their local genome. Watson *et al.* developed a similar system, dubbed "embodied evolution" [26]. Their population consists of eight robots with a neural net controller with four weights and evolution is employed to obtain appropriate weights for a phototaxis task in a small rectangular arena. The essence of the system is that robots periodically broadcast their genome (NN weights) to the other robots in a rate proportional to their fitness and recipient robots can integrate these into their own controllers. Other papers along the these lines include [24] that presents an embodied evolution system for evolving neural network controllers for obstacle avoidance in a group of six Khepera robots and [19] where two small mobile robots evolve controllers for several different tasks (phototaxis, obstacle avoidance and robot seeking) in collaboration.

In the above studies robots have a task with a quantifiable task performance that is used to define an explicit fitness function. Bredeche *et al.* investigate a group of 20 e-puck robots with no explicit fitness function or task to solve. Evolution is purely environment driven, hence the name mEDEA: a minimal Environment Driven Evolutionary Algorithm. Here again, robot controllers are neural networks and genetic material consists of NN parameters. Robots broadcast their genome to other robots and after a certain operational period a robot creates a new controller for itself by randomly selecting and mutating one of these received genomes. The system is tested in an arena with a 'sun' (light source) and although there is no specific reward for phototaxis the robots learn to aggregate near the sun for easier spreading of their genomes.

As mentioned in the Introduction, current technology limitations confine studies on evolving morphologies to software simulations. Although works based purely on simulation fall outside the present overview, the classic experiments of Sims deserve to be mentioned [22]. This system works through a traditional EA that evaluates virtual creatures one by one in a simulator, assessed by different locomotion skills, such as walking, hopping, swimming, and for the task of fighting over a block in between two organisms.[6] The virtual organisms are modular, consisting of blocks of different sizes which are connected through actuators driven by neural network controllers. A couple of other papers follow a similar approach: they evolve artificial organisms and their control structures in simulation using evolutionary algorithms [2,6,15]. These creatures are not very realistic, they cannot be directly manufactured in real hardware. The evolutionary systems are not natural either (centralized, offline), but the papers demonstrate the concept of morphology evolution.

---

[6] http://www.karlsims.com/evolved-virtual-creatures.html.

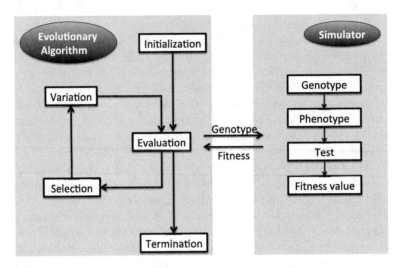

Fig. 4. Generic scheme of offline robot evolution through a conventional EA that uses a simulator for fitness evaluations.

The work of Auerbach and Bongard in [2] is especially interesting because it casts morphological evolution in a broader context of the body-mind-environment trichotomy. In particular, they study the relation between morphological, neural, and environmental complexity in an evolutionary system. They use a simple and a complex environment and evolve robots that comprise triangular meshes and are driven by neural controllers. Comparing the evolution of morphological complexity in different environments they find that "When no cost was placed on morphological complexity, no significant difference in morphological complexities between the two sets of robots evolved. However, when the robots were evolved in both environments again, and a cost was placed on complexity, robots in the simple environment were simpler than the robots evolved in the complex environment" (quote from [5]).

Figure 4 illustrates the algorithmic scheme used in these papers and others that employ offline evolution of robots or other virtual creatures. Evolution is offline, because it does not run during the operational period of the robots. In fact, robots only exist and operate for a short time when the simulator is computing their fitness. Furthermore, robots do not induce the evolutionary process 'from inside' as active participants. Everything is managed centrally by a conventional EA that decides on survival and reproduction 'from above'.

An interesting cluster of papers gets closer to reality by using simulations for evolving morphologies and constructing the end result. Lipson and Pollack used an EA and a simulator to evolve robotic organisms that consisted of bars and actuators (but no sensors) driven by a neural net for the task of locomoting over an infinite horizontal plane [16]. Three of the evolved designs were fabricated afterwards by 3D-printing the complete morphology (bars and joints) and snapping in motors by hand. Lund performed simple experiments of co-evolving robot controllers and robot body plans in a simulation of LEGO robot body plans, built the LEGO MINDSTORMS robots afterwards according to the evolved robot body plan, and transferred the evolved controller to the LEGO MINDSTORMS controller, the so-called RCX [18]. Perhaps the most interesting work in this cluster of papers is the recently developed RoboGen system [1]. RoboGen works with modular robots encoded by artificial genomes that specify the morphology and the controller of a robot, a simulator that can simulate the behavior of one single robot in a given environment, and a classic evolutionary algorithm that calls the simulator for each fitness evaluation. The system is used to evolve robots in simulation and the evolved robots can be easily constructed by 3D-printing and manually assembling their components. RoboGen was not meant and is not being used for physical robot evolution, but it could be the staring point for such a system after a number of extensions (e.g., crossover for both morphologies and controllers).

A crucial component of any EoT system is the reproduction mechanism represented by the birth/morphogenesis arrow in Fig. 3. To this end, the self-reproducing machines of Zykov et al. investigated in [28,29] are interesting. The first paper defines a physical system self-reproducing if "it can construct a detached, functional copy of itself" using a sufficient supply of material. The authors demonstrate such a system in real hardware by using actuated robot cubes with a microcontroller in each module that executes a hand-written program. They show that a robotic organism constructed from four modules is capable of making a copy of itself if the human experimenters add extra modules at particular "feeding locations".

In [29] the hand-made design is replaced by evolved design. The core idea is to define the relative replicability of a system over a period of time and use this as fitness function. Then a two-stage evolutionary process can be conducted: Stage One evolves morphologies of machines capable of reaching an area large enough to contain a detached copy of themselves and Stage Two evolves controllers to make a given morphology pick cubes from dispensers and place them at the correct positions. Both evolutionary stages are done using a centralized evolutionary algorithm in a 2D simulator. In the end, three physically plausible self-replicating machines have been found.

While the name "self-reproducing machines" may suggest otherwise these studies are not directly relevant for the EoT as discussed in this paper. First, reproduction in the EoT context requires a mechanism for constructing a new physical robot from the genetic code created by recombining/mutating the genetic codes of the parents. Having variations is essential for evolution and that is very different from making exact copies of a machine. Second, machines that could reproduce anywhere and everywhere would violate the requirement of a centralized Birth Clinic.

4   EvoSphere

EvoSphere is a specific realization of the Evolution of Things concept. It is based on the triangular decomposition of an evolutionary robot system as shown in

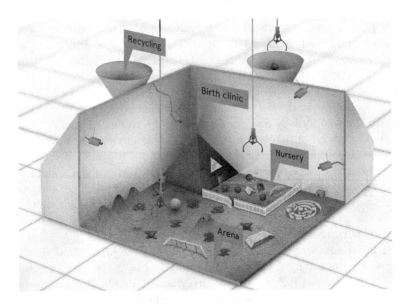

Fig. 5. Artist impression of EvoSphere showing a population of soft robots, the red entities. Note the correspondence between the three edges in the Triangle of Life in Fig. 3 and the three main EvoSphere sections: the Birth clinic, the Nursery, and the Arena.

Fig. 3. Compared to the abstract framework of the Triangle of Life, EvoSphere is a tangible design template of a complete habitat; it provides a basis for a real-world implementation, see Fig. 5. The system consists of three principal components, the Birth Clinic, the Nursery, and the Arena. These can be extended by a Recycling facility if a closed ecosystem is required. For experimental research in a laboratory some additional Monitoring infrastructure is necessary to monitor system behaviour and log the experimental data. This component is visualised by the wall-mounted cameras in Fig. 5.

The Birth Clinic is where robot phenotypes are constructed based on a given artificial genotype. Depending on the given robot morphology the Birth Clinic will consist of 'raw materials' and a production facility. In case of modular robotic organisms it should contain the parts (plenty of modules, joints, sensors, actuators) and an assembler putting these together. Further to making the bodies, the Birth Clinic also has to take care of the robot controllers. This requires the availability of processing units (computer chips, logic boards) that can be 'filled' with software code and appropriate mechanisms to implement the individual pieces of code that a newborn robot inherits from the parents.

It is important that the newborn robots start in a training arena, dubbed the Nursery, where they are trained and tested. If they pass muster after training they are declared fertile and enter the main arena; otherwise they are removed and recycled. The Nursery represents a practicable approach to solving the alignment problem of inherited bodies and minds as described in Note 2 in Sect. 2.

To this end it is essential to distinguish inheritable and learnable parts in the robot controllers and assume that lifetime learning can fine tune the working of inherited components, possibly even compensate for accidental deficiencies.[7] The condition that fertility can only be achieved after passing the Nursery test plays an important evolutionary role: it prevents reproduction of poorly performing robots. Furthermore, the Nursery can increase the chances of success in the main Arena if equipped with appropriate training facilities in a good arrangement. For instance, one could have a course for learning to locomote, followed by target following and object manipulation.

The main Arena is the place where the robots have to survive, reproduce, and perform user-defined tasks. A preprogrammed mate selection mechanism innate to each robot regulates how two robots negotiate about parenting a child. Of course, mate selection mechanisms can be made adaptable if required. If the parents agree, they transmit their genomes to the Birth Clinic that executes crossover and mutation and constructs the child; then the triangle of life can start again.

In summary, EvoSphere represents an approach towards the Evolution of Things since it forms the design template of (a certain type of) artificial evolutionary systems that work in populations of physical entities. EvoSphere satisfies all properties listed in Sect. 3: physical evolution, morphology evolution together with controller evolution, online evolution, and autonomous evolution. It is easy to imagine many different EvoSpheres depending on –among others– the type of robots (what body, what controller), the learning process in the Nursery, the details of the Arena, the presence or absence of user defined tasks, and last but not least the evolutionary operators, for instance, the details of how mate selection works.

EvoSphere brings the first real Evolution of Things system closer by representing a target installation. To this end it is relevant to recall the six main challenges identified in [9]:

1. **Body types**: to find physical constructs that are suited to be the evolvable objects forming the population. Technically this requires that they can be produced and reproduced.
2. **How to start**, i.e., the birth problem: the implementation of birth (reproduction operators) for human engineered physical artifacts is a critical prerequisite.
3. **How to stop**, i.e., the need for a kill switch.
4. **Need for speed**, i.e., the need to have a sufficiently high rate of evolution and to make good progress in real time.
5. **Process control**, in particular, on-line monitoring and steering of a system that combines open-ended and directed evolution on-the-fly.
6. **Body+mind and learning**, i.e., to include a learning component in the system to resolve the possible discrepancy between the inherited body and mind.

---

[7] A simple example is to use NN controllers with inheritable topology and learnable weights.

EvoSphere addresses challenge number 3 and 6 directly by the Birth Clinic and the Nursery. It does not offer specific solutions for the other challenges, but by providing details of the system it helps decompose and solve these. For instance the birth problem can be broken down into assembling robot components into a body, adding a CPU as the brain, and installing a controller.[8] Furthermore, by identifying the five main system components (Birth Clinic, Nursery, Arena, Recycling, Monitoring) it defines the design space of EoT systems.

5   Are We There Yet?

At the time of writing (summer 2015) I am not aware of any robotic systems that work by the principles of EvoSphere. However, there are two studies that come close in some important aspects.

The paper published last year by our research group reports on a "Robotic Ecosystem with Evolvable Minds and Bodies" that works in an online, autonomous fashion without a centralized evolution manager 'above' the robot population [27]. The system is a genuine implementation of the ToL, instantiating all three stages, Birth, Infancy, and Mature life, in a simulated circular habitat with a radius of 15m. Robots are not required to perform any specific task and are free to move in any direction until they hit the border of the habitat. The robots have a modular morphology constructed from Roombots and a controller that is a set of parametrised cyclic splines describing the servo motor angles in the Roombot joints as a function of time (Fig. 6). Body and mind are encoded by a genome and there are appropriate crossover and mutation operators to create new genomes from given parents.

The Birth Clinic is a single facility in the middle of the habitat (Fig. 7). It takes a newly created genome as input and produces a robot as output just outside of the Clinic. Newborn robots immediately enter the Nursery which is an inner circle around the Birth Clinic with a radius of 5m; robots become fertile if they can pass its perimeter and enter the outer terrain in the habitat. Learning in the Nursery is implemented by a reinforcement learning method to generate good gaits. Learning is not restricted to the infancy period as robots continue learning for their full lifetime. During their mature life robots can reproduce by periodically sending messages within a limited range containing their genome. Each robot within this range receives the genome and can decide to use it and recombine it with its own genome. A new genome is sent to the Birth Clinic that produces the new robot. It is important to notice that robots that do not enter the mating range of any other robot cannot reproduce. Hence, the number of offspring depends on how 'active' a robot is. Given that robots have a fixed maximum lifetime, this implies that population sizes vary (between 1 and 20) depending on the number of birth and death events.

---

[8] These steps may need to be revised for radically different types of robots, for instance soft robots with novel forms of control and actuation, but there will always be a list of such steps.

Fig. 6. Examples of a robotic organisms from [27]. A real robot (right) and a simulated robot in Webots (left).

Recently, in june 2015, Brodbeck *et al.* published an experimental study about "Morphological Evolution of Physical Robots through Model-Free Phenotype Development" [7]. The overall objective is to demonstrate a "model-free implementation for the artificial evolution of physical systems, to stochastically optimize the design of real-world machines". Being model-free means that the system does not employ simulations, all robots are physically constructed. As noted by the authors this avoids the reality gap but raises two new problems: the speed problem and the birth problem (challenge 4 and challenge 2 in [9]). The system demonstrates a solution to the birth problem in real hardware based on modular robot morphologies. Two types of cubic modules (active and passive) form the 'raw material' and robot bodies are constructed from a handful of such modules. The robots do not have an onboard controller, they are driven by an external PC and their task is to locomote. The evolutionary process is conducted by a centralized evolutionary algorithm following the template shown in Fig. 4. However, the robot phenotypes are constructed in real hardware for fitness evaluation and not in a simulator. The EA runs on the external PC using a generational scheme, populations of size 10, and fitness proportional selection where fitness is the travelled distance in a given time interval. Robot genomes encode the bodies implicitly by specifying the sequence of operations to build them by a robotic arm, dubbed the mother robot. The system was designed to construct new robots autonomously. Some experiments were indeed hands-free, but in some others a human operator assisted the building process.

These papers represent important milestones towards the Evolution of Things. They demonstrate the feasibility of such systems in a complimentary manner. The first paper integrates all components of the Triangle of Life, but only in simulation. Even though the use of an existing hardware platform (Roombots) makes the system constructible, it has not been constructed in the real world. The second paper showcases a genuine hardware implementation, where the robotic manipulator (mother robot) and the given supply of modules form a Birth Clinic. However, evolution is an offline, centrally managed process, the robots do not have their own onboard controller, and evolution and learning of controllers is not included.

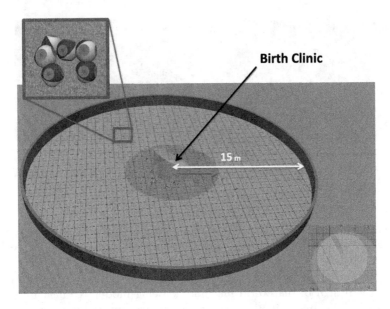

Fig. 7. Helicopter view of the whole environment in [27]. The habitat is a circle with a radius of 15m. The sliced cylinder in the centre is the Birth Clinic. The Nursery is an (invisible) inner circle with a radius of 5 m, robots become fertile if they can pass its perimeter and enter the Arena, the outer circle. This system forms the first rudimentary example of EvoSphere, albeit in simulation.

Thus, the answer to the question in the title of this section is: No, but we are getting closer. Ongoing work in research labs in Amsterdam, Cambridge, Lausanne, and Zürich (just to mention the ones I know about) already delivered promising systems and results, e.g., [1,7,27], and I am confident that these will inspire further work also elsewhere.

6   Concluding Remarks and Outlook

Constructing, studying, and utilizing artificial evolutionary systems was made possible by computer technology. The central thesis behind this paper/keynote is that advances in robot technology are about to open a new era that features artificial evolutionary systems that are physical, rather than digital. I think it is safe to predict that autonomously evolving robot populations will be possible in the future. To this end, many bits and pieces are already present and there is much know-how in the evolutionary computing, artificial life, and robotics communities. However, it will take much work in engineering as well as scientific research before the Evolution of Things can actually be realized.

EvoSphere as outlined here can be of help, because it forms a design template, i.e., a more or less tangible description of a system that can lead development efforts. When built in the real world, EvoSphere can be used as a research platform to study the evolution of intelligent machines for practical as well as theoretical purposes. On the one hand, it can be used to develop robots that are hard to obtain with traditional design and optimization techniques and it can deliver original solutions that are unlikely to be conceived by a human designer – and that without the usual drawbacks of simulations. Furthermore, advanced future versions of EvoSphere technology could be deployed outside of research labs 'in the wild'. This will enable evolving robot populations that are able to adapt to unforeseen and/or changing circumstances in inaccessible areas or uncharted territories, for instance in space.

On the other hand, EvoSphere forms an evolving ecosystem that enables fundamental research. In this respect EvoSphere can be considered as a novel scientific instrument. An analogy with cyclotrons may help explain this: while a cyclotron is a complex instrument to do research in particle physics, EvoSphere is a complex tool for research into evolution and embodied intelligence. For instance, it can be used for studying the co-evolution of body and mind or the relation between the complexity of the environment, robot morphologies, and robot controllers. Paraphrasing Pfeifer and Bongard [20] we can say that we already know how the body shapes the mind. In EvoSphere bodies become 'shapeable', hence we can also investigate how the mind shapes the body, or rather, how the two shape each other in response to various environmental conditions. In a broader context the evolving ecosystem in an EvoSphere represents a physical model of biological evolution that is more realistic than the models in related studies, e.g. [13,17,25]. By using real hardware EvoSphere can avoid the reality gap [14], guarantee that the evolved solutions are physically feasible, and ensure that the scientific findings are not grounded in simulation errors.

References

1. Auerbach, J.E., Aydin, D., Maesani, A., Kornatowski, P., Cieslewski, T., Heitz, G., Fernando, P.R., Loshchilov, I., Daler, L., Floreano, D.: Robogen: robot generation through artificial evolution. In: Sayama, H., Rieffel, J., Risi, S., Doursat, R., Lipson, H. (eds.) Artificial Life 14: Proceedings of the Fourteenth International Conference on the Synthesis and Simulation of Living Systems, pp. 136–137. The MIT Press (2014)
2. Auerbach, J.E., Bongard, J.C.: Environmental influence on the evolution of morphological complexity in machines. PLOS Comput. Biol. 10(1), e1003399 (2014)
3. Bentley, P., Corne, D.: Creative Evolutionary Systems. Morgan Kaufmann, San Francisco (2002)
4. Bentley, P.J. (ed.): Evolutionary Design by Computers. Morgan Kaufmann, San Francisco (1999)
5. Bongard, J.C., Lipson, H.: Evolved machines shed light on robustness and resilience. Proc. IEEE 302(5), 899–914 (2014)
6. Bongard, J.C., Pfeifer, R.: Evolving complete agents using artificial ontogeny. In: Hara, F., Pfeifer, R. (eds.) Morpho-Functional Machines: The New Species, pp. 237–258. Springer, Tokyo (2003)
7. Brodbeck, L., Hauser, S., Iida, F.: Morphological evolution of physical robots through model-free phenotype development. PLoS One 10(6), e0128444 (2015)

8. Eiben, A.E.: In Vivo Veritas: towards the evolution of things. In: Bartz-Beielstein, T., Branke, J., Filipič, B., Smith, J. (eds.) PPSN 2014. LNCS, vol. 8672, pp. 24–39. Springer, Heidelberg (2014)

9. Eiben, A.E., Kernbach, S., Haasdijk, E.: Embodied artificial evolution - artificial evolutionary systems in the 21st century. Evol. Intell. 5(4), 261–272 (2012)

10. Eiben, A.E., Smith, J.E.: Introduction to Evolutionary Computing. Natural Computing Series, 2nd edn. Springer, Heidelberg (2015)

11. Eiben, A.E., Bredeche, N., Hoogendoorn, M., Stradner, J., Timmis, J., Tyrrell, A.M., Winfield, A.: The triangle of life: evolving robots in real-time and real-space. In: Liò, P., Miglino, O., Nicosia, G., Nolfi, S., Pavone, M. (eds.) Advances In Artificial Life, ECAL 2013, pp. 1056–1063. MIT Press, (2013)

12. Eiben, A.E., Smith, J.: From evolutionary computation to the evolution of things. Nature 521(7553), 476–482 (2015)

13. Floreano, D., Keller, L.: Evolution of adaptive behaviour in robots by means of darwinian selection. PLOS Biol. 8(1), e1000292 (2010)

14. Jakobi, N., Husbands, P., Harvey, I.: Noise and the reality gap: the use of simulation in evolutionary robotics. In: Morán, F., Moreno, A., Merelo, J.J., Chacón, P. (eds.) Advances in Artificial Life. Lecture Notes in Computer Science, pp. 704–720. Springer, Heidelberg (1995)

15. Komosinski, M.: The framsticks system: versatile simulator of 3d agents and their evolution. Kybernetes 32(1/2), 156–173 (2003)

16. Lipson, H., Pollack, J.B.: Automatic design and manufacture of robotic lifeforms. Nature 406, 974–978 (2000)

17. Long, J.: Darwin's Devices: What Evolving Robots Can Teach Us About the History of Life and the Future of Technology. Basic Books, New York (2012)

18. Lund, H.: Co-evolving control and morphology with LEGO robots. In: Hara, F., Pfeifer, R. (eds.) Morpho-functional Machines: The New Species, pp. 59–79. Springer, Tokyo (2003)

19. Nehmzow, U.: Physically embedded genetic algorithm learning in multi-robot scenarios: the pega algorithm. In: Prince, C.G., Demiris, Y., Marom, Y., Kozima, H., Balkenius, C. (eds.) Proceedings of The Second International Workshop on Epigenetic Robotics: Modeling Cognitive Development in Robotic Systems, Number 94 in Lund University Cognitive Studies, LUCS, Edinburgh, UK, August 2002

20. Pfeifer, R., Bongard, J.: How the Body Shapes the Way We Think. MIT Press, Cambridge (2006)

21. Simoes, E.D.V., Dimond, K.R.: An evolutionary controller for autonomous multi-robot systems. In: IEEE International Conference on Systems, Man, and Cybernetics, 1999. IEEE SMC 1999 Conference Proceedings, vol. 6, pp. 596–601. IEEE (1999)

22. Sims, K.: Evolving 3D morphology and behavior by competition. In: Artificial Life IV, pp. 28–39 (1994)

23. Sproewitz, A., Billard, A., Dillenbourg, P., Ijspeert, A.J.: Roombots - mechanical design of self-reconfiguring modular robots for adaptive furniture. In: IEEE International Conference on Robotics and Automation (ICRA 2009), pp. 4259–4264. IEEE (2009)

24. Usui, Y., Arita, T.: Situated and embodied evolution in collective evolutionary robotics. In: Proceedings of the 8th International Symposium on Artificial Life and Robotics, pp. 212–215 (2003)

25. Waibel, M., Floreano, D., Keller, L.: A quantitative test of Hamilton's rule for the evolution of altruism. PLOS Biol. 9(5), e1000615 (2011)

26. Watson, R., Ficici, S., Pollack, J.B.: Embodied evolution: distributing an evolutionary algorithm in a population of robots. Robot. Auton. Syst. **39**(1), 1–18 (2002)
27. Weel, B., Crosato, E., Heinerman, J., Haasdijk, E., Eiben, A.E.: A robotic ecosystem with evolvable minds and bodies. In: 2014 IEEE International Conference on Evolvable Systems (ICES), pp. 165–172. IEEE (2014)
28. Zykov, V., Mytilinaios, E., Adams, B., Lipson, H.: Self-reproducing machines. Nature **435**(7039), 163–164 (2005)
29. Zykov, V., Mytilinaios, E., Desnoyer, M., Lipson, H.: Evolved and designed self-reproducing modular robotics. IEEE Trans. Robot. **23**(2), 308–319 (2007)

Soft Computing

A Content-Based Recommendation Approach Using Semantic User Profile in E-recruitment

Oualid Chenni[1], Yanis Bouda[1], Hamid Benachour[2], and Chahnez Zakaria[3](✉)

[1] Ecole Nationale Supérieure d'Informatique,
BP 68M, 16309 El Harrach, Algiers, Algeria
{ao_chenni,ay_bouda}@esi.dz
[2] Laboratoire de Recherche En Intelligence Articifielle (LRIA),
USTHB, El Alia BP 32, Bab Ezzouar, Algiers, Algeria
hamid.benachour@gmail.com
[3] Laboratoire de Méthodes de Conception des Systèmes (LMCS),
Ecole Nationale Suprieure d'Informatique, 16309 El Harrach, Algiers, Algeria
c_zakaria@esi.dz

Abstract. In this paper, we propose a content-based recommendation approach in the domain of e-recruitment to recommend users with job offers that suit the most their profile and learned preferences. In order to present the best offers, we construct a semantic vocabulary of the domain from the job offers corpus and initialize a profile for each user based on his Curriculum Vitae. Our method is enriching the user profiles using triggers and statistical methods following his actions regarding the job offers. The approach we propose presents to the users job offers that are the closest to their learned needs and interests which also can be updated based on his daily actions regarding these offers.

Keywords: Profiling · Recommendation · User profile · Semantic vocabulary · Triggers · E-recuitement

1 Introduction

The recent growth of the Online Web Recruitment Market has made traditional recruitment methods all but obsolete. In a world where companies are in a constant competition to hire the best profiles and increase incomes while decreasing the risks. According to the Harvard business school, the cost of a bad hire is three to five times an employee's annualized compensation. In specialist functions it reaches 10 times an annual salary[1]. Aware of these challenges, companies today invest massively in the best e-recruitment technologies and platforms. We have a plethora of online communities involving billions of people, and businesses use them to get opinions, generate consumer insights...etc., They use the web

---

[1] http://www.eremedia.com/ere/recruitment-5-0-the-future-of-recruiting-the-final-chapter/.

© Springer International Publishing Switzerland 2015
A.-H. Dediu et al. (Eds.): TPNC 2015, LNCS 9477, pp. 23–32, 2015.
DOI: 10.1007/978-3-319-26841-5_2

to scan and watch social trends and needs. We have an explosion of data, trillions of information about customers, job seekers, employees...etc. From which we can learn everything about people and their habits. The analysis of these sets of data is the main point of the competition in recruiting. Recruiters today want to receive the "ideal" shortlist of candidates, after analysing and weighting job application based on data patterns in the cloud which regroup: skill sets, experiences, behavioural patterns....etc.

The same objective is pursued by the candidates who want to receive the job offers that correspond the best to their needs and deep interests. This is the challenge that e-recruitment faces today, it's all about personalization and reduction of mis-hire and gaining the loyalty of the users. *Emploitic.com*[2] as the leader of e-recruitment in Algeria wants to build a specific recommendation system that will be integrated in their platform. In facts, their platform users, receive offers that don't correspond all the time to their interest because it is purely based on a key-words research, and recruiters suffer from the same problem, as they receive hundreds and thousands of job applications which generally do not fit the offer, due to some aspects as the difficulty for some users to understand the job description. So, to meet the needs of the users, we proposed a solution that personalizes the results which are given by the search engine and also by the suggestion and recommendation systems.

Recommendation systems are a specific form of information filtering which aims to present information items that might be of interest to the user. In general, a recommendation system allows you to compare a user profile to other certain reference characteristics, and tries to predict the opinion of a user [1]. [12] explain the recommendation systems as systems that collect opinions of a user's community, about items (job offers, TV programs...etc.) in order to use these opinions and likes to recommend interesting items to other users of this community.

In this paper, we describe the approach that we built to answer the needs of the users. We made a solution that creates a personalized profile for each user of the platform then enriches it through the use of the job offers corpus and the user's actions monitoring. The body of this paper is organized as follows: Section 2 discusses the related work. Section 3 presents the approach built. Section 4 presents the evaluation of the results obtained with the system. Finally, Section 5 is about our perspectives and a conclusion to our work.

2   Related Work

Basically, recommendation systems are divided into 4 categories: The collaborative filtering approach which predicts the interest of the user to an item by using a database of a group of other users preferences. This approach is itself divided into two subcategories: The Memory-based collaborative filtering which predicts the interests of the user by assigning him first to a group of similar users,through similarity or correlation measures, then it uses the weighted-notations of the

---

[2] http://www.emploitic.com.

same-group users regarding the items [4]; Model-based collaborative filtering on its side uses the predicted values of a user's notation regarding an item, based on the knowledge that the system has about the user. For example: using previous notations for other items [4], this model uses several different models as the cluster model or the Bayesian networks.

The second approach is the content-based filtering, which focuses on the content similarity between an item and the other items that the user has previously liked [2]. Systems that are based on this approach have a two-steps process: the user's profiling and the items representation. On one hand, they build the profile through the extraction, gathering and representation of its characteristics automatically through the monitoring of his actions regarding the items that are of interest to him. On the other hand, the items representation is made through structured data [2]. The third one is the knowledge based approach which suggests to the user, items based on the inference of his needs and preferences through the construction of a strong knowledge about the field [5], e.g.: e-recruitment. Finally, the Hybrid approach is the combination of the three previous approaches by using different technologies, we can find among them the weighted hybrid approach or meta-level hybrid systems....etc., [6].

Of course, as e-recruitment becomes more and more strategic and important, several approaches have been used in e-recruitment platforms to build personalized recommendation systems that provide better satisfaction to the user. Thus, within the sphere of job recommendation systems, we can find a lot of work that has been done using the different approaches listed above.

The common point between all the existing systems is the profile construction, an entity that represents the basis of every recommendation system. Some systems use only personal information like abilities or academic and professional experiences [9,15]. Other systems go even further and scan the users actions on the platform e.g.: safeguard, application...etc, to detect his needs and interests and save them in a re-usable way [7,10].

The collocation words to enrich the vocabulary, are used in many domains. In the translation, it is exploited to build multilingual dictionaries [8]. In emotions recognition, it is used to capture vocabularies of emotions [16]. Few works that use the collocation words in the recommendation systems. [9] use it to enrich the user profiles and update them regarding his actions and history.

3   Building a Recommendation Approach

This work is motivated by a willing to build a solution that would meet the needs of the e-recruitment platform users, and the necessity to provide them with a recommendation approach that analyses and explores their interests, infer their needs and present them opportunities that suit the best their learned preferences.

Our recommendation solution uses a content-based approach and is structured as a two-parts process. It creates first a personalized profile for each user then enrich it through the use of the job offers corpus and the user's actions monitoring.

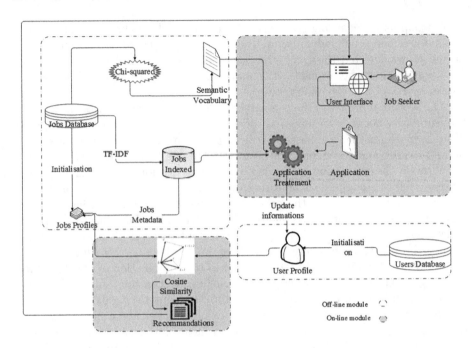

Fig. 1. Architecture of the jobs recommender.

The second part, is the recommendation module, which uses similarity metrics between the users updated profile and the different job offers available. Our solution is composed of two (02) modules:

Offline Module: Once the jobs indexed and the job profiles instantiated from jobs corpus, we initialize the user profiles from users database and establish the semantic vocabulary by searching relationships between words to enrich the profiles.

Online Module: When a user applies to a job offer in the user interface this module manages the enrichment of his profile and the recommendation of other job offers that match his updated profile (see Fig. 1).

3.1   First Challenge: Constructing the Semantic Vocabulary

Words Listing. We pull from the jobs corpus all useful unigrams, and for more efficiency we decided to consider the compound words, by using bigrams and trigrams. Then, we extract all correct bigrams B and trigrams T. To avoid redundancy, for each bigram b we take a subset T' of all trigrams t in which b is included, and tested if:

$$\sum Number\,of\,occurrences\,of\,t > \alpha \times Number\,of\,occurrences\,of\,b$$

Table 1. Bigram/Trigram detection

Bigram "b"	Occurrences	Trigrams "t"	Occurrences
Engineering Engineer	804	Electrical Engineering Engineer	309
		Mechanical Engineering Engineer	204
		Industrial Engineering Engineer	136
		Energetic Engineering Engineer	89
		Sum	738

where:

$0 < \alpha < 1$: is a value to define.

$t \in T'$: is a trigram that belongs to the subset.

The Table 1 is an example that illustrate the idea.

If we define $\alpha = 0,8$, we will find that: $804 \times 0,8 \simeq 643$ is the threshold value, and $738 > 643$ so we will assume that bigram b has no reason to exist and should be a trigram t.

Collocations. Once the list of unigrams, bigrams and trigrams is created, we build the semantic vocabulary. It is used to enrich the user profile. The idea is to find interesting relationships among words, using the triggers concept.

The triggers focus on words that often appear together. A word will probably trigger another if we can predict the second one when the first one occurs. Finding the collocation words is based on text windows or discourse units, in our case the text window is the job offer. The triggers are determined by calculating for each word(unigram, bigram and trigram) its *Chi-square measure* with each word(unigram, bigram and trigram) in the corpus. Then, only words with a high chi-square are kept used as triggered words.

$Chi-Square \mathcal{X}^2$: Pearson's chi-squared independence test is used in a text corpus to compute collocations which are, couples of words that occur together more than they should at random. It requires: a random sample and observations must be independent of each other.

The null hypothesis refers to a default position which corresponds to an absence of relationship between two words. Rejecting this hypothesis states that there is a relationship between these two words [17]:

$$\mathcal{X}^2 = \sum_{i=1}^{n} \frac{(O_i - E_i)^2}{E_i}$$

where:

O_i: the number of observations of type i.

$E_i = N \times p_i$: the expected (theoretical) frequency of type i, asserted by the null hypothesis that the fraction of type i in the population is p_i

N: total number of observations

n: the number of cells in the contingency table.

To assess the significance of the calculated value of $\mathcal{X}^2$, we refer to the standard chi-square table, with only one degree of freedom, which gives us a threshold value of 3.841 to compare with.

3.2   Second Challenge: Modelling the User Profile

Profile Schema. To modelize the user profile we considered his resume, skills, interests and activity fields. We have also modeled the job profile by its sector, title and the most significant terms in the job offer extracted with the $\mathcal{TF} \times \mathcal{IDF}$ model [14].

Considering that V_j is the vector representing the job profile, and V_u is the one representing the user profile, we have:

$Vector\_job =< Sector, Profession, Job\_Title, Meta - data\_job >$ annotated as $V_j =< S, P, T, M >$

$Vector\_user =< Sector, Profession, Cv\_Title, Skills, Meta - data\_user >$ annotated as $V_u =< S, P, T, S, M >$

Each component of these vectors is itself a vector that represents a collection of weighted words which are computed with the $\mathcal{TF} \times \mathcal{IDF}$.

Typically, the $\mathcal{TF} \times \mathcal{IDF}$ *weight* is composed by two terms:

$\mathcal{TF}$: Term Frequency, which measures how frequently a term occurs in a job offer. Since every job offer is different in length, it is possible that a term appears much more times in jobs with longer texts than those with shorter ones. To take into consideration this feature the term frequency is divided by the job offer text's length to normalize [16]:

$$\mathcal{TF}(t, d) = F(t, d)$$

where:

t: is a term

d: is a job offer

F: is the occurrence's frequency of t in d

$\mathcal{IDF}$: Inverse Document Frequency, which measures how important a term is. While computing $\mathcal{TF}$, all terms are considered equally important. However it is known that some terms, like stop words, may appear more but have less importance.

Thus we need to weigh down the frequent terms while scaling up the rare ones, by computing the following [16]:

$$\mathcal{IDF}(t, D) = \log \frac{N}{|\{d \in D : t \in d\}|}$$

where:

N: is the total number of job offers in the corpus

$|\{d \in D : t \in d\}|$: is the number of job offers in which the term t occurs.

Initialisation. To provide recommendations from the beginning, an initial profile can be used. This initial profile is automatically generated from the previously filled resume. Users are asked to fill out the resume, containing various demographic, professional data and other relevant information. The added-value of our initial profile, which uses the resume, is the fact that it allows us to avoid the cold-start. It generates recommendations from the very beginning and enables the recommender to suggest jobs according to the skills and Curriculum's content of the job seeker.

Update. Users are allowed to write applications for a specific job offer. The company, which has published the job, receives an email with the application and gains access to the user's resume. A user who applies to an offer clearly indicates an interest in this job offer. Meta-data of the user profile are updated as a consequence of his application to a job offer. For each word among the most significant ones in the job offer, we calculate its triggered terms using the semantic vocabulary. With these terms we constitue a new group of words, recompute their $\mathcal{TF} \times \mathcal{IDF}$ regarding the corpus, sort the results and take the best words to enrich the user profile. If the word is a new one, we add it, but if it is already included, we update its old value using the *Moving Average* [13]:

$$R_t = \alpha.W_t + (1 - \alpha).R_{t-1}$$

where:

R_t: is the word's weight after update
R_{t-1}: is word's weight before update
W_t: is the new weight to add pulled from $\mathcal{TF} \times \mathcal{IDF}$
$0 < \alpha < 1$: is a coefficient to define as: $\alpha = \frac{2}{N+1}$
N: is a a constant smoothing factor.

In our case, we take the average number of user visits per month which is $N = 7$, so we put $\alpha = 0,25$.

3.3 Third Challenge: Matching and Recommendations

The user and job profiles are,with all their dimensions, represented by vectors. After their construction, the cosine similarity, which is shown in the equation below, is used to compute the distance between the user profile and job profiles vectors [11]:

$$Cosine(V_u, V_j) = \frac{\sum_{i=1}^{n} V_{u_i} \times V_{j_i}}{\sqrt{\sum_{i=1}^{n} |V_{u_i}|^2 . \sum_{i=1}^{n} |V_{j_i}|^2}}$$

where:

V_u: is the user profile vector
V_j: is the job profile vector.

The smaller the angle is, the closer and more similar the job offer is to the user profile. We use this measure to compute a similarity score between the user profile and all the available offers, then we order the scores in a descending order.

3.4 Corpus

To achieve all of the steps stated above, we used a corpus of 49000 job offers, from which we removed approximatively 7000 offers written in English. We concentrated our work on the remaining 42140 offers written in French. We divided these offers in two parts. We used 42000 to search for the triggers and the remaining 140 to search for the experiments (see Table 2).

Table 2. Corpus details

Corpus size	83.238
Vocabulary size	5.032
Number of Unigrams	4.809
Number of Bigrams	169
Number of Trigrams	54

4 Evaluation

For the evaluation of our approach we proceed to a comparison between the actual recommendations service and ours. The primary goal of the experiments was to evaluate the performance of our recommendation approach, especially the contribution of the profile enrichment with triggers.

The experiment corpus is made up of 140 job offers, divided into two sets. The first one contains job offers distributed over four profiles (see Table 3). The second set has been integrated to the test corpus, in order to evaluate the real contribution of our method. It contains 48 job offers that have been randomly collected.

Table 3. Profiles

Profession	Sector	Skills
Marketing Manager	Assistantship, secretarial	Interactions
HR Director	IT, Telecom, Internet	Legal Consulting
Networks/Systems Engineer	Education, Teaching	Cisco, Configuration
Communications Manager	Telecommunications, Networks	Communication

In order to evaluate the experiment results, we used three standard metrics: *Recall, Precision* and *F-measure. Recall* is the ability of the system to return all relevant jobs, *Precision* is its ability to return only relevant jobs and *F-measure* characterizes the combined performance of *Recall* and *Precision*. Other performance metrics which are used in many fields, could measure the system's performance from its errors, namely the *False Acceptance*, where a job is wrongly accepted, and the *False Reject*, where a job is wrongly rejected. All those metrics are calculated as follows [3]:

$$Recall = \frac{Number\ of\ relevant\ jobs\ retrieved}{Number\ of\ jobs\ to\ retrieve}$$

$$Precision = \frac{Number\ of\ relevant\ jobs\ retrieved}{Number\ of\ jobs\ retrieved}$$

$$F - measure = 2 \times \frac{Precision \times Recall}{Precision + Recall}$$

$$False\ Reject = \frac{Number\ of\ False\ Rejects}{Number\ of\ jobs\ to\ retrieve}$$

$$False\ Acceptance = \frac{Number\ of\ False\ Acceptances}{Number\ of\ jobs\ retrieved}$$

Table 4 summarizes job recommendation results obtained for the four profiles. These results show that the use of triggers have allowed to improve the performance of recommendations. Indeed, the average F-measure has increased from 53 % to 75 %.

Moreover, we obtained better Recall and Precision values, for all the profiles. For "Marketing Manager", all job offers are recommended (Recall = 100 %), thus no job offer is wrongly rejected (False Reject = 0 %).

Table 4. Performances of the job recommendation

User Profile	System	Recall	Precision	F-measure	F. rejects	F. accepts.
Marketing Manager	Emploitic	0,81	0,40	0,54	0,19	0,6
	E-profiling	1,00	0,57	0,72	0,00	0,43
HR Director	Emploitic	0,88	0,76	0,81	0,12	0,24
	E-profiling	0,96	0,77	0,86	0,04	0,23
N/S Engineer	Emploitic	0,58	0,26	0,36	0,42	0,74
	E-profiling	0,85	0,71	0,77	0,15	0,29
Comm Manager	Emploitic	0,65	0,32	0,43	0,35	0,68
	E-profiling	0,90	0,50	0,64	0,10	0,50
Average	Emploitic	0,73	0,43	0,53	0,27	0,57
	E-profiling	0,93	0,64	0,75	0,07	0,36

5   Discussion and Conclusion

In this paper, we have described an approach using semantic vocabulary with an indicator of interest to personalize information retrieval in an e-recruitment environment. Our approach consists of the integration of user profile in the recommendation process after catching implicit informations about him. The user profile is described using vectors of weighted words that reflect interests and preferences. This profile is constantly updated and exploited to compute the matching with job offers. The results obtained show that our approach has achieved a good performance, greatly increasing recall and precision. In the perspectives, we propose to add other indicators of interest like: read-time of a job offer, and saving a job offer ..., We want also to use this profiling solution to optimize the search engine, and finally profile any simple visitor by creating a short term profile session.

References

1. Adomavicius, G., Zhang, J.: Stability of recommendation algorithms. ACM Trans. Inf. Syst. (TOIS) **30**(4), 23 (2012)
2. Al-Otaibi, S.T., Ykhlef, M.: A survey of job recommender systems. Int. J. Phys. Sci. **7**(29), 5127–5142 (2012)
3. Baeza-Yates, R., Ribeiro-Neto, B., et al.: Modern Information Retrieval, vol. 463. ACM Press, New York (1999)
4. Breese, J.S., Heckerman, D., Kadie, C.: Empirical analysis of predictive algorithms for collaborative filtering. In: Proceedings of the Fourteenth Conference on Uncertainty in Artificial Intelligence, pp. 43–52, Morgan Kaufmann Publishers Inc (1998)
5. Burke, R.: Integrating knowledge-based and collaborative-filtering recommender systems. In: Proceedings of the Workshop on AI and Electronic Commerce, pp. 69–72 (1999)
6. Burke, R.: Hybrid web recommender systems. In: Brusilovsky, P., Kobsa, A., Nejdl, W. (eds.) Adaptive Web 2007. LNCS, vol. 4321, pp. 377–408. Springer, Heidelberg (2007)
7. Hu, R., Pu, P.: Enhancing collaborative filtering systems with personality information. In: Proceedings of the fifth ACM Conference on Recommender Systems, pp. 197–204, ACM (2011)
8. Lavecchia, C., Smaili, K., Langlois, D., Haton, J.P.: Using inter-lingual triggers for machine translation. In: 8th Annual Conference of the International Speech Communication Association-INTERSPEECH 2007, pp. 2829–2832, ISCA (2007)
9. Lee, D.H., Brusilovsky, P.: Fighting information overflow with personalized comprehensive information access: a proactive job recommender. In: Third International Conference on Autonomic and Autonomous Systems 2007, ICAS07, pp. 21–21, IEEE (2007)
10. Rafter, R., Smyth, B.: Passive profiling from server logs in an online recruitment environment (2001)
11. Rahutomo, F., Kitasuka, T., Aritsugi, M.: Semantic cosine similarity (2012)
12. Resnick, P., Varian, H.R.: Recommender systems. Commun. ACM **40**(3), 56–58 (1997)
13. Roberts, S.: Control chart tests based on geometric moving averages. Technometrics **1**(3), 239–250 (1959)
14. Salton, G., McGill, M.J.: Introduction to Modern Information Retrieval. McGraw-Hill, Inc., New York (1986)
15. Singh, A., Rose, C., Visweswariah, K., Chenthamarakshan, V., Kambhatla, N.: Prospect: a system for screening candidates for recruitment. In: Proceedings of the 19th ACM International Conference on Information and Knowledge Management, pp. 659–668, ACM (2010)
16. Zakaria, C., Curé, O., Salzano, G., Smaïli, K.: Formalized conflicts detection based on the analysis of multiple emails: an approach combining statistics and ontologies. In: Meersman, R., Dillon, T., Herrero, P. (eds.) OTM 2009, Part I. LNCS, vol. 5870, pp. 94–111. Springer, Heidelberg (2009)
17. Zibran, M.F.: Chi-squared test of independence. Department of Computer Science, University of Calgary, Alberta, Canada (2007). Accessed 12 Aug 2010

A Genetic Algorithm for Evolving Plateaued Cryptographic Boolean Functions

Luca Mariot$^{(\boxtimes)}$ and Alberto Leporati

Dipartimento di Informatica, Sistemistica e Comunicazione,
Università degli Studi Milano - Bicocca, Viale Sarca 336/14, 20126 Milano, Italy
luca.mariot@disco.unimib.it, alberto.leporati@unimib.it

Abstract. We propose a genetic algorithm (GA) to search for plateaued boolean functions, which represent suitable candidates for the design of stream ciphers due to their good cryptographic properties. Using the spectral inversion technique introduced by Clark, Jacob, Maitra and Stanica, our GA encodes the chromosome of a candidate solution as a permutation of a three-valued Walsh spectrum. Additionally, we design specialized crossover and mutation operators so that the swapped positions in the offspring chromosomes correspond to different values in the resulting Walsh spectra. Some tests performed on the set of pseudo-boolean functions of $n = 6$ and $n = 7$ variables show that in the former case our GA outperforms Clark et al.'s simulated annealing algorithm with respect to the ratio of generated plateaued boolean functions per number of optimization runs.

Keywords: Evolutionary computing · Cryptography · Genetic algorithms · Simulated annealing · Boolean functions · Walsh transform · Spectral inversion · Nonlinearity · Resiliency

1 Introduction

The security of a symmetric cryptosystem often depends on the choice of the underlying *boolean functions*. For instance, in the *combiner model* for stream ciphers the boolean function $f : \mathbb{F}_2^n \to \mathbb{F}_2$ used to combine the outputs of n *Linear Feedback Shift Registers* (LFSRs) should satisfy several cryptographic criteria in order to resist to specific attacks. These properties include, among others, *balancedness*, high *algebraic degree* and *nonlinearity*, and high order of *resiliency*. When searching for good cryptographic boolean functions, a way to overcome the combinatorial explosion resulting from increasing the number of variables is to use *heuristic techniques*, such as *Genetic Algorithms* [7], *Simulated Annealing* [4], *Genetic Programming* (both basic and *Cartesian* GP [9,10]) and *Particle Swarm Optimization* [6]. These methods usually represent a candidate boolean function by either its *truth table* or by a tree encoding one of its possible algebraic expressions.

Clark, Jacob, Maitra and Stanica [3] proposed the *spectral inversion technique* for designing good cryptographic boolean functions, in which a candidate

© Springer International Publishing Switzerland 2015
A.-H. Dediu et al. (Eds.): TPNC 2015, LNCS 9477, pp. 33–45, 2015.
DOI: 10.1007/978-3-319-26841-5_3

solution is represented as a *permutation* of a *Walsh spectrum* that encodes a particular set of cryptographic properties. In general, by applying the *inverse Walsh transform* to such a spectrum, a *pseudoboolean function* $f : \mathbb{F}_2^n \to \mathbb{R}$ is obtained. Thus, the objective function becomes the *deviation* of f from being a boolean function, and in [3] Simulated Annealing (SA) was adopted to minimize it.

The goal of this paper is to investigate the application of *permutation-based Genetic Algorithms* for evolving cryptographic boolean functions by spectral inversion, a method which was conjectured to be more efficient than SA in [3].

In particular, we design a GA in which the chromosomes of the evolved solutions are Walsh spectra of *plateaued pseudoboolean functions*. The motivation for this choice is twofold. First, spectra of plateaued pseudoboolean functions are three-valued, hence they have an easy combinatorial characterization. Second, plateaued *boolean functions* are considered suitable candidates for cryptographic applications, since they satisfy with equality the bounds on maximum achievable algebraic degree and nonlinearity for a given resiliency order, respectively proved by Siegenthaler [11] and Tarannikov [12]. Since our GA manipulates permutations of *repeated* values, we propose a crossover and a mutation operator which ensure that the modified genes in the offspring correspond to different values in the Walsh spectrum.

Let us note that, as the number of boolean functions of n variables is 2^{2^n}, exhaustively searching for plateaued boolean functions (or, more in general, cryptographically relevant boolean functions) becomes unfeasible for $n > 5$. For this reason, we assess the performance of our GA in generating plateaued boolean functions of $n = 6$ and $n = 7$ variables. The results show that our GA outperforms Simulated Annealing in finding plateaued boolean functions of $n = 6$ variables, while for $n = 7$ SA still yields better average fitness values, even if neither technique was able to generate a plateaued boolean function in this case. This would seem to suggest that combining the global search capabilities of our GA and the local exploration of SA could lead to better results for higher numbers of variables.

The remainder of this paper is organised as follows. Section 2 gives a brief introduction about boolean functions and their cryptographic properties. Section 3 describes our permutation-based Genetic Algorithm, defining the solution encoding, the fitness function and the adopted genetic operators. Section 4 presents the results obtained by our GA on the optimization of pseudoboolean plateaued functions for $n = 6$ and $n = 7$ variables, and compares them with the results achieved by the SA algorithm described in [3]. Finally, Sect. 5 summarises the contributions of this paper and points out some possible future developments on the subject.

2   Preliminaries on Boolean Functions

In this section, we recall some basic definitions and facts about boolean functions and their cryptographic properties. For further details on the subject, we refer the reader to Carlet [2].

2.1 Representations of Boolean Functions

A *boolean function of n variables* is a mapping $f : \mathbb{F}_2^n \to \mathbb{F}_2$, where $\mathbb{F}_2 = \{0, 1\}$ is the finite field of two elements. Once an ordering of the input variables $x_1, \cdots, x_n$ has been fixed, the *truth table representation* of f is a vector $\Omega_f \in \mathbb{F}_2^{2^n}$ which specifies for all $i \in \{0, \cdots, 2^n - 1\}$ the value of $f(bin(i))$, where $bin(i)$ denotes the n-bit binary expansion of i. The *algebraic normal form* (ANF) represents a boolean function f as a sum of products over $\mathbb{F}_2$. Specifically, given $f : \mathbb{F}_2^n \to \mathbb{F}_2$, $N = \{1, \cdots, n\}$ and $\mathcal{P}(N)$ the power set of N, the ANF of f is defined by the following polynomial:

$$f(x) = \bigoplus_{I \in \mathcal{P}(N)} a_I \left(\prod_{i \in I} x_i \right). \tag{1}$$

The *polar form* $\hat{f} : \mathbb{F}_2^n \to \{-1, 1\}$ of f is the function defined as $\hat{f}(x) = (-1)^{f(x)}$ for all $x \in \mathbb{F}_2^n$. Denoting by $\omega \cdot x = \omega_1 x_1 \oplus \cdots \oplus \omega_n x_n$ the *scalar product* modulo 2 of the two vectors $\omega, x \in \mathbb{F}_2^n$, the *Walsh transform* of $f : \mathbb{F}_2^n \to \mathbb{F}_2$ is the function $\hat{F} : \mathbb{F}_2^n \to \mathbb{R}$ defined for all $\omega \in \mathbb{F}_2^n$ as

$$\hat{F}(\omega) = \sum_{x \in \mathbb{F}_2^n} \hat{f}(x) \cdot (-1)^{\omega \cdot x}. \tag{2}$$

The vector of Walsh coefficients $\mathcal{S}_f = \left(\hat{F}(bin(0)), \cdots, \hat{F}(bin(2^n - 1)) \right) \in \mathbb{R}^{2^n}$ of f is also called the *Walsh spectrum* of f, while the maximum absolute value among all Walsh coefficients $W_{max}(f)$ is called the *spectral radius* of f. One important property of the Walsh spectrum is *Parseval's identity*, which states that the sum of all squared Walsh coefficients is constant for every boolean function $f : \mathbb{F}_2^n \to \mathbb{F}_2$:

$$\sum_{\omega \in \mathbb{F}_2^n} \hat{F}(\omega)^2 = 2^{2n}. \tag{3}$$

Given a spectrum $\mathcal{S}_f$ of a boolean function f, it is possible to recover the original (polar) function by applying the *inverse Walsh transform*:

$$\hat{f}(x) = 2^{-n} \sum_{\omega \in \mathbb{F}_2^n} \hat{F}(\omega) \cdot (-1)^{\omega \cdot x}. \tag{4}$$

Notice that not all possible real-valued Walsh spectra correspond to boolean functions: in general, by applying the inverse Walsh transform to a random spectrum $\mathcal{S} \in \mathbb{R}^{2^n}$ the outcome will be the polar truth table of a *pseudoboolean function* $f : \mathbb{F}_2^n \to \mathbb{R}$.

2.2 Cryptographic Properties of Boolean Functions

The Walsh spectrum is used to characterize several cryptographic properties of boolean functions. In particular, given $f : \mathbb{F}_2^n \to \mathbb{F}_2$ along with is Walsh spectrum $\mathcal{S}_f$ and spectral radius $W_{max}(f)$, we considered the following cryptographic properties for our optimization problem:

- *Balancedness:* f is balanced if its truth table Ω_f is composed of an equal number of 0s and 1s. Equivalently, f is balanced if and only if $\hat{F}(\underline{0}) = 0$, where $\underline{0}$ denotes the null vector of $\mathbb{F}_2^n$.
- *Algebraic Degree:* the algebraic degree d of f is defined as the degree of its ANF. Functions of degree 1 are also called *affine functions*.
- *Nonlinearity:* the nonlinearity nl of f is the Hamming distance of f from the set of all affine functions. Equivalently, the nonlinearity of f can also be computed as $nl = \frac{1}{2}(2^n - W_{max}(f))$.
- *Resiliency:* function f is said to be *m-resilient* if, by fixing at most m input variables, the resulting restrictions of f are all balanced. Equivalently, f is m-resilient if and only if $\hat{F}(\omega) = 0$ for all $\omega \in \mathbb{F}_2^n$ having *Hamming weight* at most m, that is, the Walsh transform vanishes for all vectors $\omega \in \mathbb{F}_2^n$ which have at most m nonzero coordinates. Notice that 0-resiliency corresponds to balancedness.

In order to be suitable for cryptographic purposes (for instance, to be used in the combiner model), a boolean function f should be balanced, have high algebraic degree and nonlinearity, and be resilient of high order. However, functions which fully satisfy all these four criteria simultaneously do not exist. In particular, *Siegenthaler's bound* [11] and *Tarannikov's bound* [12] respectively limit the reachable values of algebraic degree and nonlinearity for a given order of resiliency:

- *Siegenthaler's Bound:* $d \leq n - m - 1$
- *Tarannikov's Bound:* $nl \leq 2^{n-1} - 2^{m+1}$

In what follows, by (n, m, d, nl) we denote the *profile* of a balanced boolean function of n variables having resiliency order m, algebraic degree d and nonlinearity nl.

Among the various classes of boolean functions which can be characterized in terms of cryptographic properties, *bent functions* are the ones reaching the highest possible values of nonlinearity. Specifically, $f : \mathbb{F}_2^n \to \mathbb{F}_2$ is bent if $\hat{F}(\omega) = \pm 2^{\frac{n}{2}}$ for all $\omega \in \mathbb{F}_2^n$. However, these functions exist only for even values of n, and moreover they are not balanced since $\hat{F}(0) = \pm 2^{\frac{n}{2}}$. Hence, bent functions are not suitable for cryptographic applications.

A broader class which includes bent functions is the set of *plateaued functions*, originally introduced by Zhang and Zheng [14]. Formally, a boolean function $f : \mathbb{F}_2^n \to \mathbb{F}_2$ is plateaued if $\hat{F}(\omega) \in \{-W_{max}(f), 0, +W_{max}(f)\}$ for all $\omega \in \mathbb{F}_2^n$. Thus, Walsh spectra of plateaued functions take at most three values. Plateaued functions are especially interesting for cryptography, since they satisfy with equality both Siegenthaler's and Tarannikov's bounds, a feature which makes them optimal with respect to all four properties mentioned above. The profile of a plateaued boolean function is of the form $(n, r - 2, n - r - 3, 2^{n-1} - 2^{r-1})$, where $r \geq \frac{n}{2}$, from which it follows that $W_{max}(f) = 2^r$. Notice that if n is even and $r = \frac{n}{2}$, then a plateaued function is bent. In what follows, we will apply our GA for evolving plateaued boolean functions.

3   Our Genetic Algorithm

3.1   Chromosomes Encoding

The main idea underlying the chromosome encoding of our GA is to represent a candidate solution as a *permutation* of a Walsh spectrum $\mathcal{S} \in \mathbb{R}^{2^n}$. This *spectral inversion* approach to heuristic design of cryptographic boolean functions was originally introduced by Clark, Jacob, Maitra and Stanica in [3].

As a first observation, notice that representing the chromosome as a permutation of the spectrum *positions* would allow us to employ classic permutation-based GA, such as those designed for the Traveling Salesman Problem [5]. However, the Walsh spectrum is generally composed of *repeated* values. This means that a position-based encoding would make the GA search into a space which is bigger than what is actually needed, since several swaps performed by permutation-based genetic operators would map to the same values in the Walsh spectrum. Hence, we represent our candidate solution directly by its Walsh spectrum *values*. From the combinatorial point of view, this representation is equivalent to performing permutations over a *multiset* $\mathcal{M}$.

Recall from the previous section that, by Parseval's identity, the sum of the squared Walsh coefficients of any n-variable boolean function equals 2^{2n}. Moreover, the values summed in the Walsh transform defined in Eq. (2) are all integers, hence we can start to model a candidate solution as a vector of 2^n integers which sum to 2^{2n}. Additionally, we are interested only in plateaued boolean functions, so that each Walsh coefficient can only take its value in the set $V = \{-2^r, 0, +2^r\}$. We thus need to determine the *multiplicities* of the elements of V in order to characterise the multiset $\mathcal{M}$ required to build the spectrum. Using the approach sketched in [3], these multiplicities can be derived from the following observations:

(1) Since a plateaued boolean function is m-resilient with $m = r-2$, all positions which correspond to input vectors having at most m nonzero coordinates must be set to zero. Therefore, in order to meet the resiliency constraint there must be *at least* $\#0_{res} = \sum_{i=0}^{m} \binom{n}{i}$ zero-valued positions in the spectrum.

(2) Each *nonzero position* in the spectrum contributes by a term of $(\pm 2^r)^2 = 2^{2r}$ in Parseval's identity. Thus, the total number of nonzero positions in the spectrum is given by $\# \pm 2^r = \frac{2^{2n}}{2^{2r}}$.

(3) From (1) and (2) we deduce that there are $\#0_{add} = 2^n - ((\# \pm 2^r) + (\#0_{res}))$ additional positions set to zero other than the ones used to satisfy m-resiliency.

(4) By setting $\hat{f}(\underline{0}) = 1$, it follows that $\sum_{\omega \in \mathbb{F}_2^n} \hat{F}(\omega) = 2^n$. Notice that this is an arbitrary assumption, since we are considering only those functions mapping the null vector to 0. However, this does not bias the final search space, since by setting $\hat{f}(\underline{0}) = -1$ we would always get plateaued functions having the same profile.

(5) By combining observations (2) and (4), we finally obtain the number of positions to be set to -2^r and $+2^r$ by solving the following system:

$$\begin{cases} (\# + 2^r) + (\# - 2^r) & = \frac{2^{2n}}{2^{2r}} \\ (\# + 2^r) - (\# - 2^r) & = 2^n \end{cases}$$

which gives

$$\begin{cases} \# + 2^r & = 2^{n-1}(2^{n-2r} + 1) \\ \# - 2^r & = 2^{n-1}(2^{n-2r} - 1) \end{cases}$$

In what follows, we denote by $x[i]$ the element at position i of vector x. Since there are $\#0_{res}$ positions in the spectrum which are set to zero for the resiliency constraint, we can restrict our representation only to those positions whose binary expansions have more than m nonzero coordinates. Let us thus consider the *restricted ordered spectrum* $\mathcal{S}_{ro} = (w_1, \cdots, w_l)$ having length $l = 2^n - \#0_{res}$ and whose first $\#0_{add}$ positions are set to zero, the next $\# - 2^r$ are set to -2^r and the final $\# + 2^r$ are set to $+2^r$. Additionally, let us denote by $P_r = (j_1, \cdots, j_l)$ the vector of positions j_i such that $hwt(bin(j_i)) > m$, where $hwt(\cdot)$ denotes the Hamming weight of the binary string passed as argument. Clearly, by permuting the components in $\mathcal{S}_{ro}$ the resulting spectrum maintains the desired cryptographic properties, since the multiplicities $\#0_{add}$, $\# - 2^r$ and $\# + 2^r$ are permutation invariant. However, we are interested only in those permutations which swap different values in the restricted spectrum. To address this problem, we employ the following equivalence relation $\sim_p$ on the symmetric group S_l: given two permutations $\pi_1, \pi_2 \in S_l$, define $\pi_1 \sim_p \pi_2$ if and only if $w_{\pi_1(i)} = w_{\pi_2(i)}$ for all $i \in \{1, \cdots, l\}$, where $w_{\pi_1(i)}, w_{\pi_2(i)}$ are components of $\mathcal{S}_{ro}$. We can thus characterize the permutations which map different values in the restricted spectrum as the representatives of the equivalence classes in the quotient set $S_l/\sim_p$. With a little abuse of notation, in what follows we write $\pi \in S_l/\sim_p$ to directly denote the representative permutation π instead of the equivalence class $[\pi]_{\sim_p}$.

The *chromosome* which encodes a candidate solution evolved by our GA is a permutation $c = (w_{\pi(1)}, \cdots, w_{\pi(l)})$ of the restricted ordered spectrum $\mathcal{S}_{ro}$, where $\pi \in S_l/\sim_p$. The *decoding* of chromosome c which yields the corresponding pseudoboolean function $f : \mathbb{F}_2^n \to \mathbb{R}$, denoted by $dec(c)$, is carried out using the following procedure:

1. Initialize the Walsh spectrum $\mathcal{S}_f$ to the null vector $(0, \cdots, 0) \in \mathbb{R}^{2^n}$.
2. For all $i \in \{1, \cdots, l\}$ set $\mathcal{S}_f[j_i] = c[i]$, where $j_i = P_r[i]$.
3. Perform *spectral inversion*: apply to $\mathcal{S}_f$ the inverse Walsh transform defined in Eq. (4) in order to obtain the polar form $\hat{f}$ of function f.

3.2   Objective and Fitness Functions

In order to measure how good a pseudoboolean function is, the authors of [3] proposed an objective function based on the distance from the *nearest boolean function*. Formally, given the polar form $\hat{f}$ of $f : \mathbb{F}_2^n \to \mathbb{R}$, the polar truth table of the nearest boolean function $\hat{b} : \mathbb{F}_2^n \to \{-1, +1\}$ is obtained for all $x \in \mathbb{F}_2^n$ as follows:

$$\hat{b}(x) = \begin{cases} +1 & \text{, if } \hat{f}(x) > 0 \\ -1 & \text{, if } \hat{f}(x) < 0 \\ +1 \text{ or } -1 \text{ (chosen randomly)} & \text{, if } \hat{f}(x) = 0 \end{cases} \tag{5}$$

Given a chromosome c and the corresponding pseudoboolean function $f = dec(c)$, the *objective function* to be minimized proposed in [3] is defined as:

$$obj(f) = \sum_{x \in \mathbb{F}_2^n} (\hat{f}(x) - \hat{b}(x))^2. \tag{6}$$

This objective function measures the *deviation* of f from being a true boolean function. Hence, an optimal solution to our problem is encoded by a chromosome c such that $obj(dec(c)) = 0$. Given how we designed the Walsh spectrum, such a solution corresponds to a plateaued boolean function.

The *fitness function* $fit(\cdot)$ maximised by our GA is simply defined as the opposite of the objective function (6), that is, $fit(f) = -obj(f)$.

3.3 Genetic Operators

Considering the chromosome encoding adopted for the candidate solutions, an appropriate crossover operator for our GA has to preserve the multiplicities $\#0_{add}$, $\#-2^r$ and $\#+2^r$ of the restricted spectrum, so that Parseval's identity and the other properties of plateaued functions are maintained. To this end, we designed a crossover operator loosely inspired by the one proposed in [7].

The main idea is to work at the loci level, and to use *counters* in order to keep track of the multiplicities of the three values 0, -2^r and $+2^r$ inserted in the offspring during the crossover phase. More precisely, given two parent chromosomes c_1 and c_2, our crossover operator builds an offspring chromosome o as follows:

1. Initialize to zero the three counters cnt_z, cnt_n and cnt_p respectively associated to the spectral values 0, -2^r and $+2^r$.
2. For all $i \in \{1, \cdots, l\}$ such that $c_1[i] = c_2[i]$, copy either $c_1[i]$ or $c_2[i]$ in $o[i]$. Depending on the copied value, update the relevant counter.
3. For all $i \in \{1, \cdots, l\}$ such that $c_1[i] \neq c_2[i]$, determine the value to be copied in $o[i]$ as follows:
   (a) If all three counters are below their maximum values (that is, $cnt\_z < \#0_{add}$, $cnt\_n < \#-2^r$ and $cnt\_p < \#+2^r$), randomly select $c_1[i]$ or $c_2[i]$ with probability $1/2$, and copy it in $o[i]$. Depending on the copied value, update the relevant counter.
   (b) If one of the three counters reached its maximum value, check if either $c_1[i]$ or $c_2[i]$ is equal to the value associated to that counter. If so, copy the gene of the other parent in $o[i]$. Otherwise, randomly select $c_1[i]$ or $c_2[i]$ with probability $1/2$, and copy it in $o[i]$. In both cases, depending on the copied value, update the relevant counter.

   (c) If two out of three counters reached their respective maximum values, copy the value associated to the remaining counter in $o[i]$.

4. Return the offspring chromosome o.

Concerning the mutation operator, we adopted a simple swap procedure which checks that the swapped values are different. In particular, let us assume that c is a chromosome of length l and that pos_0, pos_{-2^r} and pos_{+2^r} are the vectors specifying the positions of the 0s, -2^rs and $+2^r$s in c, respectively. Then, our mutation operator is applied to each locus $i \in \{1, \cdots, l\}$ of c with probability $p_\mu \in [0, 1]$, and it performs the following steps:

1. Setting $v = c[i]$, randomly select with probability $1/2$ one of the two positions vectors pos_t or pos_u, where $t \neq v$ and $u \neq v$.
2. Denoting by pos_s the selected positions vector, randomly draw with uniform probability an index j of pos_s.
3. Swap the values $c[i]$ and $c[pos_s[j]]$.
4. Swap the occurrence of i in pos_v with $pos_s[j]$.

Finally, for the selection operators we tested both *roulette wheel selection* and *deterministic tournament selection*.

3.4   Overall GA Procedure

We can now summarise the overall procedure of our GA. The input parameters for the algorithm are the number of variables n and the index $r \geq \frac{n}{2}$ of the target plateaued functions, the size of the population N (where N is even), the number of generations G to be performed, the crossover and mutation probabilities p_χ and p_μ, and the selection operator S.

1. *Initialization:* Compute the profile $(n, r - 2, n - r - 3, 2^{n-1} - 2^{r-1})$ of the target functions and the multiplicities $\#0_{res}$, $\#0_{add}$, $\# - 2^r$ and $\# + 2^r$ of the Walsh spectrum.
2. *Create Population:* For $i \in \{1, \cdots, N\}$, create a chromosome $c = (w_{\pi(1)}, \cdots, w_{\pi(l)})$ of length $l = 2^n - \#0_{res}$, where π is a random permutation of $S_l/\sim_p$, and add it to the current population $\mathcal{P}$.
3. *Initial Fitness Evaluation:* For each chromosome $c \in \mathcal{P}$, decode its respective pseudoboolean function $f = dec(c)$ and compute the fitness value $fit(f) = -obj(f)$, where $obj(\cdot)$ is defined as in Eq. (6). Set the best solution B as the individual scoring the highest fitness value.
4. *Selection Phase:* Apply N times the selection operator S on the current population $\mathcal{P}$, thus creating a candidate population $\mathcal{C}$ of (eventually repeated) N chromosomes which will produce the next generation.
5. *Crossover Phase:* For all $i \in \{1, 3, \cdots, N - 1\}$, sample a random number $r \in [0, 1]$. If $r < p_\chi$, apply the crossover operator *twice* to the pair $c_i, c_{i+1} \in \mathcal{C}$, and copy the two offspring chromosomes (o_i, o_{i+1}) in the new population $\mathcal{N}$. Otherwise, set $o_i = c_i$ and $o_{i+1} = c_{i+1}$, and copy them in $\mathcal{N}$.

6. *Mutation Phase:* For each chromosome $o \in \mathcal{N}$ and for all $j \in \{1, \cdots, l\}$, sample a random number $r \in [0, 1]$. If $r < p_\mu$, apply the mutation operator to $o[j]$.
7. *Fitness Evaluation:* For each chromosome $o \in \mathcal{N}$, compute the fitness value of $f = dec(o)$, and find the current best individual B_c having the highest fitness value in $\mathcal{N}$.
8. *Elitism:* If $fit(B_c) \leq fit(B)$, replace a random individual in $\mathcal{N}$ with B. Otherwise, update the best solution found so far by setting $B = B_c$.
9. *Population Update:* Set the current population $\mathcal{P}$ equal to $\mathcal{N}$.
10. *Termination Condition:* If the best solution found is optimal $(obj(B) = 0)$ or the maximum number of generations G has been reached, output the best solution B found by the GA. Otherwise, return to Step 4.

4 Experiments and Results

We tested our GA on the spaces of pseudoboolean functions of $n = 6$ and $n = 7$ variables, adopting in both cases index $r = 4$. This is the smallest integer value, yielding maximum nonlinearity, such that the resulting functions are not bent for $n = 6$. Table 1 reports the profiles and the multiplicities of the spectrum values for the corresponding plateaued boolean functions.

Table 1. Cryptographic profiles and spectral multiplicities for plateaued functions of $n = 6$ and $n = 7$ variables

(n, m, d, nl)	$\#0_{res}$	$\#0_{add}$	$\# - 2^r$	$\# + 2^r$
$(6, 2, 3, 24)$	22	26	6	10
$(7, 2, 4, 56)$	29	35	28	36

We limited our experimentation to these two problem instances in order to compare our GA with Simulated Annealing. As a matter of fact, the basic SA algorithm described in [3] was able to find only 5 plateaued functions with profile $(7, 2, 4, 56)$ out of 500 optimization runs, and a *change of basis* procedure [4] had to be applied in order to convert some generated sub-optimal solutions into actual boolean functions. Further, for $n = 6$ only bent functions were considered, but not generic plateaued functions. On the other hand, for higher number of variables the basic version of SA always failed to generate boolean functions, hence the authors of [3] restricted their search space to the family of *rotation symmetric boolean functions*, which we did not consider in this work.

For each value of n and selection operator considered, we performed $R = 500$ independent runs of our GA, using a population of $N = 30$ chromosomes evolved for $G = 500000$ generations. Thus, each GA run consisted of $F = 1.5 \cdot 10^7$ fitness evaluations. The crossover and mutation probabilities were respectively set to $p_\chi = 0.95$ and $p_\mu = 0.05$, while in the case where tournament selection was used we adopted a tournament size of $k = 3$.

Table 2. Statistics of the best solutions found by our GA and SA over $R = 500$ runs

n	Stat	$GA(RWS)$	$GA(DTS)$	$SA(T_1, \alpha_1)$	$SA(T_2, \alpha_2)$
6	avg_o	14.08	13.02	19.01	19.03
	min_o	0	0	0	0
	max_o	16	16	28	28
	std_o	5.21	6.23	4.89	4.81
	$\#opt$	60	93	11	10
	avg_t	83.3	79.2	79.1	79.4
7	avg_o	53.44	52.6	45.09	44.85
	min_o	47	44	32	27
	max_o	58	59	63	57
	std_o	2.40	2.77	4.39	4.18
	$\#opt$	0	0	0	0
	avg_t	204.2	204.5	180.3	180.2

Concerning the comparison with Simulated Annealing, we implemented the SA algorithm described in [3] and we tested it for $n = 6$ and $n = 7$ by setting the number of inner loops $MaxIL$ and moves within an inner loop MIL respectively to $MaxIL = 5000$ and $MIL = 3000$, thus yielding the same number $F = 1.5 \cdot 10^7$ of fitness evaluations performed by our GA. Since the authors of [3] did not mention the initial temperature which they adopted for their experiments, we tested the values $T_1 = 100$ and $T_2 = 1000$ with cooling parameter respectively set to $\alpha_1 = 0.95$ and $\alpha_2 = 0.99$. As for our GA, for each combination of parameters (n, T_0, α) we performed 500 runs of the SA algorithm.

We performed all our experiments on a 64-bit Linux machine with a Core i5 architecture and a CPU running at 2.8 GHz. For $n = 6$, a set of 500 runs of GA or SA took approximately 11.5 hours to complete, while for $n = 7$ it took about 28.3 hours and 25 hours for GA and SA, respectively. Table 2 reports the results of the experiments.

By $GA(RWS)$ and $GA(DTS)$ we denote our GA respectively with roulette wheel selection and deterministic tournament selection, while $SA(T_i, \alpha_i)$ stands for the SA algorithm run with initial temperature T_i and cooling parameter α_i, for $i \in \{1,2\}$. For each parameters combination, Table 2 reports the average (avg_o), minimum (min_o), maximum (max_o) and standard deviation (std_o) values of the objective function $obj(\cdot)$ computed on the best solutions found, along with the numbers of optimal solutions generated ($\#opt$) and the average time per run in seconds (avg_t).

For $n = 6$ it can be observed that both versions of our GA outperformed SA with respect to the ratio of generated $(6, 2, 3, 24)$ functions versus the total number of optimization runs. In particular, the adoption of tournament selection produced better results than roulette wheel selection, with 93 plateaued functions achieved using the former operator against the 60 obtained using the latter one. On the other hand, changing the initial temperature and the cooling parameter α did not seem to influence the SA performances, with only 11 plateaued functions generated by $SA(T_1, \alpha_1)$ and 10 functions generated by $SA(T_2, \alpha_2)$. Notice also that the computational overhead introduced by our GA is not very high: for example, using roulette wheel selection the average time per run of our GA was 83.3 seconds, while with tournament selection a single run took on average 79.2 seconds, which is in the same range as that employed by SA.

In the case of $n = 7$ variables, no version of our GA nor SA was able to generate a plateaued boolean function of profile $(7, 2, 4, 56)$. However, it can be seen that SA outperformed both versions of our GA. In particular, the GA obtained slightly better results using tournament selection than roulette wheel selection, but SA scored lower average objective function values than GA. The same difference can also be observed by comparing the minimum objective function values.

5 Conclusions and Directions for Further Research

In this paper, we proposed a genetic algorithm to evolve plateaued boolean functions which satisfy good cryptographic properties. Instead of searching the space of boolean functions (as it is usually done in the existing literature), we adopted the *spectral inversion* approach set forth by Clark, Jacob, Maitra and Stanica in [3], which represents a candidate solution as a Walsh spectrum already satisfying the desired cryptographic properties. The search space thus becomes the set of all plateaued pseudoboolean functions, and the objective function to be minimized is the distance of the candidate solution from the nearest boolean function. The representation adopted for the chromosomes of our GA consists in a permutation of a restricted Walsh spectrum, in which the positions related to m-resiliency are not considered, being constantly set to zero. Since the coefficients in the spectrum of a plateaued boolean function can take only three values, the chromosome actually encodes a permutation on a multiset. The decoding process first maps the loci of the chromosome to the positions in the Walsh spectrum having Hamming weight higher than m, and then the inverse Walsh transform is applied to obtain the associated pseudoboolean function. We designed a specialized crossover operator which employs counters in order to preserve the multiplicities of the three values characterizing the spectrum of plateaued functions, while for mutation we adopted a simple swap-based operator which exchanges only those positions in the chromosome corresponding to different spectral values.

The performed experiments show that in the case of $n = 6$ variables our GA achieved better results than the Simulated Annealing algorithm proposed in [3] with respect to the ratio of generated $(6, 2, 3, 24)$ boolean functions per number of optimization runs. In particular, our GA performed better when adopting deterministic tournament selection instead of basic roulette wheel selection, while modifying the initial temperature and the cooling parameter did not significantly change the SA performances. On the other hand, for $n = 7$ no heuristic technique was able to generate a $(7, 2, 4, 56)$ plateaued boolean function, but SA scored on average lower objective function values than GA.

Extending the comparison to other *direct* heuristic methods (that is, heuristics which directly explore the space of boolean functions) is not a straightforward task. The reason for this difficulty is twofold. First, there are no obvious ways to compare the sub-optimal solutions found, due to the different representations adopted. In particular, in our GA a sub-optimal solution is a pseudoboolean function which already satisfies the desired cryptographic properties, while in direct methods it is a boolean function which do not satisfy these criteria. Second, to our knowledge only two direct heuristic methods have been reported in the literature to generate $(6, 2, 3, 24)$ plateaued functions [1,4], but no information on the ratio of optimal solutions found per number of optimization runs are available. Nonetheless, these methods were also able to locate $(7, 2, 4, 56)$ functions.

The results presented in this paper, together with the above considerations on direct heuristic methods, suggest that our GA does not scale well for $n \geq 7$, the likely reason being that it gets stuck in local optima. A possible way to overcome this drawback is to combine the global search capabilities of GA with a local search technique. A straightforward method to investigate this idea could be the integration of our GA inside the SA algorithm of [3], using for example the *Genetic Annealing* framework [13]. The obvious downside to this solution, however, would be the significantly higher amount of computational resources required to carry out a single optimization run.

An alternative solution could be to add a *Hill Climbing* optimization step in our GA, similarly to the strategy adopted by Millan, Clark and Dawson in [7]. In the context of our GA, a Hill Climbing optimization step would require characterising the pairs of Walsh coefficients which, if swapped, would decrease the deviation of the resulting pseudoboolean function. Further, one could also consider substituting the classic GA by more refined evolutionary heuristics, such as the *Bacterial Evolutionary Algorithm* (BEA) [8] which could allow achieving better convergence.

An additional direction for further research would be to consider different cryptographic properties other than nonlinearity, algebraic degree and resiliency. The *propagation criterion* $PC(l)$, for instance, can be characterized by the zeros of the *autocorrelation function*, which is related to the Walsh transform by the *Wiener-Khintchine theorem* [2]. Heuristic search of boolean functions satisfying only $PC(l)$ could be done using the same basic spectral inversion method of [3]: in this case, it would suffice to evolve through our GA or SA autocorrelation spectra instead of Walsh spectra. However, finding boolean functions satisfying both Walsh-related and autocorrelation-related properties by spectral inversion would require modifying the representation of the candidate solutions, since a valid swap on the Walsh spectrum could induce an invalid swap on the autocorrelation function (and vice versa), due to the aforementioned Wiener-Khintchine theorem.

Appendix: Source Code and Experiments Data

The Java source code for the GA described in this paper and the SA algorithm proposed in [3] can be found at http://openit.disco.unimib.it/~mariot/ga_platbf, together with the data of the experiments discussed in Sect. 4.

References

1. Burnett, L., Millan, W., Dawson, E., Clark, A.: Simpler methods for generating better boolean functions with good cryptographic properties. Australas. J. Combin. **29**, 231–248 (2004)
2. Carlet, C.: Boolean functions for cryptography and error-correcting codes. In: Crama, Y., Hammer, P.L. (eds.) Boolean Models and Methods in Mathematics, Computer Science, and Engineering, pp. 257–397. Cambridge University Press, New York (2011)
3. Clark, J.A., Jacob, J.L., Maitra, S., Stanica, P.: Almost boolean functions: the design of boolean functions by spectral inversion. Comput. Intell. **20**(3), 450–462 (2004)
4. Clark, J.A., Jacob, J.L., Stepney, S., Maitra, S., Millan, W.L.: Evolving boolean functions satisfying multiple criteria. In: Menezes, A., Sarkar, P. (eds.) INDOCRYPT 2002. LNCS, vol. 2551, pp. 246–259. Springer, Heidelberg (2002)
5. Goldberg, D.E., Lingle, R.: Alleles, loci and the traveling salesman problem. In: Grefenstette, J.J. (ed.) Proceedings of the 1st International Conference on Genetic Algorithms, pp. 154–159, Lawrence Erlbaum Associates (1985)
6. Mariot, L., Leporati, A.: Heuristic search by particle swarm optimization of boolean functions for cryptographic applications. In: Laredo, J.L.J., Silva, S., Esparcia-Alcázar, A.I. (eds.) Genetic and Evolutionary Computation Conference, GECCO 2015, Companion Material Proceedings, pp. 1425–1426, ACM (2015)
7. Millan, W.L., Clark, A.J., Dawson, E.: Heuristic design of cryptographically strong balanced boolean functions. In: Nyberg, K. (ed.) EUROCRYPT 1998. LNCS, vol. 1403, pp. 489–499. Springer, Heidelberg (1998)
8. Nawa, N.E., Furuhashi, T.: Fuzzy system parameters discovery by bacterial evolutionary algorithm. IEEE Trans. Fuzzy Syst. **7**(5), 608–616 (1999)
9. Picek, S., Jakobovic, D., Golub, M.: Evolving cryptographically sound boolean functions. In: Blum, C., Alba, E. (eds.) Genetic and Evolutionary Computation Conference, GECCO 2013, Companion Material Proceedings, pp. 191–192, ACM (2013)
10. Picek, S., Jakobovic, D., Miller, J.F., Marchiori, E., Batina, L.: Evolutionary methods for the construction of cryptographic boolean functions. In: Machado, P., Heywood, M.I., McDermott, J., Castelli, M., García-Sánchez, P., Burelli, P., Risi, S., Sim, K. (eds.) EuroGP 2015. LNCS, vol. 9025, pp. 192–204. Springer, Switzerland (2015)
11. Siegenthaler, T.: Correlation-immunity of nonlinear combining functions for cryptographic applications. IEEE Trans. Inf. Theory **30**(5), 776–780 (1984)
12. Tarannikov, Y.V.: On resilient boolean functions with maximal possible nonlinearity. In: Roy, B., Okamoto, E. (eds.) INDOCRYPT 2000. LNCS, vol. 1977, pp. 19–30. Springer, Heidelberg (2000)
13. Yao, X.: Optimization by genetic annealing. In: Proceedings of the Second Australian Conference on Neural Networks, pp. 94–97, Sydney Univ. Electr. Eng (1991)
14. Zheng, Y., Zhang, X.-M.: Plateaued functions. In: Varadharajan, V., Mu, Y. (eds.) ICICS 1999. LNCS, vol. 1726, pp. 284–300. Springer, Heidelberg (1999)

Hierarchical Clustering of DNA Microarray Data Using a Hybrid of Bacterial Foraging and Differential Evolution

Muhammad Marwan Muhammad Fuad[✉]

Forskningsparken 3, Institutt for Kjemi, NorStruct,
The University of Tromsø - the Arctic University of Norway,
9037 Tromsø, Norway
marwan.fuad@uit.no

Abstract. Microarray technology is one the most important advances in bioinformatics which allows the study of the expression levels of a large number of genes simultaneously. Data mining techniques have been widely applied in order to infer useful knowledge from DNA microarray data. One of these principle techniques is clustering which groups expressed genes according to their similarity. Hierarchical clustering is one of the main clustering methods which represents data in dendrograms. In a previous work the authors used the genetic algorithms to optimize the hierarchical clustering quality based on different clustering measures. In this paper we propose another optimization method based on a hybrid of differential evolution and bacterial foraging optimization algorithm to handle the optimization problem of hierarchical clustering of DNA microarray data. We show through experiments that this hybrid optimization method is more appropriate to tackle this problem than the one which uses the genetic algorithms, as this new method gives a better clustering quality according to different clustering measures.

Keywords: Bacterial foraging optimization algorithm · Differential evolution · DNA microarray data · Genetic algorithms · Hierarchical clustering

1 Introduction

Data mining is one of the major branches of computer science. It handles several tasks, the most important of which are *classification* and *clustering*. In clustering the data are partitioned into groups so that the data objects within a group are similar to one another and dissimilar to the objects in other clusters [1]. The objective of clustering is to segment the entire dataset into relatively homogeneous subgroups or clusters [2].

In general, clustering methods can be grouped in three classes: the first one is *Partitioning Methods*. These methods divide n data objects into k partitions or clusters according to some criterion. The second class is *Hierarchical Methods*. These methods decompose the data in a top-down or a bottom-up approach, and the third class is *Model-Based Methods*, which assume that the data follow a certain probabilistic model. □

© Springer International Publishing Switzerland 2015
A.-H. Dediu et al (Eds.): TPNC 2015, LNCS 9477, pp. 46–57, 2015.
DOI: 10.1007/978-3-319-26841-5_4

The quality of clustering is measured by the error resulting from applying a certain clustering algorithm; the lower the error the higher the clustering quality, so clustering can be formulated as an optimization problem.

Optimization can be defined as follow; given a function of nbp parameters, $f:$ $U \subseteq \mathbb{R}^{nbp} \to \mathbb{R}$ which we call the *fitness function*, find the solution $\overrightarrow{X^*} = \left[x_1^*, x_2^*, \ldots, x_{nbp}^* \right]$ which satisfies $f\left(\overrightarrow{X^*} \right) \leq f(\overrightarrow{X}) \forall \overrightarrow{X} \in U$.

There have been several paradigms to tackle optimization problems. Some of them have been inspired by natural phenomena as a model or a metaphor. These bio-inspired optimization algorithms can generally be divided into two classes. The first is *Evolutionary Algorithms* (EA) which are population-based algorithms that use the mechanisms of Darwinian evolution such as selection, crossover and mutation. Of this family of optimization algorithms we mention *Genetic Algorithm* (GA), *Genetic Programming* (GP), *Evolution Strategies* (ES), and *Differential Evolution* (DE). The second family is *Swarm Intelligence* (SI). These algorithms are inspired by the collective intelligence of natural agents. Of this family we mention *Particle Swarm Optimization* (PSO), *Ant Colony Optimization* (ACO), *Artificial Bee Colony* (ABC), and *Bacterial Foraging Optimization Algorithm* (BFOA).

Bio-inspired optimization has successfully been applied to solve data mining problems such as clustering and classification [3, 4].

In [5] the authors propose using the genetic algorithms for the hierarchical clustering of gene expression data. They conduct experiments to validate their method.

In this paper we propose a hybrid optimization algorithm which is more adapted to handle this optimization problem. We show experimentally that the proposed method gives better results in terms of clustering quality compared with the one based on genetic algorithms.

The rest of the paper is organized as follows; in Sect. 2 we present related work. In Sect. 3 we present the previous method and we introduce the new hybrid method in Sect. 4. We conduct comparative experiments in Sect. 5, and we conclude in Sect. 6.

2 Background

Clustering, also called *unsupervised learning*, is one of the main data mining tasks. In clustering the data are partitioned into groups, or clusters, so that the objects within a cluster are similar to one another and dissimilar to the objects in other clusters [1]. In the language of optimization, clustering aims, simultaneously, to maximize intra-cluster similarity and to minimize inter-clusters similarity.

Clustering can be used as a tool to gain insight into the distribution of data, to observe the characteristics of each cluster, and to focus on a particular set of clusters for further analysis [1].

In computational biology and bioinformatics clustering has applications in transcriptomics, where clustering is used to build groups of genes with related expression patterns. It is also used in sequence analysis to group homologous sequences into gene families [6].

In general, clustering techniques can be divided into three main categories [7]: *Partition-Based Clustering*, *Model-Based Clustering*, and *Hierarchical Clustering*.

2.1   Partition-Based Clustering

The basis of this category of clustering methods is to minimize a certain objective function which is supposed to lead us to the discovery of the structure existing in the dataset. Typically, in this category of methods, we predefine the number of clusters and proceed with the optimization of the objective function [7].

Choosing the objective function is not an easy task as this function should reveal the underlying structure hidden in the data.

Partition-based clustering methods create an initial partitioning. They then use an iterative relocation technique that attempts to improve the partitioning by moving objects from one group to another [1].

2.2   Model-Based Clustering

This category of clustering is based on the assumption that the data follow a certain probabilistic model whose parameters are to be estimated. The structure assumes that the data are a mixture of several sources which are thought of as clusters [7].

2.3   Hierarchical Clustering

Hierarchical clustering builds a hierarchy of clusters producing a graphical representation of data called *dendrogram*. The construction of hierarchical clustering is done in three modes; the first is *bottom-up mode* in which each pattern is treated as a single-element cluster, which is then successively merged with the closest clusters. This process repeats until we get to a single cluster or reach a predefined threshold value. The second mode is *top-down mode*. This mode starts by considering the entire set as a single cluster, and then it keeps splitting it into smaller ones [7].

The third mode is *conceptual mode*. This mode consists in finding clusters that share some common property or represent a particular concept, generating a concept description for each generated class [6]. Figure 1 shows an example of hierarchical clustering.

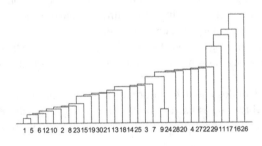

Fig. 1. Hierarchical clustering

3   Applying the Genetic Algorithms to Cluster Microarray Data

Optimization has a wide range of applications in engineering, economics, and science. Bio-inspired optimization algorithms are a large family of stochastic optimization methods inspired by nature. The largest family of bio-inspired optimization methods is Evolutionary Algorithm (EA). EA uses mechanisms derived from the theory of evolution. The most famous of the EA family is the Genetic Algorithm (GA). GA mimics the rules of Darwinian selection in that weaker individuals have less chance of surviving the evolution process than stronger ones. GA captures this concept by adopting a mechanism that preserves the "good" features during the optimization process.

In GA a population of candidate solutions, also called chromosomes, explores the search space and exploits this by sharing information. These chromosomes evolve using genetic operations (selection, recombination, mutation, and replacement). GA starts by randomly initializing a population of chromosomes inside the search space. The fitness function of these chromosomes is evaluated. According to the values of the fitness function new offspring chromosomes are generated through the aforementioned genetic operations. The above steps repeat for a number of generations or until a predefined stopping condition terminates the GA. □

Gene expression profiling is the process of determining when and where particular genes are expressed. Whereas genes and their expressions were studied one at a time, this method is not appropriate for the study of a complete genome because of the interdependence among different genes. Microarray technology is a powerful tool that allows parallel, high-throughput profiling of gene expression in a single hybridization experiment [9].

Clustering of microarray data has been widely used to identify the sets of genes which share similar expression profiles. Genes that are similarly expressed are often co-regulated and involved in the same cellular processes. Therefore, clustering suggests functional relationships between groups of genes [10].

Multi-objective optimization has been used for the fuzzy clustering of microarray gene expression data [8].

In [5] the authors propose a genetic algorithm-based method for hierarchical clustering of DNA microarray data where the chromosomes are dendrograms on a given data set. These dendrograms are built in a bottom-up mode. The authors validate their method experimentally in terms of certain cluster validity measures.

4   Using a Hybrid of Differential Evolution and Bacterial Foraging to Cluster Microarray Data

Hybridization of different optimization algorithms has been extensively used to solve different optimization problems. The main advantage that hybridization offers is that the resulting hybrid method benefits from the strengths of the two methods that constitute it, or it avoids their weaknesses.

GA has the advantage of quickly locating high performance regions of vast and complex search spaces, but it is not well suited for fine-tuning solutions [11, 12].

In order to overcome these limitations of GA we use a more powerful optimizer for the hierarchical clustering of DNA microarray data. This optimizer is a hybrid of two optimization algorithms; *Differential Evolution* and *Bacterial Foraging Optimization Algorithm.*

4.1   Bacterial Foraging Optimization Algorithm (BFOA)

The foraging bahavior of the *Escherichia coli* (*E. coli*) bacteria has inspired an optimization algorithm called *Bacterial Foraging Optimization Algorithm* (BFOA). The motivation behind BFOA is that in order to perform social foraging, an animal needs communication capabilities. Over a period of time this animal gains advantages which exploit the sensing capabilities of the whole group. This helps the group to predate on a larger prey, or it enables the individuals to get better protection against predators [13].

The basis of BFOA is that animals with poor foraging strategies tend to be eliminated by natural selection and they are either replaced by other individuals with better foraging strategies or they are shaped into ones which have these desirable strategies [14]. BFOA formulates this process as an optimization problem.

The *E. coli* bacterium moves by means of a set of flagella, each driven as a biological motor. The two types of movements the *E. coli* bacteria perform are *swimming* and *tumbling*. The former takes place when the flagella rotate in the counterclockwise direction whereas the latter is achieved by rotating the flagella in the clockwise direction. Figure 2 shows these two movement types. Together they are known as *chemotaxis* (which we will define more formally later in this section). The aim of chemotaxis is to help the bacterium approach or avoid nutrient or noxious substance gradients. This chemotaxis progress can be destroyed by sudden environmental changes that cause the elimination and dispersal of a group of bacteria.

BFOA finds the minimum of a function $f(\theta); \theta \in \mathbb{R}^{nbp}$ (*nbp* is the number of parameters) by applying four mechanisms; chemotaxis, swarming, reproduction, and elimination-dispersal.

Flagella rotating counterclockwise: swimming

Flagella rotating clockwise: tumbling

Fig. 2. The swimming and tumbling movements.

The position of each member of the population of N_b bacteria at the jth chemotactic step, k^{th} reproduction step, and l^{th} elimination-dispersal event is denoted by
$$P(i,j,k) = \{\theta^i(j,k,l)|i = 1,2,\ldots,N_b\}$$
We now describe the four mechanisms we mentioned earlier in this section:

- **Chemotaxis:** Let $\theta^i(j,k,l)$ be the ith bacterium at the jth chemotactic step, k^{th} reproduction step, and l^{th} elimination-dispersal event, then the movement of the bacterium can be represented by:

$$\theta^i(j+1,k,l) = \theta^i(j,k,l) + C(i)\frac{\Delta(i)}{\sqrt{\Delta^T(i)\Delta(i)}} \tag{1}$$

where Δ is a vector in the random direction whose elements lie in the interval $[-1,1]$

- **Swarming:** *E. coli* bacteria demonstrate a swarming behavior as they travel in rings which move up the nutrient medium when they are placed at the center of a semisolid matrix with a single nutrient chemo-effecter. When simulated by a high level of succinate the bacteria release an attractant aspartate which helps them aggregate into groups and thus move as a swarm. The cell-to-cell signal in the swam can be represented by the following function:

$$f_{cc}(\theta, P(j,k,l)) = \sum_{i=1}^{N_b} f_{cc}(\theta, \theta^i(j,k,l)) =$$
$$\sum_{i=1}^{N_b}\left[-d_{attractant}.exp\left(-\omega_{attractant}\sum_{m=1}^{nbp}(\theta_m - \theta^i_m)^2\right)\right] + \tag{2}$$
$$\sum_{i=1}^{N_b}\left[-h_{repellant}.exp\left(-\omega_{repellant}\sum_{m=1}^{nbp}(\theta_m - \theta^i_m)^2\right)\right]$$

where the coefficients $d_{attractant}$, $\omega_{attractant}$, $h_{repellant}$, $\omega_{repellant}$ are control parameters.

The objective function $f_{cc}(\theta, P(j,k,l))$ is added to the original objective function to represent a *time varying* objective function in that if many cells come close together there will be a high amount of attractant and hence an increasing likelihood that other cells will move towards the group. This produces the swarming effect [14].

- **Reproduction:** Through this process the least healthy bacteria die out and the healthier ones will replicate themselves. This guarantees that the size of the bacterial swam will remain constant.
- **Elimination and dispersal:** There might be a gradual or sudden change in the environment where the bacteria live. As a result, a small percentage of the bacteria in a certain region will be liquidated or a group might be dispersed into another location. This has two effects on chemotaxis: the first is destroying the chemotactic progress, and the second is that the new bacteria might be placed at locations with a better food source, thus assisting chemotaxis.

4.2 Differential Evolution (DE)

Differential Evolution is an evolutionary optimization algorithm which is particularly adapted to solve continuous optimization problems.

DE starts with a population of *popSize* vectors each of which is of *nbp* dimensions, where *nbp* is the number of parameters. In the next step for each individual $\vec{T}_i$ (called the *target vector*) of the population three mutually distinct individuals $\vec{V}_{r1}, \vec{V}_{r2}, \vec{V}_{r3}$ and different from $\vec{T}_i$ are chosen randomly from the population. The *donor vector* $\vec{D}$ is formed as a weighted difference of two of $\vec{V}_{r1}, \vec{V}_{r2}, \vec{V}_{r3}$ added to the third; i.e.. $\vec{D} = \vec{V}_{r1} + F(\vec{V}_{r2} - \vec{V}_{r3})$. F is called the *mutation factor*.

The *trial vector* $\vec{R}$ is formed from elements of the target vector $\vec{T}_i$ and elements of the donor vector $\vec{D}$ according to different schemes. In this paper we choose the crossover scheme presented in [15]. In this scheme an integer *Rnd* is chosen randomly among the dimensions $[1, nbp]$. Then the trial vector $\vec{R}$ is formed as follows:

$$t_i = \begin{cases} t_{i,r1} + F(t_{i,r2} - t_{i,r3}) & if \ (rand_{i,j}[0, 1[< C_r) \bigvee (Rnd = i) \\ t_{i,j} & otherwise \end{cases} \quad (3)$$

where $i = 1, \ldots, nbp$. C_r is the *crossover constant*. In the next step DE selects which of the trial vector and the target vector will survive in the next generation and which will die out. This selection is based on which of $\vec{T}_i$ and $\vec{R}$ yields a better value of the fitness function. DE continues for a number of generations n.

4.3 A Hybrid of Differential Evolution and Bacterial Foraging

Compared with other bio-inspired optimization algorithms, BFOA possesses a poor convergence behavior over multi-modal and rough fitness landscapes. Its performance is also heavily affected with the growth of problem dimensionality [16]. On the other hand, DE may suffer from *stagnation*; i.e. the inability of progressing towards global optima. DE may also suffer from premature convergence. To overcome these problems the authors of [17] proposed an optimization algorithm, called *Chemotactic Differential Evolution* (CDE), which is based on hybridizing DE and BFOA by integrating some features from both of these optimizers. This hybrid optimization is particularly appropriate for our problem of hierarchical clustering in order to avoid converge to a local optimum and reaching a global optimum.

In CDE each trial vector first undergoes an adaptive computational chemotaxis. The trial vector is viewed as an *E. coli* bacterium. During chemotaxis, the bacterium which is close to a noxious substance takes a larger chemotactic step to move towards nutrient substances. Before each move, it is ensured that the bacterium moves in the direction of increasing nutrient substance concentration; i.e. a region with smaller objective function value. After this, it is subjected to DE mutation. For the trial vector, three vectors, other than the previous one, are selected, one of which is added to a scaled difference of the remaining two. The produced vector probabilistically interchanges its components with the original vector. Offspring vector replaces the original one if the objective function value is smaller for it. The process is repeated several times over the entire population in order to obtain the optimal solution [17].

5 Experiments

The objective of our experiments is to compare the performance of CDE with that of GA on hierarchically clustering DNA microarray data where clustering is handled as an optimization problem whose outcome is the optimal hierarchical clustering of the data.

For the purpose of our experiments we use the same clustering validity measures that were used in the original paper which are *homogeneity*, *separation* and the *Silhouette index*.

Definition-1: Homogeneity of a cluster C_p is defined as:

$$h(C_p) = \frac{2}{m(m-1)} \sum_{\substack{i \neq j}}^{\frac{m(m-1)}{2}} d(i,j), \quad i,j \in C_p \tag{4}$$

Where $d(,)$ is the distance function used in the clustering, and $m = |C_p|$
The homogeneity of a clustering C is defined as:

$$H(C) = \frac{1}{k} \sum_{p=1}^{k} h(C_p) \tag{5}$$

Where $k = |C|$

The quality of clustering increases when the distances among data objects within a cluster are minimal. In other words, the lower the homogeneity value the higher the clustering quality.

We have to mention here that most researchers define homogeneity based on similarity in (Eq. 4) hence they maximize it to get a better clustering quality. But in this paper we compare our method with that presented in (3) where the authors defined (Eq. 4) based on distances, so homogeneity is to be minimized in this case to get a better clustering quality, which is what we did too in this paper.

Definition-2: Separation of a clustering C is defined as:

$$S(C) = \frac{2}{k(k-1)} \sum_{\substack{p \neq q}}^{\frac{k(k-1)}{2}} d_m(C_p, C_q), \quad p,q \in [1,k] \tag{6}$$

The quality of clustering increases when the distances among clusters are maximal. In other words, the higher the separation value the higher the clustering quality.

Definition-3: The *Silhouette index* (SI) was proposed in [18]. It is defined as follows [19]: given a dataset $\{X_1, X_2, \ldots, X_N\}$ which is partitioned into k clusters $\{C_1, C_2, \ldots, C_k\}$. The silhouette width of the ith vector in cluster C_j is given by:

$$S_i^j = \frac{b_i^j - a_i^j}{max\{b_i^j, a_i^j\}} \tag{7}$$

Where

$$a_i^j = \frac{1}{m_j - 1} \sum_{\substack{k=1 \\ k \neq i}}^{m_j} d(X_i^j, X_k^j), \quad i = 1, \ldots, m_j$$

And

$$b_i^j = \min_{\substack{n = 1, \ldots, K \\ n \neq j}} \left\{ \frac{1}{m_n} \sum_{k=1}^{m_n} d(X_i^j, X_k^j) \right\}, \quad i = 1, \ldots, m_j$$

The silhouette of cluster C_j is then defined as:

$$S_j = \frac{1}{m_j} \sum_{i=1}^{m_j} s_i^j \tag{8}$$

And the SI, the global Silhouette index, is given by:

$$SI = \frac{1}{K} \sum_{j=1}^{K} S_j \tag{9}$$

Greater values of SI indicate a better clustering quality. □

As for the fitness function of our hierarchical clustering optimization problem, we use the same fitness function that was used in the original paper: the dendrogram fitness function, which is defined as:

$$f_d(D) = \frac{1}{|D|} \sum_{p=1}^{|D|} f_c(C_p) \tag{10}$$

Where

$$f_c(C) = maxM + S(C) - H(C) \tag{11}$$

Where M is the proximity matrix of the clustered data points.

The Data: The dataset we are using in the experiments is the same dataset used in [5] and it is available at [20]. It is considered as a benchmark dataset for validating different clustering algorithms. The expression matrix is composed of 384 genes

Table 1. Comparison of homogeneity, separation and SI between the five best solutions given by GA and those given by CDE

Clustering Quality Measure	Optimization Algorithm									
	GA					CDE				
	S1	S2	S3	S4	S5	S1	S2	S3	S4	S5
Homogeneity	6.15	6.28	6.16	6.27	6.36	5.38	**4.95**	6.17	5.46	5.59
Separation	15.99	17.02	11.57	28.87	10.37	**31.38**	23.74	24.59	22.29	30.48
SI	36.29	36.33	36.32	37.36	36.40	39.82	38.19	**40.73**	38.90	38.28

evaluated on 17 conditions, labeled into 5 clusters of genes (ground truth) and it was normalized with mean 0 and variance 1 [5].

We use the same protocol that was used in the original paper; i.e. we perform an optimization process twice; once when the optimizer is GA and another when the optimizer is CDE, to get the solutions with the highest value of the fitness function for each optimizer. We calculate the clustering validity measures of these optimal solutions in terms of homogeneity, separation and SI given in (Eqs. 5, 6 and 9), respectively, taking into account that clustering quality increases with higher values of separation and SI and with lower values of homogeneity.

In order to make an unbiased comparison, we run the optimization process five times for each optimizer and we report the optimal solution of each run and for each optimizer (S1,...,S5 in Table 1).

As we can see in Table 1, the performance of CDE is clearly better than that of GA for the three clustering validity measures. Whereas the lowest homogeneity value of GA was 6.15, four out of the five solutions of CDE gave a better (lower) value. Two of the five solutions of CDE also gave better (higher) separation values than those of GA. An interesting remark that we see in Table 1 is the difference of the separation values given by GA which strongly indicates that the optimization algorithm converged prematurely in several cases when GA was used as an optimizer.

As for SI, we also see that all the solutions given by CDE were higher than their GA counterparts.

6   Conclusion

In this work we proposed a hybrid optimization method of differential evolution and bacterial foraging optimization algorithm to optimize the hierarchical clustering quality of DNA microarray data. This clustering quality was measured by using three well-known clustering validity measures which are homogeneity, separation and the Silhouette index. We compared the proposed hybrid method with one proposed in a previous work which uses the genetic algorithms as an optimizer. We showed experimentally how the new hybrid method gives better results on all three clustering validity measures, which makes the hybrid method more adapted to solve this optimization problem for its ability to avoid premature convergence and also in approaching the global optimum.

In the future we plan to tackle this problem as a multi-optimization problem that optimizes the three aforementioned clustering validity measures directly. We believe that the main challenge of this multi-objective problem will be the high computational cost.

References

1. Han, J., Kamber, M., Pei, J.: Data Mining: Concepts and Techniques, 3rd edn. Morgan Kaufmann, San Francisco (2011)
2. Larose, D.T.: Discovering Knowledge in Data: An Introduction to Data Mining. Wiley, New York (2005)
3. Muhammad Fuad, M.M.: Differential evolution-based weighted combination of distance metrics for k-means clustering. In: Dediu, A.-H., Lozano, M., Martin-Vide, C. (eds.) TPNC 2014. LNCS, vol. 8890, pp. 193–204. Springer, Heidelberg (2014)
4. Muhammad Fuad, M.M.: Applying non-dominated sorting genetic algorithm II to multi-objective optimization of a weighted multi-metric distance for performing data mining tasks. In: Mora, A.M., Squillero, G. (eds.) EvoApplications 2015. LNCS, vol. 9028, pp. 579–589. Springer, Heidelberg (2015)
5. Castellanos-Garzón, J., Miguel-Quintales, L.: Evolutionary techniques for hierarchical clustering applied to microarray data. In: Corchado, J.M., De Paz, J.F., Rocha, M.P., Riverola, F.F. (eds.) The 2nd International Workshop on Practical Applications of Computational Biology and Bioinformatics (IWPACBB 2008), vol. 49, pp. 118–127. Advances in Soft Computing 2009 (2009)
6. Gorunescu, F.: Data mining: Concepts, Models and Techniques. Blue Publishing House, Cluj-Napoca (2006)
7. Krzysztof, J.C., Pedrycz, W., Swiniarski, R.W., Kurgan, L.A.: Data Mining: A Knowledge Discovery Approach. Springer-Verlag New York, Inc., Secaucus (2007)
8. Muhammad Fuad, M.M.: Multi-objective optimization for clustering microarray gene expression data - a comparative study. In: Jezic, G., Howlett, R.J., Jain, L.C. (eds.) The 9th International KES Conference on Agents and Multi-Agent Systems: Technologies and Applications - KES-AMSTA-15, June 17–19, 2015, Sorrento, Italy, vol. 38, pp. 123–133. Published in Smart Innovation, Systems and Technologies, Springer, Switzerland (2015)
9. Elloumi, M., Zomaya, A.Y.: Algorithms in Computational Molecular Biology. Wiley, New York (2011)
10. Maulik, U., Bandyopadhyay, S., Mukhopadhyay, A.: Multiobjective Genetic Algorithms for Clustering: Applications in Data Mining and Bioinformatics. Springer, Heidelberg (2011)
11. Gendreau, M., Potvin, J.: Metaheuristics in combinatorial optimization. Ann. Oper. Res. **140**(1), 189–213 (2005)
12. Kazarlis, S., Papadakis, S., Theocharis, J., Petridis, V.: Solving goal programming problems using multi-objective genetic algorithms. IEEE Trans. Evol. Comput. **5**(3), 204–217 (2001)
13. Kim, D.H., Abraham, A., Cho, J.H.: A hybrid genetic algorithm and bacterial foraging approach for global optimization. Inf. Sci. **177**(18), 3918–3937 (2007)
14. Passino, K.M.: Biomimicry of bacterial foraging for distributed optimization and control. IEEE Control Syst. Mag. **22**(3), 52–67 (2002)

15. Feoktistov, V.: Differential Evolution: In Search of Solutions (Springer Optimization and Its Applications). Springer- Verlag New York Inc., Secaucus (2006)
16. Biswas, A., Dasgupta, S., Das, S., Abraham, A.: Synergy of PSO and bacterial foraging optimization-a comparative study on numerical benchmarks. In: Corchado, E., Corchado, J. M., Abraham, A. (eds.) Innovations in Hybrid Intelligent Systems ASC, vol. 44, pp. 255–263. Springer, Heidelberg (2007)
17. Biswas, A., Dasgupta, S., Das, S., Abraham, A.: A synergy of differential evolution and bacterial foraging algorithm for global optimization. Neural Netw. World 17(6), 607–626 (2007)
18. Rousseeuw, P.J.: Silhouettes: a graphical aid to the interpretation and validation of cluster analysis. J. Comp. Appl. Math. 20, 53–65 (1987)
19. Petrovic, S. : A comparison between the silhouette index and the davies-bouldin index in labelling IDS clusters. In: Proceedings of the 11th Nordic Workshop of Secure IT Systems (2006)
20. http://faculty.washington.edu/kayee/cluster

Fault Classification of a Centrifugal Pump in Normal and Noisy Environment with Artificial Neural Network and Support Vector Machine Enhanced by a Genetic Algorithm

Abtin Nourmohammadzadeh[(✉)] and Sven Hartmann

Department of Informatics, Clausthal University of Technology,
Clausthal-Zellerfeld, Germany
{abtin.nourmohammadzadeh,sven.hartmann}@tu.clausthal.de
https://www.in.tu-clausthal.de/

Abstract. Fault diagnosis and detection play a crucial role in every system for its safe operation and long life. Condition monitoring is an applicable and effective method of maintenance techniques in the fault diagnosis of rotating machinery. In this paper two outstanding heuristic classification approaches, namely Artificial Neural Network (ANN) and Support Vector Machine (SVM) with four different kernel functions are applied to classify the condition of a real centrifugal pump belonging to petroleum industry into five different faults through six features which are: flow, temperature, suction pressure, discharge pressure, velocity and vibration. To increase the power of our classifiers, they are trained and tuned by Genetic Algorithm (GA) which is an effective evolutionary optimisation method. The experiments are done once with normal data and another time with noisy data in order to examine how robust the approaches are. Finally, the classification results of ANN-GA, SVM-GA, pure ANN and SVM (without GA enhancements) along with other two practical classification algorithms, namely K-Nearest Neighbours (KNN) and Decisions Tree, are compared together in terms of different aspects.

Keywords: Artificial Neural Network (ANN) · Support Vector Machine (SVM) · Genetic Algorithm (GA) · Fault diagnosis · Centrifugal pump

1 Introduction

The role of centrifugal pumps is of great importance in many industries. Hence, condition monitoring of them is absolutely necessary to prevent early failure, production line breakdown and to improve plant safety, efficiency and reliability. Furthermore, pumps, compressors and piping are causes of the major equipment failure in oil and gas plants. Centrifugal pumps are sensitive to: (1) variation in liquid condition (i.e. viscosity, specific gravity, and temperature), (2) Suction variation, such as pressure and availability of a continuous volume of fluid, and (3) variation in demand. Some of failure reasons are induced by captivation,

ⓒ Springer International Publishing Switzerland 2015
A.-H. Dediu et al. (Eds.): TPNC 2015, LNCS 9477, pp. 58–70, 2015.
DOI: 10.1007/978-3-319-26841-5_5

hydraulic instability, or other system related problems. Others are the direct result of improper maintenance, maintenance-related problems, improper lubrication, misalignment, unbalance, seal leakage, and a variety of others in which machine reliability is periodically affected.

In this research, we use the data of a real centrifugal pump used in a petroleum industry located in the south of Iran. The data consists of 7 columns, the first six are features, i.e. flow, temperature, suction pressure, discharge pressure, velocity and vibration. The last column i s the fault class related to those features ranged from 1 to 5. Table 1 shows an example of the given data and our problem of fault classification.

Table 1. A row of the given data sheet containing values of the six features and the related fault type and under that a row of features without the fault type which should be diagnosed by us.

Flow	Temperature	Suction pressure	Discharge pressure	Velocity	Vibration	Fault type
57	96	20	700	3.5	7.67	3
a	b	c	d	e	f	?

Considering the above explanations, our problem is to devise precise intelligent approaches which receive a number of data sheet's rows, learn the pattern behind the features and given fault types, and finally, are themselves able to detect faults by giving them only the features' values afterwards. Obviously, approaches with less errors or misclassification are more favourable. Due to the fact that failure diagnosis by human is time consuming and human errors may happen, using artificial intelligence and machine learning classification methods has gained popularity to develop a diagnostic scheme. Artificial Neural Networks (ANNs), which are inspired from the biological nervous systems, have been widely used by researchers in the field of classification. Support Vector Machine (SVM) presented by *Vapnik 1995* [15] is a strong classification method based on the Structural Risk Minimisation (RSM). The application of SVM in classification is called Support Vector Classification (SVC). Hence, SVM and SVC mean exactly the same in this paper.

The reminder of this paper is organised as follows: In Sect. 2 a review of the related literature and different methods used for fault classification of pumps and similar devices are presented. Our ANN and SVC approaches are described in Sect. 3. Section 4 contains the results and comparisons of the all methods applied. Finally, conclusions and a recommendation for future research are covered in Sect. 5.

2   Related Work

In this section we aim at presenting an overview of the methods applied to classifying and clustering faults in centrifugal pumps and the likes. Researchers of this field have widely used Artificial Intelligence (AI) due to its applicability and capability in learning complicated patterns and accurate classification. *Sun et al. 2012* [13] review Computational Intelligence (CI) approaches for oil-immersed power transformer maintenance by discussing historical developments and by presenting state-of-the-art fault diagnosis methods.

ANNs, which are of prominent approaches in AI, have been chosen as classifier in many papers. As some examples: *Unal et al. 2014* [14] propose an ANN based fault estimation algorithm verified with experimental tests and promising results. Their ANN model was modified using a genetic algorithm providing an optimal skilful fast-reacting network architecture with improved classification results. In *Azadeh et al. 2013* [2] a unique flexible algorithm is proposed for condition monitoring of a centrifugal pump into two different states based on ANN and SVM with hyper-parameters optimisation.

SVM has gained a considerable popularity among the surveys done in recent years. In *Bacha et al. 2012* [3] an intelligent fault classification with a SVM approach is applied to power transformer Dissolved Gas Analysis (DGA). An application of the SVM in multiclass gear-fault diagnosis is studied by *Bansal et al. 2013* [4]. *Bordoloi & Tiwari 2014* [5] attempt the multi-fault classification of gears by SVM learning technique using frequency domain data. *Fai & Zhang 2014* [6] applied support vector machine with genetic algorithm to fault diagnosis of a power transformer in which genetic algorithm is used to select appropriate free parameters of SVM.

An improved Ant Colony Optimisation (IACO) algorithm is proposed in *Li et al. 2013* [9] to determine the parameters of SVM and then it is applied to the rolling element bearing fault detection. *Gryllias and Antoniadis* [7] propose a hybrid two stage one-against-all SVM approach for the automated diagnosis of defective rolling element bearings. In *Muralidharan et al. 2014* [12] the application of SVM algorithm in the field of fault diagnosis and condition monitoring are discussed. *Wang et al. 2014* [16] develop a noise-based intelligent method for Engine Fault Diagnosis (EFD), so-called HHT–SVM model based on the techniques of Hilbert-Huang Transform (HHT) and Support Vector Machine (SVM). *Zhu et al. 2014* [19] train a multi-class SVM to achieve a prediction model by using Particle Swarm Optimisation (PSO) to seek the optimal parameters.

Other methods are used in this area as well. For instance: The survey of *Lei et al. 2013* [8] summarises the recent research and development of Empirical Mode Decomposition (EMD) in fault diagnosis of rotating machinery. *Azadeh et al. 2010* [1] provide a correct and timely diagnosis mechanism of pump failures by knowledge acquisition through a fuzzy rule-based inference system which could approximate human reasoning. The study of *Muralidharan & Sugumaran 2013* [11] uses vibration signals for fault diagnosis of centrifugal pumps using wavelet analysis. *Zhang and Nadi 2007* [18] propose three Genetic Programming based approaches for solving multi-class classification problems in roller bearing fault detection.

At last it is worth mentioning that although rarely but clustering approaches are used in the field of fault detection. *Zogg et al. 2006* [20] is an example that simplifies known clustering techniques and introduces new vector clustering techniques for faults of heat pumps.

3   Description of the Applied Methods

In this section detailed explanations on the structure of our employed ANN and SVC (SVM) methods are given. Afterwards, we describe how GA is combined with these two classification approaches and illustrate the overall procedure of the devised integrated ANN-GA and SVC-GA algorithms.

3.1   The ANN-GA Framework

In machine learning, Artificial Neural Networks are a family of statistical learning algorithms inspired by biological neural networks. They are mainly used for function approximation, pattern recognition and classification. ANNs are presented as systems of interconnected "neurons" which can compute values and the combination of them leads to a network that can learn a complicated pattern between inputs and outputs. An ANN consists of nodes as neurons in different layers. Each node transmits a final value to nodes of the next layer. This value can be obtained by a function in the node called the activation function. The first layer has neurons equal to the number of inputs, whereas the last layer has neurons equal to the outputs. Between these two layers some hidden layers may exist to boost the ability of the ANN. For our classification problem we need an ANN that receives the values of six features as inputs and diagnoses the fault type based on them. Figure 1 depicts the structure of the applied ANN with nodes and the activation functions to convert a series of features to a fault type. The Network is fed by the six inputs and send them to all of the 3 neurons considered for the next layer. In each neuron i of the middle layer the weighted sum of inputs plus a constant number b_i is computed which is called T_i of the neuron, $T_i = w_{i1}x_1 + w_{i2}x_2 + ... + w_{i6}x_6 + b_i$. The three values resulted from this layer are sent to the last layer consisted of only one neuron. This last neuron acts exactly like the neurons of the previous layer and returns the weighted sum of the received values added by a constant b_4, $E = \sum_{i=1}^{3} l_i T_i + b_4$. Finally E goes through a step function, which determines the final output of the network or the fault class based on the amounts of c_i.

We summarise the main parameters of this network, which have a crucial effect on its performance in matrices:

$$W = \begin{vmatrix} w_{1,1} & w_{1,2} & w_{1,3} \\ w_{2,1} & w_{2,2} & w_{2,3} \\ w_{3,1} & w_{3,2} & w_{3,3} \end{vmatrix}$$

$$B = [b_1, b_2, b_3, b_4] \ , \ L = [l_1, l_2, l_3,] \ , \ C = [c_1, c_2, c_3, c_4].$$

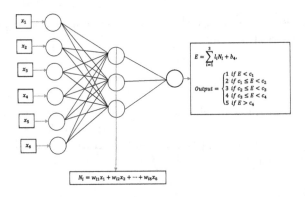

Fig. 1. The structure of the applied ANN for fault classification

Choosing the best amounts for the above parameters can improve the classification performance of the ANN but it is a very difficult task to adjust them on the best or optimal values. Hence, besides the conventional training methods, we apply Genetic Algorithm, which is a powerful evolutionary optimisation algorithm and is able to obtain solution of good qualities in real time. For detailed explanation of GA, readers are referred to *M.D. Vose 1999* [10]. Due the fact that these parameters are continuous, we use the continuous version of GA in which the values of the parameters are considered as genes and they constitute a chromosome together. The initial population is generated by producing 200 chromosomes. The fitness of each chromosome is evaluated based on the below function:

$$Fitness\ function = 1 - percentage\ of\ correct\ predicted\ classes = 1 - \frac{N_c}{N_T}$$

Where N_c is the number of correct predicted faults and N_T is the total number of predictions. The algorithm seeks to minimise the above fitness function iteration by iteration to reach a near optimal solution in the end. The main characteristics of the applied GA are as follows: *Population size* $= 200, Crossover\ percentage = 0.7, Mutation\ percentage = 0.3, Maximum\ of\ Iterations = 100$

Figure 2 illustrates the procedure of our combined ANN-GA algorithm. According to the figure, firstly, the initial amounts of (W, B, L, C) are set. The data sheet is divided to training data set and testing data set. GA begins to optimise the amount of parameters by its selection, crossover and mutation operators. The algorithm terminates by reaching the maximum of iterations and determines the best found values for ANN parameters. Then these values are used for fault detections afterwards.

3.2 The SVM-GA Framework

In SVM (SVC), we have a set of training input $D = \{(x_1, x_2), ..., (x_i, y_i)\}$, where $x \in R^d$ and $y \in \{-1, 1\}$ is the class label, $i = 1, ..., l$. The method seeks to find

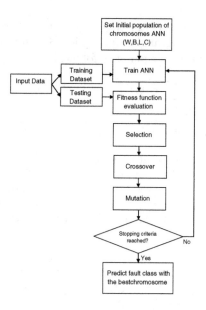

Fig. 2. The procedure of the applied ANN-GA algorithm

a separating hyper plane that maximises the distance to the nearest data points of each class. This goal is met by minimising the following objective function:

$$Max\ \frac{1}{2}\|w\|^2 + C\sum_{i=1}^{l}\varepsilon_i \tag{1}$$

$$Subject\ to\ \ y_i[W^T.\Phi(x_i)] \geq 1 - \varepsilon_i \tag{2}$$

$$\varepsilon_i \geq 0, i = 1, ..., l$$

This model is called soft margin SVM and ε_i handles misclassification, w is a weight vector, b is bias and C is the misclassification penalty to trade-off between the model complicity and training error. In equation (2), $\Phi(x_i)$ is a non-linear function and maps the input data to a high dimensional feature space where data can be separated linearly. Considering necessary condition for optimality, one can turn the above minimization problem into the following dual form:

$$Max\ \sum_{i=1}^{l}\alpha_i - \frac{1}{2}\sum_{i=1}^{l}\sum_{j=1}^{l}\alpha_i\alpha_j K(x_i, x_j) \tag{3}$$

$$Subject\ to\ \sum_{i=1}^{l}\alpha_i y_i = 0 \tag{4}$$

$$0 \leq \alpha_i \leq C, i = 1, ..., l,$$

where $K(x_i, x_j)$ is a kernel function representing the inner product of $\langle \Phi(x_i), \Phi(x_j) \rangle$ and α_i is a Lagrangian multiplier. Solving the dual problem leads to the optimal separating hyper plane as following:

$$\sum_{SV} \alpha_i y_i K(x_i, x_j) + b = 0. \tag{5}$$

The optimal classifying rule is:

$$f = sgn(b + \alpha_i [y_i K(x_i, x_j)]), \tag{6}$$

where SV is the set of support vectors that the corresponding Lagrangian multipliers are positive for them. Figure 3 shows how a soft margin SVM with linear separating hyper plane divides the data into two classes.

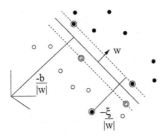

Fig. 3. Linear seperating hyper planes in soft margin SVM

We used the following kernel functions in our SVC for the fault diagnosis of the centrifugal pump:

$$Polynomial : K(x_i, x_j) = (\gamma. <x_i, x_j> +s)^d \tag{7}$$

$$Gaussian\ basis\ function : K(x_i, x_j) = -\gamma.\|x_i - x_j\|^2 \tag{8}$$

$$Linear : K(x_i, x_j) =<x_i, x_j> \tag{9}$$

$$Quadratic : K(x_i, x_j) = (<x_i, x_j> +1)^2 \tag{10}$$

As the parameters, i.e. C, γ, s, of SVM like those of ANN can strongly affect its performance, properly adjusting them can considerably improve it. Hence, other than conventional methods, these parameters are determined with the GA used for ANN. Considering the fact that SVM can only divide the data into two groups and there are 5 fault classes in our problem to be classified, we should implement SVM four times after each other. Each run of SVM classifies one fault from the remaining ones and has its own training process. Figures 4 and 5

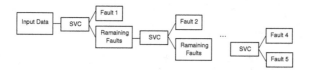

Fig. 4. SVM approach to obtain 5 classes

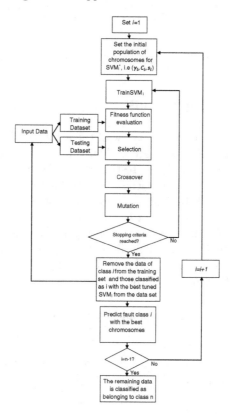

Fig. 5. The procedure of the applied SVM-GA

illustrate the framework of our SVM-GA algorithm. As it is shown by Fig. 5, the initial parameters of SVM are set at first. Then the GA searches in the space of parameter amounts for each of the 4 runs separately and as it terminates for each, it begins with the parameter setting of the next one. Finally, when the parameters have been tuned for all the runs, the procedures ends with the best values found.

Figure 6 illustrates the fitness function values of SVM-GA with Gaussian kernel function from the first up to the last iteration of GA.

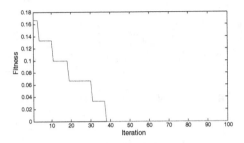

Fig. 6. Fitness function values of SVC-Gaussian-GA

4   Results and Comparisons

In this section we present a brief overview of the achieved results. We have altogether 100 rows of data. For feeding the algorithms, 70 % of data are randomly considered for training and 30 % as testing data. To make the data noisy for testing the robustness of the approaches, 0.1 is added to 30 % of columns 1, 3, and 6 of the data sheet. Table 2 shows percentage of correct fault diagnosis of pure GA and SVM methods without GA improvements and Fig. 7 depicts this amounts visually. SVM-Gaussian has the best performance and a good robustness. SVC-Linear is in the second position but it has the highest robustness among all. SVC-Quadratic, ANN and SVC-Polynomial are in the next ranks. It is worth mentioning that ANN has the worst robustness.

Table 2. Correct diagnosis proportion of the pure ANN and SVM

	ANN	SVM			
		Linear	Quadratic	Gaussian	Polynomial
Normal	0.8	0.866	0.833	0.933	0.8
Noisy	0.7	0.8333	0.766	0.866	0.733

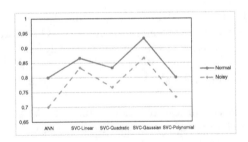

Fig. 7. Correct diagnosis of the pure ANN and SVM with Normal and Noisy Data

To show the superiority of our ANN-GA and SVM-GA, the diagnosis experiments are also done with K-Nearest Neighbours (KNN) and Decision Tree, which are of high rated classification methods. Table 3 and Fig. 8 show these performance comparisons. According to the results, SVM-Gaussian has again the best performance among all and GA enhancement has enabled it to detect faults in all cases correctly both in normal and noisy environment. Therefore, it is the most robust as well, together with SVM-GA-linear. ANN-GA performs worse than SVM-GA with all the kernels in terms of correctness, and considering robustness, SVM-GA is superior except for the case of polynomial function which results almost the same as ANN-GA. Finally, the worst diagnosis performances belong to KNN and Decision Tree.

Table 3. Correct diagnosis proportion of ANN-GA, SVM-GA, KNN and Decision Tree with Normal and Noisy Data

	ANN-GA	SVM-GA				KNN	Decision Tree
		Linear	Quadratic	Gaussian	Polynomial		
Normal	0.866	0.9	0.833	0.933	1	0.9	0.666
Noisy	0.733	0.9	0.866	1	0.766	0.533	0.5

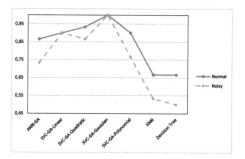

Fig. 8. Correct diagnosis proportion of ANN-GA, SVM-GA, KNN and Decision Tree with Normal and Noisy Data

To show the GA effects on ANN and SVM, the performance improvements are depicted by Fig. 9. The largest improvement is for SVM-Gaussian in noisy condition and lowest for SVM-Polynomial in noisy condition.

For Comparisons of the methods in detail, McNemar's tests are executed and the results are tabulated as Table 4 to examine which model outperforms the others significantly. McNemar's is a nonparametric statistical test for two related nominal samples with a null hypothesis of marginal homogeneity in 2×2 contingency tables. A detailed explanation on McNemar's test is provided in *Webb et al. 2011* [17]. If the significance level is set to 10%, then a p-value

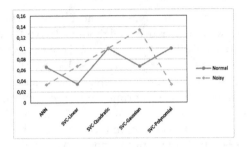

Fig. 9. The improvement of methods by GA

less than 0.1 shows that models vary significantly. The tests for SVC and SVC-GA are done with their best kernel function which is Gaussian according to the accuracy results.

Table 4. MCNemar's test results (p-values)

	ANN-GA	SVM	ANN	Decision Tree	KNN
Normal environment					
SVC-GA	0.1336	0.4795	0.0412	0.0044	0.0044
ANN-GA		0.6171	0.4795	0.0771	0.0412
SVC			0.1336	0.0133	0.0133
ANN				0.1138	0.0771
Decision Tree					0.7518
Noisy environment					
SVC-GA	0.1333	0.1336	0.0077	0.0003	0.0003
ANN-GA		0.2207	1	0.0455	0.0771
SVC			0.1306	0.0026	0.0044
ANN				0.771	0.1824
Decision tree					1

At the end of this section, we perform 10-fold cross-validation to evaluate the validity of models. For this sake, the data sheet is divided into 10 even subsets, then each of them is once used as the test dataset and the other 9 as training dataset. Finally, the averages of models' accuracies (proportion of correct predicted fault types) are considered for models' validity evaluation. The average of models' accuracies are presented in Table 5.

5   Conclusion

In this paper we presented fault classification algorithms by combination of two intelligent machine learning methods, namely ANN and SVM, with Genetic

Table 5. Average of accuracies in 10 fold

	Normal environment	Noisy environment
SVC-GA	0.95	0.95
SVC	0.9	0.85
ANN-GA	0.85	0.75
ANN	0.85	0.8
KNN	0.6	0.6
Decision tree	0.6	0.5

Algorithm. The results showed that GA can significantly improve the performance of the classifiers. The performances of all employed algorithms, i.e. ANN, ANN-GA, SVC, SVC-GA, KNN and Decision Tree, were compared by different tests in normal and noisy condition. The comparisons showed that SVM with Gaussian kernel function had the best accuracy in correct fault diagnosis and an excellent robustness against noise. It was also observed that SVM is superior to ANN in most of the cases. For future research in this direction, testing the ability of other optimisation algorithms to improve ANN, SVM and other classification methods is recommended.

References

1. Azadeh, A., Ebrahimipour, V., Bavar, P.: A fuzzy inference system for pump failure diagnosis to improve maintenance process: the case of a petrochemical industry. Expert Syst. Appl. 37(1), 627–639 (2010). http://dx.doi.org/10.1016/j.eswa.2009.06.018
2. Azadeh, A., Saberi, M., Kazem, A., Ebrahimipour, V., Nourmohammadzadeh, A., Saberi, Z.: A flexible algorithm for fault diagnosis in a centrifugal pump with corrupted data and noise based on ANN and support vector machine with hyperparameters optimization. Appl. Soft Comput. J. 13(3), 1478–1485 (2013). http://dx.doi.org/10.1016/j.asoc.2012.06.020
3. Bacha, K., Souahlia, S., Gossa, M.: Power transformer fault diagnosis based on dissolved gas analysis by support vector machine. Electric Power Syst. Res. 83(1), 73–79 (2012). http://dx.doi.org/10.1016/j.epsr.2011.09.012
4. Bansal, S., Sahoo, S., Tiwari, R., Bordoloi, D.: Multiclass fault diagnosis in gears using support vector machine algorithms based on frequency domain data. Measurement 46(9), 3469–3481 (2013). http://www.sciencedirect.com/science/article/pii/S0263224113002078
5. Bordoloi, D.J., Tiwari, R.: Optimum multi-fault classification of gears with integration of evolutionary and SVM algorithms. Mech. Mach. Theor. 73, 49–60 (2014). http://dx.doi.org/10.1016/j.mechmachtheory.2013.10.006
6. Fei, S.W., Zhang, X.B.: Fault diagnosis of power transformer based on support vector machine with genetic algorithm. Expert Syst. Appl. 36(8), 11352–11357 (2009). http://dx.doi.org/10.1016/j.eswa.2009.03.022

7. Gryllias, K.C., Antoniadis, I.A.: A support vector machine approach based on physical model training for rolling element bearing fault detection in industrial environments. Eng. Appl. Artif. Intell. 25(2), 326–344 (2012). http://dx.doi.org/10.1016/j.engappai.2011.09.010

8. Lei, Y., Lin, J., He, Z., Zuo, M.J.: A review on empirical mode decomposition in fault diagnosis of rotating machinery. Mech. Syst. Sig. Process. 35(1–2), 108–126 (2013). http://dx.doi.org/10.1016/j.ymssp.2012.09.015

9. Li, X., Zheng, A., Zhang, X., Li, C., Zhang, L.: Rolling element bearing fault detection using support vector machine with improved ant colony optimization. Meas. J. Int. Meas. Confederation 46, 2726–2734 (2013)

10. Voser, M.D.: The Simple Genetic Algorithm: Foundation and Theory. MIT Press, Cambridge (1999)

11. Muralidharan, V., Sugumaran, V.: Rough set based rule learning and fuzzy classification of wavelet features for fault diagnosis of monoblock centrifugal pump. Measurement: Journal of the International Measurement Confederation 46(9), 3057–3063 (2013). http://dx.doi.org/10.1016/j.measurement.2013.06.002

12. Muralidharan, V., Sugumaran, V., Indira, V.: Fault diagnosis of monoblock centrifugal pump using SVM. Int. J. Eng. Sci. Technol. 17(3), 1–6 (2014). http://linkinghub.elsevier.com/retrieve/pii/S2215098614000275

13. Sun, H.C., Huang, Y.C., Huang, C.M.: Fault Diagnosis of power transformers using computational intelligence: a review. Energy Procedia 14, 1226–1231 (2012). http://dx.doi.org/10.1016/j.egypro.2011.12.1080

14. Unal, M., Onat, M., Demetgul, M., Kucuk, H.: Fault diagnosis of rolling bearings using a genetic algorithm optimized neural network. Measurement 58, 187–196 (2014). http://linkinghub.elsevier.com/retrieve/pii/S0263224114003601

15. Vapnik, V.N.: The Nature of Statistical Learning Theory. Springer, New York (1995)

16. Wang, Y.S., Ma, Q.H., Zhu, Q., Liu, X.T., Zhao, L.H.: An intelligent approach for engine fault diagnosis based on Hilbert-Huang transform and support vector machine. Appl. Acoust. 75, 1–9 (2014)

17. Webb, A.: Statistical Pattern Recognition. Wiley, New York (2011)

18. Zhang, L., Nandi, A.K.: Fault classification using genetic programming. Mech. Syst. Sig. Process. 21(3), 1273–1284 (2007)

19. Zhu, K., Song, X., Xue, D.: A roller bearing fault diagnosis method based on hierarchical entropy and support vector machine with particle swarm optimization algorithm. Measurement 47, 669–675 (2014). http://www.sciencedirect.com/science/article/pii/S0263224113004569

20. Zogg, D., Shafai, E., Geering, H.P.: Fault diagnosis for heat pumps with parameter identification and clustering. Control Eng. Pract. 14(12), 1435–1444 (2006)

Evolutionary Approach for Finding Correlation Immune Boolean Functions of Order t with Minimal Hamming Weight

Stjepan Picek[1], Sylvain Guilley[2,3], Claude Carlet[4,5],
Domagoj Jakobovic[6]([✉]), and Julian F. Miller[7]

[1] ESAT/COSIC and IMinds, KU Leuven, Kasteelpark Arenberg 10,
Bus 2452, 3001 Leuven-heverlee, Belgium
[2] TELECOM-ParisTech, 46 rue Barrault, 75634 Paris Cedex 13, France
[3] Secure-IC S.A.S., ZAC des Champs Blancs, 15, rue Claude
Chappe - Bât. B, 35510 Cesson-Sévigné, France
[4] LAGA, UMR 7539, CNRS, Department of Mathematics, University of Paris 8,
2 Rue de la Liberté, 93526 Saint-Denis Cedex, France
[5] LAGA, UMR 7539, CNRS, Department of Mathematics,
University of Paris 13, Villetaneuse, France
[6] Faculty of Electrical Engineering and Computing,
University of Zagreb, Zagreb, Croatia
`domagoj.jakobovic@fer.hr`
[7] Department of Electronics, University of York, York, UK

Abstract. The role of Boolean functions is prominent in several areas like cryptography, sequences and coding theory. Therefore, various methods to construct Boolean functions with desired properties are of direct interest. When concentrating on Boolean functions and their role in cryptography, we observe that new motivations and hence new properties have emerged during the years. It is important to note that there are still many design criteria left unexplored and this is where Evolutionary Computation can play a distinct role. One combination of design criteria that has appeared recently is finding Boolean functions that have various orders of correlation immunity and minimal Hamming weight. Surprisingly, most of the more traditionally used methods for Boolean function generation are inadequate in this domain. In this paper, we concentrate on a detailed exploration of several evolutionary algorithms and their applicability for this problem. Our results show that such algorithms are a viable choice when evolving Boolean functions with minimal Hamming weight and certain order of correlation immunity. This approach is also successful in obtaining Boolean functions with several values that were known previously to be theoretically optimal, but no one succeeded in finding actual Boolean functions with such values.

Keywords: Boolean functions · Cryptography · Correlation immunity · Hamming weight · Evolutionary algorithms

© Springer International Publishing Switzerland 2015
A.-H. Dediu et al. (Eds.): TPNC 2015, LNCS 9477, pp. 71–82, 2015.
DOI: 10.1007/978-3-319-26841-5_6

1 Introduction

One usual source (although not the only one) of nonlinearity in ciphers are Boolean functions. In block ciphers, the nonlinearity often comes from Substitution Boxes or S-boxes which are actually a number of Boolean functions (hence, also the name vectorial Boolean functions). On the other hand, in stream ciphers the nonlinearity comes from Boolean functions. Both of those scenarios, while not the only ones, show us the prominent role of Boolean functions in cryptography. Finding Boolean functions fitting all the criteria and analyzing the best possible trade-offs between these criteria are still crucial questions today.

Historically, Boolean functions have been dominantly used in conjunction with Linear Feedback Shift Registers (LFSRs). Two commonly used models are filter generators and combiner generators. In a combiner generator, several LFSRs are used in parallel and their output is the input for a Boolean function. On the other hand, in a filter generator, the output is obtained by a nonlinear combination of a number of positions in a longer LFSR [3]. To be effective such Boolean functions need to be balanced, have high nonlinearity, large algebraic degree, large algebraic immunity, and high correlation immunity (in the case of combiner generators).

To obtain such functions, there exist a number of construction methods. Those methods can be roughly divided into algebraic constructions, random search, heuristics and combinations of those methods [19]. In this paper, we examine one branch of heuristics, more precisely Evolutionary Algorithms (EAs), in order to evolve Boolean functions. It is worth mentioning that EAs can be used either as the primary or the secondary construction method. In primary constructions one obtains new functions without using known ones. In secondary constructions, one uses already known Boolean functions to construct new ones (either with different properties or sizes) [3].

We said that a Boolean function needs to be balanced (among other criteria) to be suitable for cryptography. Indeed, this is true, but only when we consider the role of Boolean functions in filter and combiner generators. However, recently one more application emerged where we are actually interested in Boolean functions that have minimal Hamming weight and are therefore as far as possible from being balanced. Such Boolean functions can be used to help resist side-channel attacks.

Side-channel attacks do not rely on the security of the underlying algorithm, but rather on the implementation of the algorithm in a device [13]. One class of countermeasures against side-channel attacks are masking schemes. In masking schemes one randomizes the intermediate values that are processed by the cryptographic device. One obvious drawback of such an approach is the masking overhead which can be substantial in embedded devices or smart cards.

Correlation immune Boolean functions can reduce the masking overhead either by applying leakage squeezing method [4,6] or with Rotating S-box masking [5]. We emphasize that a number of construction methods (primarily algebraic constructions) are not suitable for these design criteria since they produce balanced Boolean functions.

Up to now, there has been almost no work to examine how to evolve Boolean functions with various orders of correlation immunity and minimal Hamming weight. This is the gap this paper aims to rectify. In order to do so, we experiment with several algorithms, both from the single objective and the multi-objective optimization area. More precisely, we use Genetic Algorithms (GAs), Genetic Programming (GP), Cartesian Genetic Programming (CGP), and NSGA-II. Our investigation has a twofold impact since we offer a detailed examination of the EAs performance on the aforementioned problem. Furthermore, we find values previously completely unknown for certain Boolean function sizes and orders of the correlation immunity property.

1.1   Related Work

There exist a number of works that examine Boolean functions in cryptography and their generation with Evolutionary Computation (EC) techniques. Here, we give only a small subset of works related to our investigation.

Millan et al. work with GAs in order to evolve Boolean functions with high nonlinearity [15]. Burnett in her thesis uses GAs to evolve both Boolean functions and Substitution boxes [2]. McLaughlin and Clark use simulated annealing to evolve Boolean functions that have several cryptographic properties with optimal values [14]. Picek, Jakobovic and Golub experiment with GP and GAs to find Boolean functions that have several optimal properties [18]. Picek et al. experiment with both heuristics and heuristics in conjunction with algebraic construction to evolve Boolean functions with high nonlinearity [20]. Picek et al. use CGP to evolve Boolean functions with eight inputs and high nonlinearity [19]. Finally, Picek et al. investigate several EAs in order to evolve Boolean functions with different values of the correlation immunity property. In the same paper, the authors also discuss the problem of finding correlation immune functions with minimal Hamming weight, but they experiment only with Boolean functions that have eight inputs [17].

The remainder of this paper is organized as follows. In Sect. 2, we describe relevant cryptographic properties and representations of Boolean functions. Section 3 represents the techniques for using Boolean functions in masking schemes as well as our motivation for this research. In Sect. 4, experimental setup and the algorithms we use are given. Section 5 presents the results and a short discussion. Finally, Sect. 6 concludes and gives some suggestions for future work.

2   Introduction to Boolean Functions and Their Properties

Let n, m be positive integers, i.e. $n, m \in \mathbb{N}^+$. The set of all n-tuples of the elements in the field $\mathbb{F}_2$ is denoted as $\mathbb{F}_2^n$ where $\mathbb{F}_2$ is the Galois field with 2 elements. The inner product of two vectors a and b is denoted as $a \cdot b$ and equals $a \cdot b = \oplus_{i=1}^{n} a_i b_i$. Here, "$\oplus$" represents addition modulo two (bitwise XOR). The Hamming weight (HW) of a vector a, where $a \in \mathbb{F}_2^n$, is the number of non-zero positions in the vector.

An (n, m)-function is any mapping F from $\mathbb{F}_2^n$ to $\mathbb{F}_2^m$. If m equals 1 then the function f is called a Boolean function.

A Boolean function f on $\mathbb{F}_2^n$ can be uniquely represented by a truth table (TT), which is a vector $(f(\mathbf{0}), ..., f(\mathbf{1}))$ that contains the function values of f, ordered lexicographically, i.e. $\mathbf{a} \leq \mathbf{b}$ [3].

The support $supp(a)$ of a vector a is the index set of the non-zero positions in a, i.e. $supp(a) = \{i : a_i \neq 0\}$, and the support $supp(f)$ of a Boolean function f is the vector set of the non-zero entries in the truth table (TT) representation of f, i.e. $supp(f) = \{x : f(x) \neq 0\}$ [3]. The HW of a Boolean function f is the cardinality of its support.

The Walsh-Hadamard transform W_f is a second unique representation of a Boolean function that measures the correlation between $f(\mathbf{x})$ and the linear function $\mathbf{a} \cdot \mathbf{x}$ [3]:

$$W_f(\mathbf{a}) = \sum_{\mathbf{x} \in \mathbb{F}_2^n} (-1)^{f(\mathbf{x}) \oplus \mathbf{a} \cdot \mathbf{x}}. \tag{1}$$

A Boolean function f is correlation immune of order t (in brief, $CI(t)$) if the output of the function is statistically independent of the combination of any t of its inputs [21]. For the Walsh-Hadamard spectrum it holds equivalently [10]:

$$W_f(\mathbf{a}) = 0, \text{ for } 1 \leq HW(\mathbf{a}) \leq t. \tag{2}$$

3   Boolean Functions and Masking

Some applications manipulate sensitive data, such as cryptographic keys. Obviously, these should remain secret. However, skillful attackers might try to probe bits within a processor or a memory; they often succeed, unless countermeasures are implemented [9].

To protect secrets from probing attempts, it is customary to implement a countermeasure known as masking. It consists in changing randomly the representation of the key (and of any other data which depends on the key), so as to deceive the attacker. For example, if each bit k_i, $1 \leq i \leq n$ of a key k is masked with a random bit m_i, then an attacker could probe $k_i \oplus m_i$. However, provided m_i is uniformly distributed, the knowledge of $k_i \oplus m_i$ does not disclose any information on bit k_i, unless of course the attacker can also probe separately m_i, in which case a higher order masking would be necessary.

However, for implementation reasons, it is often impractical to mask each bit individually. Indeed, the generation of random numbers is costly, thus it is desirable to limit the number of random bits required. Furthermore, masking each bit of a vector of length n would correspond to choosing the global mask in the whole set of 2^n possible masks, which may be too costly.

Specifically, on the example of the AES cipher, some key bytes are mixed with plaintext bytes before entering a Substitution box. Generating all the 256 Substitution boxes suitable for all possible masks in $\mathbb{F}_2^8$ is too expensive for embedded systems. Hence, by restricting the number of possible masks, the overhead incurred by the countermeasure becomes more affordable.

Let us consider the simple example of masking one byte ($n = 8$). This can be achieved by using two complementary masks, such as $m_0 = (00000000)_2$ and $m_1 = (11111111)_2$. An attacker who measures one bit of the masked byte cannot derive any information about the corresponding unmasked bit. If we define by f the Boolean function $\mathbb{F}_2^8 \rightarrow \mathbb{F}_2$ whose support is $\{m_0, m_1\}$, then f plays its masking role as it is balanced: any bit can take value 0 and 1 with equal probability. In general, any Boolean function which is $CI(1)$ is a valid masking.

Let us now consider a stronger attacker who is able to probe two bits simultaneously. In this case, some information can be recovered. Typically, if the two masked bits are equal, then so are the two unmasked bits. So, by testing all pairs of bits, the attacker can recover the whole key (or its complement). It happens that, against such "second-order attacker", it would be desirable that the masks be the support of a $CI(2)$ Boolean function [6]. But clearly, this support must have a cardinality strictly greater than 2. Hence, masking can be summarized as the problem of finding Boolean functions whose support is a set of masks with the two following constraints:

1. it should have small Hamming weight, for implementation reasons, and
2. it should have high correlation immunity t, in a view to resist an attacker with multiple ($\leq t$) probes.

Clearly, there is a tradeoff. This motivates the research for low Hamming weight high correlation immunity Boolean functions.

Some work on this topic has been summarized by Hedayat, Sloane and Stufken in their book [11]. However, in this book, some entries (minimum Hamming weight for a given pair (n, t)) are expressed as non-tight bounds. Recently, the exact value for entries corresponding to ($n = 9, t = 4$), and ($n = 10, t \in \{4, 5\}$) have been obtained by Carlet and Guilley in [6]. Still, the exact values $(n, t) \in \{(11, 4 - 5), (12, 4 - 6), (13, 4 - 7)\}$ that are of practical interest, have remained unknown until this research.

4   Experimental Setup

In this section, we briefly present the algorithms we use as well as the experimental setup and fitness functions.

4.1   Single Objective Optimization

Genetic Algorithm. The GA represents the individuals as strings of bits representing truth tables of Boolean functions. We use a simple GA with elimination tournament selection with size 3 [8]. A mutation is selected uniformly at random between a simple mutation, where a single bit is inverted, and a mixed mutation, which randomly shuffles the bits in a randomly selected subset. The crossover operators are one-point and uniform crossover, performed uniformly at random for each new offspring. For each of the fitness functions we experiment with population sizes of 50, 100, 500, and 1 000 and mutation probabilities of 0.1, 0.3, 0.5, 0.7, and 0.9.

Genetic Programming. GP uses a representation where individuals are trees of Boolean primitives which are then evaluated according to the truth table they produce. The function set for GP in all experiments is OR, XOR, AND, XNOR, and AND with one input inverted. Terminals correspond to n Boolean variables. Boolean functions may be represented with only XOR and AND operators, but it is quite easy to transform it from one notation to the other. GP uses a tournament selection with tournament size 3 [12]. We use a simple tree crossover with 90 % bias for functional nodes and a subtree mutation. We experiment with tree depth sizes of 5, 7, 8, and 9 and population sizes of 100, 200, 500, 1 000, and 2 000.

Cartesian Genetic Programming. The function set n_f for the CGP is the same as for the GP. Setting the number of rows to be 1 and levels-back parameter to be equal to the number of columns is regarded as the best and most general choice [16]. We experiment with genotype sizes of 500, 1 000, 2 000, and 3 000 and mutation rates of 1 %, 4 %, 7 %, 10 %, and 13 %. The number of input connections n_n for each node is two and the number of program output connections n_o is one. The population size for CGP equals five in all our experiments. For CGP individual selection we use a $(1 + 4)$-ES in which offspring are favored over parents when they have a fitness better than or equal to the fitness of the parent. The mutation operator is one-point mutation where the mutation point is chosen with a fixed probability. The number of genes mutated is defined as fixed percentage of the total number of genes. CGP solutions are directed graphs with Boolean primitives as nodes, that are also evaluated using the truth table they produce.

Fitness Function. The following fitness function for single objective optimization is obtained after a set of experiments where we determined which one performed best on average. The goal is **maximization**:

$$fitness = (MAX\_HW - supp) - MAX\_HW \times |CI - TARGET\_CI|. \quad (3)$$

Here, MAX_HW represents the Hamming weight of a Boolean function that has all ones in its truth table (i.e. $HW = 2^n$, where n represents the number of inputs of a Boolean function), $TARGET\_CI$ represents the order of correlation immunity we want to find and finally, $supp$ represents the cardinality of the support of a Boolean function. The function consists of two parts: the first part rewards Boolean functions with smaller support, while the second part acts as a penalty for solutions with a correlation immunity that differs from the target. The penalty part is multiplied with maximum value of the reward part, so that any solution with the right CI is always better than any other solution with different CI. This way, the distance to the target CI is regarded as a constraint, and the support as a secondary objective.

4.2 Multi-Objective Optimization

Since the goal of the function design includes two criteria, it can be formulated as a multi-objective optimization problem. The first objective is attaining a desired target correlation immunity, and the second one is the minimization of the support. Following these criteria, a multi-objective problem can be formulated as:

$$fitness_A = |CI - TARGET\_CI|; \tag{4}$$
$$fitness_B = MAX\_HW - supp, \tag{5}$$

where the first criteria, $fitness_A$, is **minimized**, while the second criteria, $fitness_B$, is **maximized**.

In our experiments we applied the well known NSGA-II algorithm for multi-objective optimization [7]. Note that NSGA-II can be paired with any of the Boolean representations (i.e. truth table in GA, tree in GP and graph in CGP), but based on the performance in the initial round of experiments, we only present the results of tree representation (GP) with multi-objective evolution.

4.3 Common Parameters

The number of independent runs for each experiment is 50. The function set n_f for both GP and CGP in all the experiments is OR, XOR, AND, XNOR, and AND with one input inverted. For stopping condition we use the number of evaluations which we set to 1 000 000.

5 Results and Discussion

We report the performance of the selected algorithms, and additionally present the best obtained values in order to compare EC with the existing results. For the first part, the evolutionary algorithms are compared with each other using basic statistical indicators to assess their performance. The comparison between EAs is carried out using the parameter combinations that fill the gaps in the recent work [6], i.e. for functions with the number of bits n and correlation immunity t in the set $(n, t) \in \{(11, 4 - 5), (12, 4 - 6), (13, 4 - 7)\}$.

For the second part, we only select the single best results obtained by any algorithm and compare it with the values found in the related literature. Since there is a large number of experiments, we conduct a parameter tuning phase for a medium sized Boolean function of nine inputs and the correlation immunity order of two. Parameter tuning phase has a stopping condition of 500 000 evaluations. Later we use the best obtained set of parameters for all test scenarios. Due to the lack of space, we do not present exhaustively the tuning phase results.

5.1 Genetic Algorithm

The results for GA in this application were very poor; in the tuning phase, where we test different parameters for Boolean functions of 9 bits and target correlation immunity equal to the value of two, we were unable to obtain a single solution with the desired correlation immunity for any of the parameter settings. The GA with the truth table representation does succeed in finding the desired values, but only for very small problem sizes (e.g. for up to six variables), where the size of the solution is not large. However, since those cases are not representative to the problem, we do not experiment with GA in the rest of the paper.

5.2   Genetic Programming

Based on the results of the parameter tuning phase, the best performance for GP was obtained with a maximum tree depth of five, whereas there were practically no differences with regards to the population size. Based on this, we continued with depth five and the population size of 1 000.

However, since the tuning was performed on 9 bit functions, we note that for larger sizes (e.g. 12 or 13 bits), the maximum depth of five may simply be not enough to represent the desired behavior. Indeed, while with the depth of seven and the same number of evaluations we obtain *statistically* worse solutions in general, there were cases where a single best solution was reached with a depth of 7. This is further explored in Sect. 5.5, while for the algorithm comparison we remain with the depth of 5 where the results are given in Table 1.

Table 1. Results for GP (single objective, maximization)

n \ t	4	5	6	7
11	1 830.4/1 920/15	1 643.52/1 792/21		
12	3 840/3 840/50	3 507.2/3840/5	2 928.64/3 072/43	
13	7 680/7 680/50	7 383.04/7 680/37	6021.12/6144/47	5 324.8/6 144/30

The results for each combination of n and t are reported in the form of $avg/max/\#hits$, where avg represents the average best fitness value over 50 runs, max is the single best fitness value, and $\#hits$ is the number of runs in which the best value was reached. We chose this simple statistic because the fitness often assumes negative values (due to the penalty part in the fitness function) which are not very indicative, and since the observed algorithms often reach the same maximum value.

5.3   Cartesian Genetic Programming

In the case of CGP, the best parameters after the tuning phase were mutation probability of 13 % and the genotype size of 500. The results of CGP with the obtained parameter settings are given in Table 2, with the same nomenclature as in Table 1. Negative value means that on average most of the runs did not succeed in finding any solutions with the $TARGET\_CI$ value. This suggests that the number of evaluations was too low for those problem instances.

Table 2. Results for CGP (single objective, maximization)

t / n	4	5	6	7
11	1218.56/1 792/4	901.12/1 536/6		
12	2 549.76/3 584/9	1 515.52/3 072/6	-532.48/2 048/28	
13	4 587.52/7 168/2	1 638.4/6 144/8	-819.2/4 096/20	-3 604.48/4 096/3

5.4 Multi-objective Genetic Programming

In the last phase, we used NSGA-II multi-objective algorithm to try to reach the desired output while regarding both correlation immunity and Hamming weight as independent objectives. Although the name implies a genetic algorithm, in this work the multi-objective approach is used with tree-based representation of GP, since it exhibited the best performance.

The results for the multi-objective approach were disappointing; in most cases, the algorithm was unable to reach the desired target CI value, while the secondary objective was very bad even in the other cases. We found solutions only in cases when $n = 12$ and $CI = 4$ where the support equals 2 048 and when $n = 13$ and $CI = 4$ with the support equal to 4 096. In the first case the value was found three times, and in the second, only once.

5.5 Discussion

Finally, we combine all the single best values we obtained with any evolutionary algorithm and present them in Table 3. In this table the values are not represented with our fitness function, in which the expression $(MAX\_HW - supp)$ was maximized, but rather only as the resulting support ($supp$), since this form was used in the existing work (note that in this case the smaller values are the better ones). These best EC results are equal to those presented in Tables 1 and 2, with the exception of 13 bits and correlation immunity 6, where GP with depth 7 obtained a better result.

This paper reports results for Boolean functions which were previously unknown. These are indicated using gray cells in Table 3. When discussing the optimality of those results, we follow the conjectures from [1].

Here, $w_{n,t}$ represents the lowest weight of $CI(t)$ nonzero function of n variables. The conjecture was made in [1, Sec. C.2] that the values in each column of Table 3 are non-decreasing. The values for $(n, t) \in \{(11, 4 - 5)\}$ in Table 3 are interesting from this viewpoint: if the conjecture is true then they are optimal since they cannot be smaller than for $(n, t) \in \{(10, 4 - 5)\}$, but the conjecture may be false; further investigations are needed to clarify this point. If $(n, t) \in \{(11, 4 - 5)\}$ represent the minimal possible values; then since it is known from [1, Sec. C.1] that $w_{n,t} \geq 2w_{n-1,t-1}$, then the solution for $n = 12$ and $t \in \{5, 6\}$ has also a minimal Hamming weight. Finally, for $n = 13$, by following the same reasoning, Hamming weights for $t \in \{6, 7\}$ are again the optimal

Table 3. Best obtained results.

n \ t	1	2	3	4	5	6	7	8	9	10	11	12	13
5	2	8	16	16	32								
6	2	8	16	32	32	64							
7	2	8	16	64	64	*128*	128						
8	2	*16*	16	64	128	128	*256*	256					
9	2	*16*	*32*	128	128	256	256	*512*	512				
10	2	*16*	*32*	128	256	512	512	x	*1 024*	1 024			
11	2	*16*	*32*	128	256	512	1 024	1 024	x	2 048	2 048		
12	2	16	*32*	256	256	1 024	1 024	x	x	x	*4 096*	4 096	
13	2	16	32	*256*	*512*	1 024	2 048	4 096	4 096	x	x	*8 192*	8 192

values, if the Hamming weight for $n = 11$ and $t = 4, 5$ is optimal. Actually, the value $w_{13,6} = 1\,024$ was already known (see Table 12.1 at page 319 in [11]), hence it does not appear as a gray cell in Table 3. However, there are cases in which we were unable to obtain the target correlation immunity value, which are denoted with an x. There are also instances in which none of the EAs we implemented was able to reach a previously known optimal value, and those are marked in italic. We note that some of those optimal values are actually trivial to obtain and by slight adjustments in the fitness functions we could reach those levels. However, we decided to follow a 'black-box' principle where we do not use specifics about the problem. It is obvious that for some combinations of the number of bits and correlation immunity, the optimization problem as formulated in this work, becomes very hard. In these cases the fitness function is unable to lead the population in the desired direction, which merits further research on both the design of the fitness function and properties of the underlying fitness landscape, as well as the use of different representations and genetic operators. Besides the comparisons based solely on the obtained results, it is also possible to consider the speed of the procedure. Indeed, in [1], authors report that with the SMT solver, the resolution of the problem can last several days. Obtaining the optimal values for the largest Boolean function size of 13 inputs, with our approach lasted on average 30 minutes.

The failure of a GA with a bit-string representation to reach any meaningful results may be explained with two causes: the first one relates to the problem size, and its rapid increase with the number of bits. While the size of the truth table grows exponentially with the number of bits, the size of the search space grows with an even larger rate, which quickly renders a standard GA unusable. The second reason could be a high epistasis of the problem since the bits in the truth table are not independent. This in the conjunction with the fact that the correlation immunity property is concerned with the statistical independence of the bits on the output/input, could lead to a reason why higher values of correlation immunity present difficulty for GA in bitstring representation. This phenomenon can be also observed on the results from [17].

The multi-objective approach has also failed to produce competitive results. Although the nature of the problem suggests different criteria may be optimized independently, the NSGA-II explores a large region in the search space that is of no interest to the final goal. In this application, the stated objectives can clearly be regarded as a primary and a secondary one; first try to reach a desired correlation immunity, and then reduce the Hamming weight as much as possible. While the fitness function we presented may obviously be defined in many different ways, it is apparent that in the current form it is more effective than the multi-objective approach. There are undoubtedly more applications in cryptography where multi-objective optimization may prove useful, where a trade-off between different properties is sought by the system designer.

6   Conclusion and Future Work

In this paper we investigated the evolution of Boolean functions with minimal Hamming weight and various orders of the correlation immunity property. An approach based on Genetic Programming proved to be very successful since we obtained very good results for all Boolean function sizes from five to thirteen inputs. We emphasize that this approach also yielded previously unknown values, where for the most of those it is possible to show they represent global optima. In our future work, we plan to concentrate on even larger Boolean functions in an attempt to find more unknown values as well as the practical upper limit for the use of EAs for the evolution of Boolean functions.

References

1. Bhasin, S., Carlet, C., Guilley, S.: Theory of masking with codewords in hardware: low-weight dth-order correlation-immune boolean functions. Cryptology ePrint Archive, Report 2013/303 (2013). http://eprint.iacr.org/
2. Burnett, L.D.: Heuristic optimization of boolean functions and substitution boxes for cryptography. Ph.D. thesis, Queensland University of Technology (2005)
3. Carlet, C.: Boolean functions for cryptography and error correcting codes. In: Crama, Y., Hammer, P.L. (eds.) Boolean Models and Methods in Mathematics, Computer Science, and Engineering, 1st edn, pp. 257–397. Cambridge University Press, New York (2010)
4. Carlet, C., Danger, J.-L., Guilley, S., Maghrebi, H.: Leakage squeezing of order two. In: Galbraith, S., Nandi, M. (eds.) INDOCRYPT 2012. LNCS, vol. 7668, pp. 120–139. Springer, Heidelberg (2012)
5. Carlet, C., Guilley, S.: Side-channel Indistinguishability. In: Proceedings of the 2nd International Workshop on Hardware and Architectural Support for Security and Privacy, HASP 2013, pp. 9:1–9:8. ACM, New York (2013)
6. Carlet, C., Guilley, S.: Correlation-immune boolean functions for easing counter measures to side-channel attacks (Chapter 3). In: Niederreiter, H., Ostafe, A., Panario, D., Winterhof, A. (eds.) Algebraic Curves and Finite Fields Cryptography and Other Applications. Radon Series on Computational and Applied Mathematics, vol. 16, pp. 41–70. De Gruyter, Berlin (2014)
7. Deb, K., Pratap, A., Agarwal, S., Meyarivan, T.: A fast and elitist multiobjective genetic algorithm: NSGA-II. IEEE Trans. Evol. Comput. **6**(2), 182–197 (2002)
8. Eiben, A.E., Smith, J.E.: Introduction to Evolutionary Computing. Springer, Heidelberg (2003)

9. Gammel, B.M., Mangard, S.: On the duality of probing and fault attacks. J. Electron. Test. 26(4), 483–493 (2010). http://dx.doi.org/10.1007/s10836-010-5160-0
10. Guo-Zhen, X., Massey, J.: A spectral characterization of correlation-immune combining functions. IEEE Trans. Inf. Theor. 34(3), 569–571 (1988)
11. Hedayat, A.S., Sloane, N.J.A., Stufken, J.: Orthogonal Arrays—Theory and Applications. Springer Series in Statistics. Springer, New York (1999)
12. Koza, J.R.: Genetic Programming: On the Programming of Computers by Means of Natural Selection. MIT Press, Cambridge (1992)
13. Mangard, S., Oswald, E., Popp, T.: Power Analysis Attacks: Revealing the Secrets of Smart Cards (Advances in Information Security). Springer, Secaucus (2007)
14. McLaughlin, J., Clark, J.A.: Evolving balanced Boolean functions with optimal resistance to algebraic and fast algebraic attacks, maximal algebraic degree, and very high nonlinearity. Cryptology ePrint Archive, Report 2013/011 (2013). http://eprint.iacr.org/
15. Millan, W.L., Clark, A.J., Dawson, E.: Heuristic design of cryptographically strong balanced boolean functions. In: Nyberg, K. (ed.) EUROCRYPT 1998. LNCS, vol. 1403, pp. 489–499. Springer, Heidelberg (1998)
16. Miller, J.F. (ed.): Cartesian Genetic Programming. Natural Computing Series. Springer, Heidelberg (2011)
17. Picek, S., Carlet, C., Jakobovic, D., Miller, J.F., Batina, L.: Correlation immunity of boolean functions: an evolutionary algorithms perspective. In: Proceedings of the Genetic and Evolutionary Computation Conference, GECCO 2015, Madrid, Spain, pp. 1095–1102, July 11–15, 2015
18. Picek, S., Jakobovic, D., Golub, M.: Evolving cryptographically sound boolean functions. In: Proceedings of the 15th Annual Conference Companion on Genetic and Evolutionary Computation, GECCO 2013 Companion, pp. 191–192. ACM, New York (2013)
19. Picek, S., Jakobovic, D., Miller, J.F., Marchiori, E., Batina, L.: Evolutionary methods for the construction of cryptographic boolean functions. In: Proceedings of Genetic Programming - 18th European Conference, EuroGP 2015, Copenhagen, Denmark, April 8–10, 2015, pp. 192–204 (2015)
20. Picek, S., Marchiori, E., Batina, L., Jakobovic, D.: Combining evolutionary computation and algebraic constructions to find cryptography-relevant boolean functions. In: Bartz-Beielstein, T., Branke, J., Filipič, B., Smith, J. (eds.) PPSN 2014. LNCS, vol. 8672, pp. 822–831. Springer, Heidelberg (2014)
21. Siegenthaler, T.: Correlation-immunity of nonlinear combining functions for cryptographic applications (corresp.). IEEE Trans. Inf. Theor. 30(5), 776–780 (2006)

Generation of Linguistic Advices for Saving Energy: Architecture

Gracian Trivino[✉] and Daniel Sanchez-Valdes

European Centre for Soft Computing, Gonzalo Gutierrez Quiros. sn,
33600 Mieres, Spain
{gracian.trivino,daniel.sanchezv}@softcomputing.es
http://www.softcomputing.es/ldcp

Abstract. Automatic generation of natural language is a challenging multidisciplinary research field. This paper presents some first results in the NATCONSUMERS European project. The goal of this project is the generation of natural language recommendations that are tailored to each specific consumer characteristics for promoting more sustainable behaviors of consumption.

Here, we present a multidisciplinary research that consists in merging a classical architecture for natural language generator systems, proposed in the field of Computational Linguistics, together with results of our previous research in the field of Computing with Perceptions. We present a general view of the architecture of the NATCONSUMERS natural language generator system and we include an example of implementation.

Keywords: Linguistic description of data · Computing with perceptions · Computing with words · Fuzzy Logic

1 Introduction

Residential energy consumption represents the 28 % of all EU consumption and if we consider commercial buildings this percentage increases to 40 % (36 % of EU CO_2 emissions). In this context, the reduction of consumption in the residential sector should play an important role in energy efficiency programs and policies as is stated in the recent Energy Efficiency Directive 2012/27/EU.

Inefficient everyday energy consuming behaviors are largely habitual and therefore the potential of energy savings at home with actions focused in consumer behavior are really promising.

A central goal of NATCONSUMERS [1] is the definition of a feedback framework based in the provision of personalized recommendations in natural language tailored to each consumer group for promoting more sustainable behaviors. Our approach relies in the complete characterization of EU energy consumers, and the design of specific personalized actions tailored to each detected consumer pattern.

© Springer International Publishing Switzerland 2015
A.-H. Dediu et al. (Eds.): TPNC 2015, LNCS 9477, pp. 83–94, 2015.
DOI: 10.1007/978-3-319-26841-5_7

Designing and developing natural language generators is a complex Software Engineering project. An important component of this type of projects is the system architecture. Currently, a definition of a computational architecture that is suitable to NATCONSUMERS necessities is not available. Therefore it is needed to analyze the scientific and technical literature to find some fundamentals and extended these ideas to design it.

In Software Engineering, one well known methodology is the so called Unified Process [3]. Unified Process is an iterative and incremental development process, i.e., the project cycle of life is based in the development of use cases with increasing complexity degree. In this methodology, the architecture has a central role and it is one of the first elements that must be defined. In addition, the Unified Process requires the project team to focus on addressing the most critical risks as soon as possible in the project life cycle. Although Unified Process provides a solid framework for developing the NATCONSUMERS architecture, the methodology must be particularized to this specific family of projects.

Looking for solutions to the NATCONSUMERS architecture in the field of Computational Linguistics, we have found that a good starting point is the classical book by Reiter and Dale, "Building Natural Language Generation Systems" [6]. This book presents a general view of architecture for this type of computational systems but it must be strongly customized to each practical application, as the authors explain.

In previous papers, we have described several computational systems for generating linguistic descriptions of different phenomena, e.g., the beauty of the double stars [2], the Mars planet surface [8] and, recently, the behavior of electricity consumers [4]. Nevertheless, in these works we have not developed an architecture so complete as the needed in NATCONSUMERS, e.g., these works do not consider the need of identifying the communication goals and the need of performing an important classification of types of user.

In this paper, we contribute to the field of Natural Language Generation by describing an architecture for computational systems able to generate linguistic advices aimed to modify the electricity consumers behavior.

We provide descriptions of all the components of the new architecture, but since the Unified Process is an iterative and incremental methodology, this is a first version that we will modify along the project scope by extending and detailing these components along the project.

We include a first demonstration pilot using a small database of input data and a first corpus analysis considering a first consumers classification.

The rest of this paper is organized as follows. Section 2 briefly introduces the Reiter's architecture for natural language generators. Section 3 presents our approach to the NATCONSUMERS architecture. Sections 4 and 5 describe the concepts of Granular Linguistic Model of Phenomena and Message Template that are important elements in our approach. Section 6 contains the experimentation and discussion of results. Finally, Sect. 7 contents the conclusions.

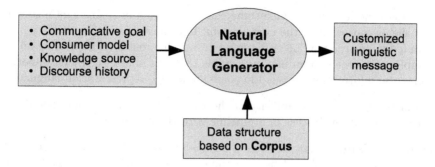

Fig. 1. Basic architecture of a natural language generation system

2 Architectural Framework

Reiter and Dale [6] describe a methodology and architectural framework for building natural language generation systems (NLGS). Here, we summarize the main ideas of this architecture, focusing on the goal of our research. Figure 1 shows the main components.

The basic task in the requirements analysis for NLGS is the determination of the inputs the system will be provided with, the output texts it is expected to produce, and what information is needed to produce those outputs. This collection of input and output data is called *Corpus*. After the requirements analysis task is finished, it will be an agreed-upon corpus of representative target texts which contains the range of outputs that can be expected of the system. Many times, including NATCONSUMERS project, the output text presents information that has to be derived from the input data after some computation, involving also other data sources.

After the development stage, we should obtain, from the *Corpus* analysis, a data structure that contains all the possible linguistic messages organized as a tree of choices. See *Data structure based on Corpus* in Fig. 1. The NLGS uses the input data to choose the best suitable message among the set of available possibilities, i.e., the generated message is an instance of these possibilities.

The set of input data elements are described by Reiter and Dale as follows:

Communicative goal. The production of a linguistic message can be viewed as a goal-driven communication process. It can be seen as an attempt to satisfy some *communicative goal* that the speaker has.

User Model is a characterization of the hearer or intended audience for whom the text is to be generated. Among the many things that might be included in a *user model* are information about the user's expertise, task, and preferences.

Discourse history is a model of the previous interactions between the user and the NLGS. In its simplest form, a discourse history may be no more than a list of the entities that have been mentioned in the discourse so far, thus providing a means of controlling the generation of anaphoric forms; more complex models will provide some characterization of the semantic content of the discourse up to the current point in order to avoid repetition.

Knowledge source may be represented in very different ways depending on the application: one system may use simple tables of numbers, whereas another may use information encoded in some knowledge representation language.

In order to face the complexity of the whole NLGS, Reiter and Dale divide the Text Generation Process in a pipeline with three components:

Document Planner that produces a *document plan*. This module must decide what information should be communicated in the output text and also to provide order and structure over the information to be conveyed.

Micro planner that produces a *text specification*. This module solves the problem of choosing content words, nouns, verbs, adjectives and adverbs for the generated text. Also the linguistic aggregation that involves the use of linguistic resources to build sentences which communicate several pieces of information at once.

Surface realizer that produces the *final text*. Linguistic realization is generally viewed as the problem of applying some characterization of the rules of grammar to some more abstract representation in order to produce a text which is syntactically and morphologically correct.

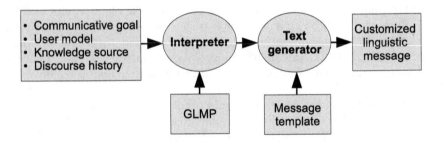

Fig. 2. Architecture for NATCONSUMERS

3   NATCONSUMERS Architecture

The architectural framework represented above provides a general view that must be customized when we deal with implementing practical applications (Fig. 2).

During a first analysis stage, we explored a set of possible **communicative goals**, i.e., different ways of improving the efficiency in electrical energy consumption. In a first approach we considered the following list:

– To use low consumption bulbs.
– To reduce the general consumption by comparing with similar householders.

- To reduce the consumption in stand-by, e.g., switch off the computer during nights.
- To move the time of the washing machine from a peak to a valley zone of consumption.
- To change the old appliances by more efficient ones.
- To improve the building thermal isolation.

The problem of modeling (characterizing) the different types of European electricity consumers is likely one of the hardest problems in NATCONSUMERS. We have created our pilot prototype using a first classification of consumers (**user model**) based on their attitudes as consumers of electricity, that can be briefly described as follows:

- Consumption oriented users (Cluster 1): Averagely innovative. Not concerned about the environment. Savings are not important. Very positive about shopping.
- Modern and passive people (Cluster 2): Innovative. Concerned about the environment, but only on opinion level. Non saver. Not concerned about their energy usage.
- Modern and active people (Cluster 3): Innovative. Strongly concerned on environmental issues, both attitudinal and behavioral level. Cost sensitive. Concerned about their energy usage.
- Traditional savers (Cluster 4): Non innovative. Not concerned about the environment. Saving is the most important for them. They are interested in their energy consumption, but not the environmental issues.

Note that this is a first quite limited classification that must be improved by considering additional data like the size of the household (1, 2, 3 and 4+), the structure of the household (single pensioner/double pensioner/single adult/double adult/family with children etc.), the housing type (block of flats/flats/semi-detached house/detached house), etc.

The **source of knowledge** are the energy consumption data that are obtained thanks to the recently installed electrical energy counters in many European households. These new energy meters provide us with:

- Profiles of consumption of householders, i.e., the receivers of messages.
- Profile of consumption of other householders to generate comparative descriptions.
- Feedback about the obtained results, i.e., we could know if we are provoking some modification of behavior.

For the sake of simplicity, in this first approach we have decided do not take into account the **discourse history**.

In our approach, we have implemented the *Natural Language Generator* and the *Data structure based on Corpus* using two modules with their associated data structures. More specifically, the *Document Planner* is implemented by using the *Interpreter* module that produces an instantiated *Granular Linguistic Model of Phenomena*, that we relates with the Reiter's *document plan*. The *Micro planner* and the *Surface realizer* are implemented by using the *Text Generator* that produces an instance of the *Text template*.

In order to demonstrate how to apply this architecture, in the next sections we describe all the elements that are needed for implementing a use case. Here, we focused on generating reports addressed to modern and active people (cluster 3) with the goal of achieving a general reduction of consumption, including specific hourly consumption and consumption in standby.

4   Granular Linguistic Model of Phenomena

The Granular Linguistic Model of Phenomena (GLMP) is a useful paradigm for developing computational systems able to generate linguistic descriptions of data [7,8,10]. The main element of this structure is known as Computational Perception (CP), which is the computational model of a unit of information (granule) acquired by the designer at certain granularity degree. It is based on the concept of linguistic variable developed by Zadeh [11]. A CP is defined by the tuple $(A, W, R) = \{(a_1, w_1, r_1), (a_2, w_2, r_2), \ldots, (a_n, w_n, r_n)\}$. A represents the set of natural language sentences that linguistically describes the perception (e.g., *"Your electrical consumption in the morning is {low | medium | high}"*); $W \in [0, 1]$ are the validity degrees of each sentence in A to represent the current state of the described phenomenon; and $R \in [0, 1]$ are the relevancy degrees of each sentence according with the user (the receiver of the linguistic message) interests.

The GLMP is a network of Perception Mappings (PMs), which are the elements used to create and aggregate CPs. Here, the designed GLMP is shown in Fig. 3. It receives as input data the electrical consumption of the analyzed household, the electrical consumption of other households with similar characteristics (cluster), and the curve of electricity consumption per hours. This information is aggregated and combined by means of the corresponding PMs, obtaining the following CPs:

- CP_{GC}: compares the general consumption (hourly average load profile) of the analyzed household with respect to the general consumption of its cluster.
- CP_{SB}: compares the standby consumption of the household (the consumption of electronic appliances, specially the fridge, when they are in standby mode) with respect to the standby consumption of its cluster.
- CP_{HT}: represents the specific consumption of the household attending to the different parts of the day, i.e., dawning, morning, midday, afternoon, evening, and night.
- CP_{CT}: represents the specific consumption of the cluster attending to the different parts of the day.
- CP_{SC}: compares the specific consumption of the household with respect to the specific consumption of its cluster.
- CP_{CS}: represents the relevant shifts in the electrical consumption attending to the electricity cost and the household consumption. Energy cost is different depending on which part of the day it is consumed. The goal is to analyze

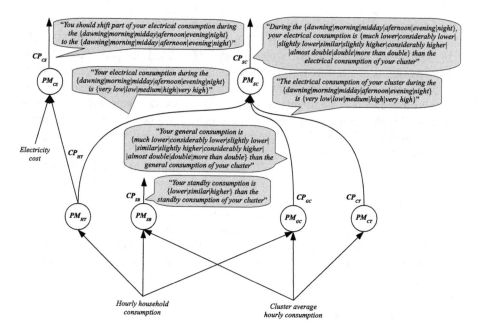

Fig. 3. GLMP that linguistically describes the electrical consumption

the load profile and to suggest the user to shift the energy consumption from some parts of the day to others with lower energy cost.

In order to explain how the information is aggregated by the PMs in the GLMP, we will explain the details of PM_{GC} as an example. The rest of PMs follow the same procedure (for a more detailed information, please see our previous works [9,10]).

4.1 General Consumption (PM_{GC})

A PM is a tuple (U, y, f, g, T) where each component is explained as follows:

U is set of numerical values or input CPs. Here, it is a vector composed by two inputs: the hourly energy consumption of the analyzed household and the average hourly energy consumption of its cluster.

y is the output $CP_{GC} = (A_{GC}, W_{GC}, R_{GC})$, where $A_{GC} = (Much\ lower\ (q_1)$, Considerably lower (q_1), Slightly lower (q_3), Similar (q_4), Slightly higher (q_5), Considerably higher (q_6), Almost double (q_7), Double (q_8), More than double (q_9)).

f is the validity function $W_{GC} = f()$. We compute the ratio between the daily household consumption and the average daily consumption of the cluster. We obtain W_{GC} by means of a set of trapezoidal membership functions forming a strong fuzzy partition. The linguistic labels of A_{GC} were uniformly distributed and they are defined by their vertices as follows: {*Much lower* (0, 0.25, 0.25, 0.5), *Considerable lower* (0.25, 0.5, 0.5, 0.75), *Slightly lower* (0.5, 0.75, 0.75, 1), *Similar* (0.75, 1, 1, 1.25), *Slightly higher* (1, 1.25, 1.25, 1.5), *Considerably higher* (1.25, 1.5, 1.5, 1.75), *Almost double* (1.5, 1.75, 1.75, 2), *Double* (1.75, 2, 2, 2.25), *More than double* $(2, 2.25, 2.25, \infty)$}. Note that Fuzzy Logic provides many other forms of aggregation functions, e.g., we can aggregate the values of several CPs using a set of fuzzy rules to generate a new CP based on them.

g is the function that calculates the matrix of relevance degrees $R_y = g()$. In this case, the relevance values are set by the designer in function of the user characteristics as follows: R_{GC} =(1, 1, 0.8, 0.5, 0.5, 0.7, 0.8, 1, 1). Note that, here, we have considered that the extreme values are more relevant than the intermediate ones.

T is a basic text generation algorithm, a template, that produces linguistic expressions as follows: *"Your general consumption is {much lower | considerably lower | slightly lower | similar | slightly higher | considerable higher | almost double | double | more than double} than the general consumption of your cluster".*

5   Report Template

The top of the report contains a linguistic description about the consumption of the user attending to three different aspects: *general, specific* and *standby consumption* (see, e.g., Fig. 4). As stated in Sect. 3, in this first demonstration example, we generate reports addressed to modern and active people, so we used everyday natural language and we have accompanied the text with the image of a virtual agent that interacts with the user in a friendly and emotional way, increasing the effectiveness and acceptance of the advices. The use of emotions plays a significant role in the human decision-making process as an important aspect of the human intelligence. Sensitivity and expressiveness are very important in human interaction and transmit valuable information [5]. The computational model of the emotions of the virtual agent used in this application is explained in [4]. This virtual agent changes its mood, linguistic and facial expressions according with the type of consumption in order to improve the empathy with the user.

At the bottom, the Report Template contains two graphics that represents the load profile of a household during the two analyzed months and a comparison between his/her consumption in low, medium and high cost zones with respect to the cluster.

6   Experimentation

In this first pilot, we analyzed the energy consumption of 12 households randomly selected, that were previously classified in four groups or clusters, according to the classification explained in Sect. 3. We work with two datasets. First one contains the hourly consumption data of each household during one year, from 01.01.2014 to 31.12.2014. The second dataset contains the average consumption

General consumption: Ups... your average consumption is considerably higher with respect to households similar than you. If you reduce it, you will improve your energy efficiency. Go it!

Specific consumption: You are consuming the most part of the electricity during those periods in which the electricity cost is higher. If you want to save money on your bill, you should shift part of your electrical consumption during the morning (high cost) to the dawning (low cost).

Standby consumption: Your standby consumption is similar with respect to households similar than you. If you reduce it, you could save money on your bill. Yes, you can!

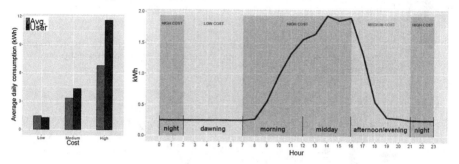

Fig. 4. Energy consumption report for user id.144283

data for the four clusters during one year, for the same period. Each household was identified by an id. number.

6.1   Results and Discussion

Figures 4, 5 and 6 show the energy consumption reports for three households of the same cluster, specifically, cluster 1. It represents the potential and adaptability of the developed tool, since these households present three totally different consumption profiles. We will explain each report in detail:

- Figure 4 represents the report of a household whose energy consumption is considerably higher than the average consumption of its cluster. In this sense, the avatar looks somewhat worried and sad, and it is reflected both in its facial gesture and its expressions. In addition, we can see that this household consumes the most part of the electricity during those periods in which the electricity cost is higher, so the avatar recommends to shift part of the electrical consumption from morning to dawning.
- Figure 5 represents the report of a household whose energy consumption is similar than the average consumption of its cluster. In this case, the avatar looks neutral, since this report corresponds to the first report of the year and it does not have historical data to compare trends.
- Finally, Fig. 6 represents the report of a household whose energy consumption is much lower than the average consumption of its cluster. In addition, the consumption in high cost zone is low. Here, the avatar looks happy and

relaxed. Even so, the avatar gives some advices and recommendations to the consumer, in order to keep the good habits and improve, even more, its energy consumption.

General consumption: Well, your average consumption is similar with respect to households similar than you. If you reduce it, you will improve your energy efficiency. Come on!

Specific consumption: You are consuming the most part of the electricity during those periods in which the electricity cost is lower, so you are saving money on the bill. Nevertheless, if you could shift part of the electrical consumption during the morning (high cost) to the dawning (low cost), you could even save more money.

Standby consumption: Your standby consumption is lower with respect to households similar than you. Well done! We encourage you to keep it up and save even more money.

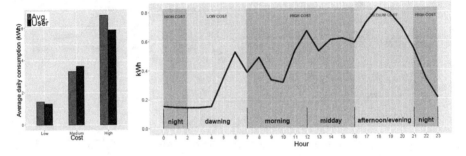

Fig. 5. Energy consumption report for user id.146660

General consumption: Hello! your average consumption is much lower with respect to households similar than you. Well done!

Specific consumption: You are consuming the most part of the electricity during periods in which the electricity cost is higher. If you want to save money on your bill, you should shift part of your electrical consumption during the morning (high cost) to the dawning (low cost).

Standby consumption: Your standby consumption is lower with respect to households similar than you. Well done! We encourage you to keep it up and save even more money.

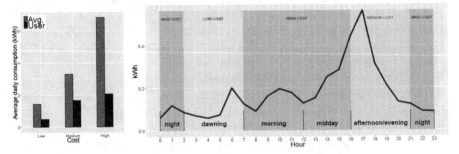

Fig. 6. Energy consumption report for user id.144502

7   Conclusions

This paper presents our first results in NATCONSUMERS project. We describe the first version of an architecture for computational systems able to generate linguistic advices aimed to modify the electricity consumers behavior. It is a multidisciplinary research where we merge ideas from two fields that currently are not closely connected, namely, Computational Linguistics and Computing with Perceptions.

It is a two years long project and many tasks are pending. With the collaboration of all the partners, we need to develop a suitable model of the European consumer of electricity. We need to elaborate a more complete list of communication goals than the presented here. We need to create a Corpus with as many as possible examples of input data combinations and the expected linguistic expression as output.

In this paper we contribute to the field of Natural Language Generation by opening opportunities of collaboration between two currently isolated fields. We provide very practical results that will be used as the kernel from where developing the NATCONSUMERS natural language generation system.

Acknowledgments. We thank our partners in NATCONSUMERS project for their help in performing this research. We thank especially our Hungarian partners Ariosz ltd. that have provided us with the data base and the classification of consumers that we have used in this first work. This project has received funding from the European Union Horizon 2020 research and innovation program under grant agreement No 657672. Also this research was partially funded by the Spanish Ministry of Economy and Competitiveness under project TIN2014-56633-C3-1-R.

References

1. Natconsumers. http://www.natconsumers.eu. Accessed 28 Aug 2015
2. Arguelles, L., Trivino, G.: I-struve: Automatic linguistic descriptions of visual double stars. Eng. Appl. Artif. Intell. **26**(9), 2083–2092 (2013)
3. Booch, G., Rumbaugh, J., Jacobson, I.: The Unified Software Development Process. Addison-Wesley Professional, Reading (1999)
4. Menendez, C., Eciolaza, L., Trivino, G.: Generating advices with emotional content for promoting efficient consumption of energy. Int. J. Uncertainty Fuzziness Knowl.-Based Syst. **22**(5), 677–697 (2014)
5. Picard, R.: Affective Computing. MIT Press, Cambridge (1997)
6. Reiter,   E.,   Dale,   R.:   Building   Natural   Language   Generation   Systems,   vol.   33.   Cambridge   University   Press, Cambridge (2000)
7. Sanchez-Valdes, D., Trivino, G.: Computational perceptions of uninterpretable data. A case study on the linguistic modeling of human gait as a quasi-periodic phenomenon. Fuzzy Sets Syst. **253**, 101–121 (2014)
8. Sanchez-Valdes, D., Alvarez-Alvarez, A., Trivino, G.: Linguistic description about circular structures of the mars surface. Appl. Soft Comput. **13**(12), 4738–4749 (2013)

9. Sanchez-Valdes, D., Alvarez-Alvarez, A., Trivino, G.: Dynamic linguistic descriptions of time series applied to self-track the physical activity. Fuzzy Sets Syst. (2015). http://dx.doi.org/10.1016/j.fss.2015.06.018
10. Sanchez-Valdes, D., Alvarez-Alvarez, A., Trivino, G.: Walking pattern classification using a granular linguistic analysis. Appl. Soft Comput. **33**, 100–113 (2015)
11. Zadeh, L.A.: The concept of a linguistic variable and its application to approximate reasoning. Parts I, II, and III. Inf. Sci. **8, 8, 9**, 199–249, 301–357, 43–80 (1975)

Computing Architectures

A Model for the Emergence of Coded Life

Ilana Agmon[1,2] and Tal Mor[3]($\boxtimes$)

[1] Schulich Chemistry Department, Technion, Haifa, Israel
chilana@tx.technion.ac.il
[2] Fritz Haber Research Center for Molecular Dynamics, Hebrew University,
Jerusalem, Israel
[3] Computer Science Department, Technion, Haifa, Israel
talmo@cs.technion.ac.il

Abstract. In the conceptualization presented here, a possible scenario concerned with the emergence of coded life in nature is inferred from a model that merges computer science concepts with prebiotic chemistry. In this ("digital") model, sets of strings composed of letters, such that each letter represents a molecular building block, are located within compartments. Some of the sets of strings (together with their reactions) form "autocatalytic sets". Some of the strings in the autocatalytic sets play the role of catalysts of reactions and others play the role of templates for replication processes.

We find several unique sets of strings, comprised of two types of letters (r_i and p_j) representing nucleotides and amino acids (respectively), with some inherent asymmetry in their properties, that prompt the emergence of a code. By identifying such "code prompting" autocatalytic sets, our abstract model suggests novel models for artificial life, and a possible explanation for the emergence and the fixation of the genetic code in life as we know it.

Keywords: Self-organizing systems · Autocatalytic sets · Artificial life · Evolution · Origin of life · Universal replicator · Genetic code · System biology · Translation

1 Introduction

There is still no standard definition of the term "Life" [19], and there is no "standard model" of the origin of life [7,25]. Life as we now know it is too complex to assume it had spontaneously emerged in a non-biological world. Yet, there is a general agreement that RNA preceded DNA, and that "it all started" from a prebiotic primordial soup of molecules. It is also generally accepted that evolution occurred first in populations of complex molecules [28], and only later in "proto-organisms", the hypothetical ancestors of LUCA[1].

When and how genetically-coded proto-organisms first appeared along the line of evolution is not yet clear. Although various different models concerned

---

[1] LUCA is the Last Universal Common Ancestor of all currently living organisms.

© Springer International Publishing Switzerland 2015
A.-H. Dediu et al. (Eds.): TPNC 2015, LNCS 9477, pp. 97–108, 2015.
DOI: 10.1007/978-3-319-26841-5_8

with the emergence of life, e.g. [6,8,14,17,23,24,27,28,30], resulted in a significant progress in the last few decades in understanding the possibilities regarding the origin of life, none of the models presents a complete scenario for the emergence of life. In particular, the emergence of the genetic code remained a major open question (see for example [18,21,31]).

"Indeed[2], it stands to reason that any scenario of the code origin and evolution will remain vacuous if not combined with understanding of the origin of the coding principle itself and the translation system that embodies it. At the heart of this problem, is a dreary vicious circle: what would be the selective force behind the evolution of the extremely complex translation system before there were functional proteins? And, of course, there could be no proteins without a sufficiently effective translation system."

The contemporary genetic code is the set of rules by which information encoded in genetic material (DNA or RNA sequences) is "translated" into proteins (long sequences of amino acid) in living cells. The code-dictionary maps tri-nucleotide sequences (called codons) to amino acids via a process called "translation". Every triplet of nucleotides in a nucleic acid sequence that has a coding function specifies a single amino acid; e.g., the word CAG encodes the amino acid glutamine [where U, A, C, G are the four letters, namely nucleotides, building the RNA]. The contemporary genetic code is essentially common to all living organisms, indicating that it must have preceded LUCA. Therefore, clarifying its inception in the prebiotic world, and its fixation, are of critical importance to our ability to shed light on the emergence of life.

Although there is currently no consensual definition of the term "Life", it is agreed that in order to be considered as "living", the set of molecules must allow for a stable replication of its constituents. Originally two methods, template replication and Auto Catalytic Sets (ACS), were presented as competitive models for basic evolution from the prebiotic soup, into a much richer organic prebiotic environment. ACS was first suggested as a model for replication of peptides [15] (peptides are short sequences of amino acids), while the template replication is a model for replication of RNA. However, once ribozymes, i.e. molecular catalysts made out of RNA, were found [9,20] ACS of RNA strings were also considered. Additionally, variants of both models (e.g., [21]) explored a world in which RNA and small peptides evolved together (see also [24]).

Here we present a model that outlines an evolutionary path that leads from the prebiotic world to a code-prompting self-replicating set of molecules. Our model is based on the notion of autocatalytic sets; see [12,13,15,28] and see some references to experimental support in [16]. ACS are sets of food-molecules and strings, along with reactions — reactions generating the strings and catalyzed by them, such that no outside help is required for the strings replication from the food-molecules that are assumed to be available whenever needed.

Our model follows the well established ACS model, and then goes one step beyond it. First, as the ACS model, our model is also a "letters-and-strings" abstraction that enables us to ignore almost all the physical and chemical details

---

[2] This is a quote from Koonin and Novozhilov [18].

of the molecules involved. Second, as in the ACS model [15], as well as in other models [17], our letters and strings live and evolve inside compartments. We then deal with the following question: under what circumstances could the sets of letters and strings be thought of as extremely simplified "coded entities", that potentially preceded biological proto-organisms? We find such entities — **CO**de-**P**rompting **ACS** — COPACS. These may explain the emergence and the fixation of the genetic code, while also proposing a candidate for the first code word (the first peptide generated by the translation process).

The requirements established for this set (the COPACS) to be formed and for the code to be fixated may apply also to the artificial life of nano-robots or autonomous agents, or to the field of artificial cells.

In Sect. 2 we discuss the origin of life from computer science point of view. In Sect. 3 we present the rules dictating the behavior of the letters and strings in our model; We then present ACS, template replication and the conditions under which the molecules involved in template replication form an ACS. We also define the notion of universal replicators. Our models for the emergence of a code, developed in Sect. 4, present three code-prompting autocatalytic sets of strings. We also explicitly identify what could have been the <u>first</u> code word. We finally provide some conclusions in the last section.

2 Modelling the Origin of Life – Computer Science Point of View

Methods and concepts from computer science (and maybe also from information theory) may be important for research into the origin of life. The main method we use here is the "digital abstraction". In general, "abstraction" is a method of treating complex things at several different levels. In understanding and designing complex communication and computing systems, such as the internet, or a microprocessor, people commonly use the abstraction method; e.g. people use the TCP/IP model for the internet.

For explaining how a computer works people use several levels of abstraction. These include as the physical (the lowest level), the electronic (voltages, currents, continuous time), the digital (bits, discrete times when the logical values "0" and "1" are well defined, Boolean operations, etc.), the machine language, the high-level language, and the algorithm levels. Levels that are not next to each other should, in general, not be mixed.

Similarly we suggest to consider at least four levels of abstraction for the concept of life, that may be useful (or even vital) for understanding life and for deepening into its origins: the physical level (mainly quantum physics), the molecular level (chemistry), the "digital" level which is what we consider here, and the code level (the genotype and the related phenotype), which is only relevant for understanding later stages leading to LUCA. [Clearly, the code level cannot be relevant to the prebiotic stages of "life"/"proto-life", prior to the emergence of the genetic code]. For designing some types of artificial life the chemistry level might be replaced by electronics as when designing a computer or a computer network system; Note however that artificial life in which one is satisfied with making use of "man-made code", will (probably) not benefit much from the results of the current work as we do not assume the pre-existence of a code.

Here, we use the letters and strings abstraction, and binary operations (a yes/no for a reaction, etc.) — the digital level, to see how a code may have emerged in a prebiotic world. We notice that it is actually vital to go beyond strings: E.g., folding of strings and strings attachment into two dimensional or three dimensional structures probably played an important role in the origin of life. We fully ignore here the lowest level, (quantum) physics, and (as always is done when using an abstraction), we do consider the middle level, chemistry, but rather briefly, when needed, and mainly as a tool to define the set of characteristics of our letters and rules for generating our strings.

Several other concepts from computer and information sciences are related to the abstraction of the origin of life, and in particular to our COPACS model:

1. compartmentalization, leading to a subsystem having a distinct molecular environment,
2. replication — autocatalytic sets of strings/molecules, and reactions catalyzed by these molecules,
3. coding — giving meaning to meaningless combinations of basic building blocks; in our case, strings (RNA) containing ordered triplets of nucleotides lead to ordered strings of amino acids (peptides) and some of these RNA strings and peptides are words that have an operational meaning,
4. evolutionary algorithms before, during and after the emergence of a code.
5. error correction, entropy reduction, active transport and related issues. [This last item, involving "input/output" through the compartment walls, is only relevant at stages of evolution much later than the ones discussed here].

In the journal paper we intend to give more details regarding the five concepts enumerated above.

3   Autocatalytic Sets, Template Replication, and Universal Replicators

We deal here with a simple abstract model in which two types of letters, r_i and p_j, exist within a compartment[3]. We define the following characteristics for these letters:

1. Both types of letters have the capability of being combined into directed strings, Rk made of r letters, and Pm made of p letters. Both types of letters have directionality which can be described as having a head and a tail, such that while forming a string the head of one letter is connected

---

[3] We assume a small number of different letters: there are four r letters and (for example) just four [10,14] or just ten [22] p letters. See also [11].

to the tail of a second letter of the same type. We shall call the connection between neighboring letters along the strings "backbone connection" for both types of strings. These connections are assumed to be strong, allowing the sustainability of the one dimensional string. Within each R string, each r letter can form backbone connections with any other r letter, such that the sequence of r_i's in a string can be completely random. Similarly, the sequence of p_j's letters in each P string can be random too.

2. We assume that long random R strings of up to 100 r_i's can be found in the environment. In contrast, P strings do not form easily and only single p letters or very short strings (up to 2–3 p letters) are expected in the environment.

3. In addition to their ability to be combined into strings, the Rk and Pm strings can generate more complex structures, by forming bonds perpendicular to the string direction, namely perpendicular to the direction of the backbone connections. These connections will be named "perpendicular connections" and they are assumed to be weaker than the backbone connection. Thus, an R string or a P string has the potential to form 2-dimensional (2D) and 3D structures. Such structures are highly relevant here due to the requirement to act as catalysts for specific chemical reactions.

   – In contrast to the backbone connections, the perpendicular connections of the r letters belonging to an R string are specific. Thus, an R string has the potential to attract specific r letters or another R string to generate a ladder-like structure; We shall examine two cases (Fig. 1): a. r_i within a string can form a perpendicular connection only with a single "complementary letter" from the set of letters. b. r_i within a string can form perpendicular connections only with an identical r_i.

   – Non-specific perpendicular connections are assumed between p letters belonging to different P strings.

4. Potentially there exists an attraction (called the stereochemical attraction [29]) between any p_i letter and a specific triplet of r_j letters. Such a triplet of r_j letters is the same coding triplet mentioned earlier, which is specific per the letter p_i.

5. A bond (a strong connection) can be form, with the help of a catalyst, between any specific p letter and the last letter of a specific type of R strings (that we call tR). The resulting string is called a "charged" tR string — a tR string which carries at its end a p letter.

While long R strings and very short P strings with random composition are assumed to naturally exist within the compartment, the appearance of non-random R and P strings, have been explained mainly via two models: template replication and the formation of autocatalytic sets.

Both template replication and ACS models rely on catalyzed reactions. A catalyst is a substance which increases the rate of a "chemical reaction" (e.g. forming a connection) by many (even 6–7) orders of magnitude, without being changed by the reaction. Catalysis majorly enhances the rate of a reaction, thus essentially abolishing the opposite process, i.e. from the product to the reactants. We assume here that both types of strings, R and P, are capable of acting as

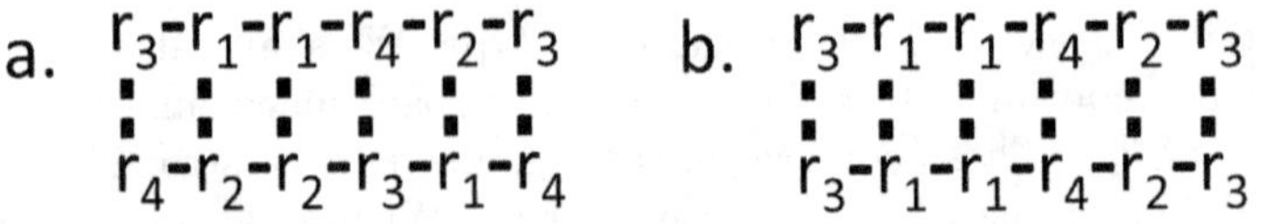

a. $r_3\text{-}r_1\text{-}r_1\text{-}r_4\text{-}r_2\text{-}r_3$ b. $r_3\text{-}r_1\text{-}r_1\text{-}r_4\text{-}r_2\text{-}r_3$
$\vdots \quad \vdots \quad \vdots \quad \vdots \quad \vdots \quad \vdots$ $\vdots \quad \vdots \quad \vdots \quad \vdots \quad \vdots \quad \vdots$
$r_4\text{-}r_2\text{-}r_2\text{-}r_3\text{-}r_1\text{-}r_4$ $r_3\text{-}r_1\text{-}r_1\text{-}r_4\text{-}r_2\text{-}r_3$

Fig. 1. Two possible ladder structures formed by R strings: a. **Cross templating:** Each r_i recognizes only the complementary r in the perpendicular direction [in this case (r_1,r_2) are complementary, and (r_3,r_4) are complementary]. b. **Self templating:** Each r_i recognizes only an identical r_i in the perpendicular direction.

catalysts, if a specific 2D or 3D structure is formed, by their folding, stabilized by the perpendicular connections.

3.1 Template Replication

We shall describe a model of "self-templating" of R strings in which each r letter in a string R attracts from the environment an identical letter, to form a perpendicular bond, and to build a ladder structure (see Fig. 1b). If these newly added letters are bonded via backbone connections, a second string R, identical to the original one, is obtained, that is – the string R acted as a self-template to generate a copy of itself.

The string replication has a much higher probability of occurrence if it is aided by a particular catalyst C. The catalyzed reaction is written as: $R + F \xrightarrow{C} R + R$. The letter F, which stands for Food, relates to all r_i letters and possibly to short R strings (e.g. various combinations of two-three r_i letters) which are assumed to be common in the environment. During the replication process the template string (the original R string) does get modified, by forming perpendicular bonds to new r_i letters, yet by the end of the template replication, once separated from the newly-generated string and "released" from being held by the catalyst, the template string returns to its original form.

A second model for template replication is the "cross templating" based on the ladder structure shown in Fig. 1a, where each letter in the original string R specifically interacts with its complementary letter, and a string complementary to R is formed. While in life as we know it, only cross-template replication exists, we stick here to the self-template replication, for simplicity.

3.2 Autocatalytic Sets

ACS is a (complete) catalytic set of molecules and reactions. Intuitively speaking, the set of molecules of an ACS includes some given food-molecules, and in addition, some non-food molecules such that all of them are generated from that given set of food-molecules, and such that no outside "help" is required for the generation of all non-food molecules in the set. Non-catalyzed processes are commonly excluded from the set [15] (since catalysis increases the rate of processes significantly), hence each reaction in the ACS must be catalyzed by at least one molecule in the ACS. See [13] for more formal detail about ACS. Following [13,28] we present two basic examples of ACS[4] in Fig. 2: item "a" shows a "single non-food molecule ACS", and item "b" shows "two non-food molecules ACS". Such ACSs potentially result in exponential growth of the products [28]. Note that the general model of catalysis in ACS [12,13,15] is the "binary polymer model" where a reaction is either catalyzed or not catalyzed by a given molecule.

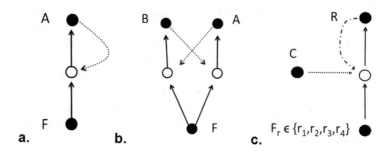

Fig. 2. a. A single (non-food) molecule ACS, catalyzing its own formation. Black dots are used here for molecules, empty dots for reactions. Full lines indicate input and output of a reaction, and the dotted line – a catalytic process. b. molecules A and B catalyze the formation of each other. This is the simplest non-trivial ACS. c. Template-replication of R using R itself as a template, and C as a catalyst. Dash-dot-dash-dot line indicates a templating process. Note that unless the molecule C is a food molecule, this set is not autocatalytic.

Template Replication Viewed as ACS: The set of molecules and reactions composing the process of templating is shown in Fig. 2c. Note that this set is not sufficient for claiming that we obtain an ACS; if C is not a food-molecule then another reaction, catalyzing the formation of C, must be added. To avoid incorporating an additional molecule into the ACS, the catalytic capabilities of a molecule that belongs to the ACS (namely by R, by C itself, or by a food-molecule) must be used, e.g. via the reaction $F_c \xrightarrow{R} C$.

3.3 Universal Catalysts and Replicators

Some catalysts may be universal. As an example, suppose that we have a family of strings Rk, and suppose that one catalyst, say C, catalyzes the self-templating process $Ri + F \xrightarrow{C} Ri + Ri$, for template-replicating each of the Ri's from the relevant food F, using the already existing Ri.

Definition (informal): molecule C, in the above example is called a "universal replicator" for the family of strings whose replication is catalyzed by it via the (self) templating process.

---

[4] As is clarified in [28], there are several non-identical definitions of the term ACS; We use here the term ACS to mean precisely what is named "RAF-ACS" in [13].

4   The Emergence of a Code

4.1   Toy Model 1: The Emergence of a Code

In this subsection we present the emergence of a code using a (non-realistic, yet inspiring) toy model. Consider a world of R strings and P strings, such that three strings are unique: First, a (universal catalyst) string $P0$ that catalyzes the self-template replication of any R string that interacts with it. Second, a unique string R_{mes} is assumed (for now) to be random. Last, there is a unique string $R0$ that plays a unique role: If a string R_{mes} passes through it, every coding triplet in R_{mes} moves through a "reading" position in $R0$. When the triplet is in the reading position, it can attract a relevant p letter from the environment. Once this occurs, $R0$ catalyzes the bonding of this p letter to the previously attracted p letters, to form (step by step) a string P. After the letter p is bonded, $R0$ enables the string R_{mes} to move further, so that the next incoming triplet arrives at the reading position.

The attraction that acts between each p_i letter and a specifically assigned triplet of r_i letters is called the "stereochemical" attraction [29]. The P string built by that "translation" process is random in sequence, but it is uniquely dictated by the string R_{mes} (three letters after three, etc., in R_{mes}). In some sense, the string R_{mes} acts as a template for building a specific string P, hence we name it $R_{mes}(P)$. Let us refer to this type of templating operation as "translation", the term actually used in biochemistry for the same operation.

In most cases the strings $R_{mes}(P)$ (and hence also the resulting P strings) are random. Suppose that just one time, by pure chance, the string R_{mes} had a specific sequence, such that the resulting P string was $P0$ mentioned above. Let's call this R_{mes} string $R_{mes}(P0)$ to keep track of the P string it encodes.

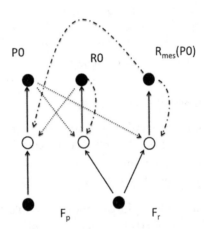

Fig. 3. Template replication via "translation" of $P0$ using R_{mes} as a template and $R0$ as a catalyst; if a specific R_{mes} that we call $R_{mes}(P0)$ exists, a universal replicator for all R strings ($P0$) is generated, resulting in a COPACS.

This scenario now leads to the emergence of a code! $R_{mes}(P0)$ is the code-word that contains the information concerned with the sequence of the p_i letters in the $P0$ string. The set $P0$, $R0$, and that unique $R_{mes}(P0)$, form an autocatalytic set (see Fig. 3): $P0$ will be generated by $R0$ and $R_{mes}(P0)$, while the replication of these R strings will be catalyzed by $P0$, as these two R strings are expected to be in the vicinity of $P0$. Once such a COPACS is built, it becomes more and more prevalent [28], inside the compartment; by diffusion [5], the environment as well as neighboring compartments, can be potentially enriched with these three strings.

The biochemical equivalents of $P0$, R_{mes} and $R0$ are the (proto-)polymerase [26] the messenger RNA and the (proto-)ribosome [1,2,4], respectively; We extend the description of those molecules in the journal version of this paper [3], where we suggest that our last two models (once modified to be using cross-template replication of R strings) could be related to the real prebiotic chemistry relevant for the emergence of proto-life.

4.2   The Main Idea – The (More Realistic) Emergence of a Code: Toy Model 2

Toy model 1 relies on the possibility that p_i letters, attracted by their assigned triplets in R_{mes} and then accommodated in a specific location in $R0$, can interact with each other to form backbone connections, resulting in the formation of a P string. Although toy model 1 provides a feasible COPACS, the biochemical equivalents do not comply with the suggested mechanism.

A more realistic scenario relies on the perpendicular weak bonds described in the self-template process in addition to the stereochemical attraction. A new type of players is introduced, R-p strings that bridge between the p letter and R_{mes}. These strings are formed from several r letters plus exactly one letter p

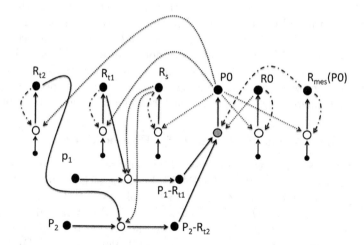

Fig. 4. Model 2, simplified to make use of just two tR strings — R_{t1} and R_{t2}.

located at the end of the string. Each R string is assigned to a particular p_i, by having at a specific location along the string, a triplet of r letters that is identical to the triplet assigned to the p_i letter on R_{mes}. As an example let us assume that there are four r letters in the compartment, and that the triplet in R_{mes} coding for a specific p_i, is $(r_2 r_4 r_1)$. The R-p_i string is then composed of an R string which at a particular place displays the triplet $(r_2 r_4 r_1)$, and p_i attached to its end.

The full set of strings in our second model now contains, in addition to the strings described in toy model 1, also a specific set of R strings and a related set of R-p strings. We will term these specific R strings tR and those attached to the matching p letter, p_i-tRi. While being attached to its assigned coding triplet on R_{mes}, the p_i at the end of the R string still has the freedom to interact with other p letters, which are specifically attached via tR strings to the neighboring triplets on R_{mes}. If this interaction occurs (e.g., at a dedicated site on $R0$), and $R0$ catalyzes the formation of a backbone connection between p letters, a P string, which is a translation of the information in R_{mes}, can be formed.

The above model is not complete yet, it does not form an ACS, hence also not a COPACS: While the addition of the tRi to the ACS is easy — they are generated via self-template replication process (catalyzed by $P0$), the attachment of the letter p_i to each tRi must also be catalyzed. To resolve this, let a special R string named sR catalyze the attachment of each p_i letter to its specific tRi string. The attachment process generates a string p-tR which we call a "charged tR string". As with the other R strings, the string sR is also self-template replicated by $P0$. This completes an ACS, which includes a code string $R_{mes}(P0)$, thus also a COPACS.

We assume that sR is non-specific, but it accommodates p_i and tRj only if they arrive together, "combined" by the stereochemical attraction of the p_i to its coding triplet in tRj — hence $i = j$. The string sR is therefore a universal catalyst for the bonding of a p letter to a tR string. In Fig. 4 we present the COPACS describing model 2, but with just two tR strings; Both charging processes are catalyzed by the single sR string. Note that when several charged tR strings are involved in the translation process of building $P0$, we need to clarify that the buildup of $P0$ potentially does not require all of them, in contrast to all other processes (denoted by empty circles) in all figures till now and here as well, where two (or more) lines defining a process are always needed together. To denote that difference we use grey circle for the generation of $P0$ in that case.

4.3   Toy Model 3: The Emergence of a Fixated Code

Let us assume that the single (universal catalyst) string sR has been gradually replaced, due to evolution of the COPACS, by a set of non-universal catalyst strings sRj, such that each sRj selectively catalyzes only the attachment of the letter p_j to the string tR_j. The resulting COPACS now includes a single P catalyst, $P0$, that copies all the R strings in the set via template replication, and an R catalyst, $R0$, which translates $R_{mes}(P0)$ into $P0$. The COPACS also includes a set of sR strings, such that each of them catalyzes the formation of a specific p-tR string. $R0$ then catalyzes the formation of $P0$: it accommodates the relevant charged string (according to the coding triplets in $R_{mes}(P0)$), catalyzing the formation of a backbone connection between each incoming p letter and the already formed portion of $P0$.

Let us now describe the fixation of the code-dictionary. The emergence of the COPACS in toy models 1 and 2 relied on the stereochemical attraction between specific p_i and the relevant triplets of r letters. Then, after sR evolved into a set of selective string sRj, the importance of the stereochemical attraction ceases to exist: Each Rp molecule p_j-tRj can, in toy model 3, be formed even if there is no attraction between p_j and tRj! This leads to the following outcome: The resulting set remains a COPACS even if now it migrates and is captured in a compartment with somewhat different internal conditions and stereochemical attraction — the code-dictionary got fixated.

5   Summary and Conclusions

We presented here two COPACSs that may be related to the origin of life: In toy model 2, the COPACS constituted of a single peptide (or a protein) — the proto-polymerase ($P0$), along with several RNA components; the proto-ribosome ($R0$), mRNApolymerase ($R_{mes}(P0)$), aa-proto-tRNAs (p_i-tRi) and a non-specific proto-synthetase (sR). Further evolution (presented in our model 3) of the non-specific proto-synthetase (sR) into specific catalysts (sRi), would have detached the ACS from possible environmental dependence, leading to a fixated code-dictionary that could have migrated into other compartments, potentially eliminating any previous code that might have existed there.

We leave for the journal version of the paper deeper analyses of the involved molecules. We leave for future examination the identity of the second code word.

Acknolwledgments. TM thanks the Israeli Ministry of Defense Research and Technology Unit. We thank Yuval Elias for fruitful discussions, we thank Yuval Elias and Erez Mor for a lot of help with the Figures, and we thank Itay Fayerverker for several useful comments.

References

1. Agmon, I.: The dimeric proto-ribosome: structural details and possible implications on the origin of life. Int. J. Mol. Sci. **10**, 2921–2934 (2009)
2. Agmon, I., Bashan, A., Yonath, A.: On ribosome conservation and evolution. Isr. J. Ecol. Evol. **52**, 359–374 (2006)
3. Agmon, I., Elias, Y., Mor, T.: On the emergence of the genetic code. On preparation
4. Bokov, K., Steinberg, S.V.: A hierarchical model for evolution of 23S ribosomal RNA. Nature **457**, 977 (2009)
5. Chen, I.A., Nowak, M.A.: From prelife to life: how chemical kinetics become evolutionary dynamics. Acc. Chem. Res. **45**, 2088–2096 (2012)
6. Crick, F.H.C.: The origin of the genetic code. J. Mol. Biol. **38**, 367–379 (1968)

7. Dyson, F.J.: Origins of Life. Cambridge University Press, Cambridge (1985)
8. Gilbert, W.: Origin of life: the RNA world. Nature **319**, 618 (1986)
9. Guerrier-Takada, C., Gardiner, K., Marsh, T., Pace, N., Altman, S.: The RNA moiety of ribonuclease P is the catalytic subunit of the enzyme. Cell **35**, 849–857 (1983)
10. van der Gulik, P., Massar, S., Gilis, D., Buhrman, H., Rooman, M.: The first peptides: the evolutionary transition between prebiotic amino acids and early proteins. J. Theor. Biol. **261**, 531–539 (2009)
11. Harada, K., Fox, S.W.: Thermal synthesis of natural amino-acids from a postulated primitive terrestrial atmosphere. Nature **201**, 335–336 (1964)
12. Hordijk, W., Hein, J., Steel, M.: Autocatalytic sets and the origin of life. Entropy **12**, 1733–1742 (2010)
13. Hordijk, W., Kauffman, S.A., Steel, M.: Required levels of catalysis for emergence of autocatalytic sets in models of chemical reaction systems. Int. J. Mol. Sci. **12**, 3085–3101 (2011)
14. Ikehara, K.: Possible steps to the emergence of life: the [GADV]-protein world hypothesis. Chem. Rec. **5**, 107–118 (2005)
15. Kauffman, S.: Autocatalytic sets of proteins. J. Theor. Biol. **119**, 1–24 (1986)
16. Kauffman, S.: Approaches to the origin of life on earth. Life **1**, 34–48 (2011)
17. Koonin, E.V., Martin, W.: On the origin of genomes and cells within inorganic compartments. TRENDS Genet. **21**, 647–654 (2005)
18. Koonin, E.V., Novozhilov, A.S.: Origin and evolution of the genetic code: the universal enigma. IUBMB Life **61**, 99–111 (2009)
19. Koshland, D.E.: The seven pillars of life. Science **295**, 2215–2216 (2002)
20. Kruger, K., Grabowski, P.J., Zaug, A.J., Sands, J., Gottschling, D.E., Cech, T.R.: Self-splicing RNA: autoexcision and autocyclization of the ribosomal RNA intervening sequence of tetrahymena. Cell **31**, 147–157 (1982)
21. Kunin, V.: A system of two polymerases - a model for the origin of life. Orig. Life Evol. Biosph. **30**, 459–466 (2000)
22. Miller, S.L., et al.: A production of amino acids under possible primitive earth conditions. Science **117**, 528–529 (1953)
23. Orgel, L.E.: Evolution of the genetic apparatus. J. Mol. Biol. **38**, 381–393 (1968)
24. Rouch, A.: Evolution of the first genetic cells and the universal genetic code: a hypothesis based on macromolecular coevolution of RNA and proteins. J. Theor. Biol. **357**, 220–244 (2014)
25. Schroedinger, E.: What is Life?: The Physical Aspect of the Living Cell. Cambridge University Press, Cambridge (1944)
26. Seckbach, J.: Life in the Universe: From the Miller Experiment to the Search for Life on Other Worlds, vol. 7. Springer, Cham (2004)
27. Segré, D., Ben-Eli, D., Deamer, D.W., Lancet, D.: The lipid world. Orig. Life Evol. Biosph. **31**, 119–145 (2001)
28. Vasas, V., Fernando, C., Santos, M., Kauffman, S., Szathmáry, E.: Evolution before genes. Biol. Direct **7**, 1–14 (2012)
29. Woese, C.R.: On the evolution of the genetic code. Proc. Natl. Acad. Sci. USA **54**, 1546 (1965)
30. Woese, C.R.: The Genetic Code: The Molecular Basis for Genetic Expression. Harper and Row, New York (1967)
31. Yarus, M., Caporaso, J.G., Knight, R.: Origins of the genetic code: the escaped triplet theory. Annu. Rev. Biochem. **74**, 179–198 (2005)

Five-Card Secure Computations Using Unequal Division Shuffle

Akihiro Nishimura[1]([✉]), Takuya Nishida[1], Yu-ichi Hayashi[2],
Takaaki Mizuki[3], and Hideaki Sone[3]

[1] Sone-Mizuki Laboratory, Graduate School of Information Sciences,
Tohoku University, 6-3 Aramaki-Aza-Aoba, Aoba, Sendai 980-8578, Japan
akihiro.nishimura.p3@dc.tohoku.ac.jp
[2] Faculty of Engineering, Tohoku Gakuin University,
1-13-1 Chuo, Tagajo, Miyagi 985-8537, Japan
[3] Cyberscience Center, Tohoku University, 6-3 Aramaki-Aza-Aoba,
Aoba, Sendai 980-8578, Japan
tm-paper+card5cop@g-mail.tohoku-university.jp

Abstract. Card-based cryptographic protocols can perform secure computation of Boolean functions. Cheung et al. recently presented an elegant protocol that securely produces a hidden AND value using five cards; however, it fails with a probability of $1/2$. The protocol uses an unconventional shuffle operation called unequal division shuffle; after a sequence of five cards is divided into a two-card portion and a three-card portion, these two portions are randomly switched. In this paper, we first show that the protocol proposed by Cheung et al. securely produces not only a hidden AND value but also a hidden OR value (with a probability of $1/2$). We then modify their protocol such that, even when it fails, we can still evaluate the AND value. Furthermore, we present two five-card copy protocols using unequal division shuffle. Because the most efficient copy protocol currently known requires six cards, our new protocols improve upon the existing results.

Keywords: Cryptography · Card-based protocols · Card games · Cryptography without computers · Real-life hands-on cryptography · Secure multi-party computations

1 Introduction

Suppose that Alice and Bob have Boolean values $a \in \{0,1\}$ and $b \in \{0,1\}$, respectively, each of which describes his/her private opinion (or something similar), and they want to conduct secure AND computation, i.e., they wish to know only the value of $a \wedge b$. In such a situation, a card-based cryptographic protocol is a convenient solution. Many such protocols have already been proposed (see Table 1), one of which can be selected by them for secure AND computation. For example, if they select the six-card AND protocol [6], they can securely produce

© Springer International Publishing Switzerland 2015
A.-H. Dediu et al. (Eds.): TPNC 2015, LNCS 9477, pp. 109–120, 2015.
DOI: 10.1007/978-3-319-26841-5_9

a hidden value of $a \wedge b$ using six playing cards, e.g., ♣♣♣♡♡♡, along with a "random bisection cut."

Recently, Cheung et al. presented an elegant protocol that securely produces a hidden AND value using only five cards (♣♣♣♡♡); however, it fails with a probability of 1/2 [2] (we refer to it as *Cheung's AND protocol* in this paper). The protocol uses an unconventional shuffling operation that we refer to as "unequal division shuffle"; after a sequence of five cards is divided into a two-card portion and a three-card portion, these two portions are randomly switched. The objective of this paper is to improve Cheung's AND protocol and propose other efficient protocols using unequal division shuffle.

This paper begins by presenting some notations related to card-based protocols.

Table 1. Known card-based protocols for secure computation

	# of colors	# of cards	Type of shuffle	Avg. # of trials	Failure rate
∘ *Secure AND in a non-committed format*					
den Boer [1]	2	5	RC	1	0
Mizuki-Kumamoto-Sone [5]	2	4	RBC	1	0
∘ *Secure AND in a committed format*					
Crépeau-Kilian [3]	4	10	RC	6	0
Niemi-Renvall [8]	2	12	RC	2.5	0
Stiglic [10]	2	8	RC	2	0
Mizuki-Sone [6]	2	6	RBC	1	0
Cheung et al. [2] (§2.3)	2	5	UDS	1	1/2
∘ *Secure XOR in a committed format*					
Crépeau-Kilian [3]	4	14	RC	6	0
Mizuki-Uchiike-Sone [7]	2	10	RC	2	0
Mizuki-Sone [6]	2	4	RBC	1	0

RC = Random Cut, RBC = Random Bisection Cut,
UDS = Unequal Division Shuffle

1.1 Preliminary Notations

Throughout this paper, we assume that cards satisfy the following properties.

1. All cards of the same type (black ♣ or red ♡) are indistinguishable from one another.
2. Each card has the same pattern ? on its back side, and hence, all face-down cards are indistinguishable from one another.

We define the following encoding scheme to deal with a Boolean value:

$$\boxed{\clubsuit}\,\boxed{\heartsuit} = 0, \quad \boxed{\heartsuit}\,\boxed{\clubsuit} = 1. \tag{1}$$

Given a bit $x \in \{0,1\}$, when a pair of face-down cards $\boxed{?}\,\boxed{?}$ describes the value of x with encoding scheme (1), it is called a *commitment* to x and is expressed as

$$\underbrace{\boxed{?}\,\boxed{?}}_{x}. \tag{2}$$

For a commitment to $x \in \{0,1\}$, we sometimes write

$$\underbrace{\boxed{?}}_{x^0} \quad \underbrace{\boxed{?}}_{x^1}$$

instead of expression (2), where $x^0 := x$ and $x^1 := \overline{x}$. In other words, we sometimes use a one-card encoding scheme, $\boxed{\clubsuit} = 0, \boxed{\heartsuit} = 1$, for convenience.

Given commitments to players' private inputs, a card-based protocol is supposed to produce a sequence of cards as its output. The *committed* protocols listed in Table 1 produce their output as a commitment. For example, any AND protocol outputs

$$\underbrace{\boxed{?}\,\boxed{?}}_{a \wedge b}$$

from input commitments to a and b. On the other hand, *non-committed* protocols produce their output in another form.

Hereafter, for a sequence consisting of $n \in \mathbb{N}$ cards, each card of the sequence is sequentially numbered from the left (position 1, position 2, ..., position n), e.g.,

$$\overset{1}{\boxed{?}}\,\overset{2}{\boxed{\clubsuit}}\,\overset{3}{\boxed{\heartsuit}} \cdots \overset{n}{\boxed{?}}.$$

1.2   Our Results

As mentioned above, given commitments to Alice's bit a and Bob's bit b together with an additional card $\boxed{\clubsuit}$, Cheung's AND protocol produces a commitment to $a \wedge b$ with a probability of $1/2$; when it fails, the players have to create their input commitments again. This paper shows that in the last step of Cheung's AND protocol, a commitment to the OR value $a \vee b$ is also obtained when the protocol succeeds in producing a commitment to $a \wedge b$. Next, we show that, even when the protocol fails, we can still evaluate the AND value (more precisely, any Boolean function) by slightly modifying the last step of the protocol. Thus, the improved protocol never fails to compute the AND value.

Furthermore, we present two five-card copy protocols using unequal division shuffle. Because the most efficient copy protocol currently known requires six

Table 2. Protocols for making two copied commitments

	# of colors	# of cards	Type of shuffle	Avg. # of trials	Failure rate
Crépeau-Kilian [3]	2	8	RC	1	0
Mizuki-Sone [6]	2	6	RBC	1	0
Ours (§4)	2	5	UDS	2	0

cards [6], our new protocols improve upon the existing results in terms of the number of required cards, as shown in Table 2. Note that our protocols require an average of two trials.

The remainder of this paper is organized as follows. Section 2 first introduces Cheung's AND protocol along with known shuffle operations and then presents a more general definition of unequal division shuffle. Section 3 describes our slight modification to the last step of Cheung's AND protocol to expand its functionality. Section 4 proposes two new copy protocols that outperform the previous protocols in terms of the number of required cards. Finally, Sect. 5 summarizes our findings and concludes the paper.

2 Card Shuffling Operations and Known Protocol

In this section, we first introduce a random bisection cut [6]. Then, we give a general definition of unequal division shuffle. Finally, we introduce Cheung's AND protocol [2].

2.1 Random Bisection Cut

Suppose that there is a sequence of $2m$ face-down cards for some $m \in \mathbb{N}$:

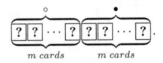

Then, a *random bisection cut* [6] (denoted by $[\cdot|\cdot]$)

$$\left[\boxed{?}\boxed{?}\cdots\boxed{?}\middle|\boxed{?}\boxed{?}\cdots\boxed{?}\right]$$

means that we bisect the sequence and randomly switch the two portions (of size m). Thus, the result of the operation will be either

$$\boxed{?}\boxed{?}\cdots\boxed{?}\boxed{?}\boxed{?}\cdots\boxed{?} \quad \text{or} \quad \boxed{?}\boxed{?}\cdots\boxed{?}\boxed{?}\boxed{?}\cdots\boxed{?},$$

where each occurs with a probability of exactly $1/2$.

The random bisection cut enables us to significantly reduce the number of required cards and trials for secure computations. See Table 1 again; the four-card non-committed AND protocol [5], the six-card committed AND protocol [6], and the four-card committed XOR protocol [6] all employ random bisection cuts. Using random bisection cuts, we can also construct a six-card copy protocol [6] (as seen in Table 2), adder protocols [4], protocols for any three-variable symmetric functions [9], and so on.

Whereas the most efficient committed AND protocol [6] currently known (that always works) uses a random bisection cut and requires six cards as stated above, Cheung et al. introduced unequal division shuffle whereby they constructed a five-card committed AND protocol that works with a probability of $1/2$. Its details are presented in the next two subsections.

2.2 Unequal Division Shuffle

Here, we present a formal definition of unequal division shuffle, which first appeared in Cheung's AND protocol [2].

Suppose that there is a sequence of $\ell \geq 3$ ($\ell \in \mathbb{N}$) face-down cards:

$$\underbrace{\boxed{?}\,\boxed{?}\cdots\boxed{?}}_{\ell \ cards}.$$

Divide it into two portions of unequal sizes, say, j cards and k cards, where $j + k = \ell$, $j \neq k$, as follows:

$$\overbrace{\underbrace{\boxed{?}\,\boxed{?}\cdots\boxed{?}}_{j \ cards}\underbrace{\boxed{?}\,\boxed{?}\cdots\boxed{?}}_{k \ cards}}^{\ell \ cards}.$$

We consider an operation that randomly switches these two portions of unequal sizes; we refer to it as *unequal division shuffle* or (j, k)-*division shuffle* (denoted by $[\cdot | \cdot]$):

$$\left[\underbrace{\boxed{?}\,\boxed{?}\cdots\boxed{?}}_{j \ cards}\Big|\underbrace{\boxed{?}\,\boxed{?}\cdots\boxed{?}}_{k \ cards}\right].$$

Thus, the result of the operation will be either

$$\underbrace{\boxed{?}\,\boxed{?}\cdots\boxed{?}}_{j \ cards}\underbrace{\boxed{?}\,\boxed{?}\cdots\boxed{?}}_{k \ cards} \ \text{or} \ \underbrace{\boxed{?}\,\boxed{?}\cdots\boxed{?}}_{k \ cards}\underbrace{\boxed{?}\,\boxed{?}\cdots\boxed{?}}_{j \ cards},$$

where each case occurs with a probability of exactly $1/2$.

We demonstrate an implementation of unequal division shuffle in Appendix A.

2.3   Cheung's AND Protocol

In this subsection, we introduce Cheung's AND protocol. It requires an additional card ♣ to produce a commitment to $a \wedge b$ from two commitments

$$\boxed{?}\,\boxed{?}\,\boxed{?}\,\boxed{?}$$
$$\underbrace{\quad}_{a}\;\underbrace{\quad}_{b}$$

placed by Alice and Bob, respectively. As mentioned in Sect. 2.2, the protocol uses unequal division shuffle, specifically $(2,3)$-division shuffle, as follows.

1. Arrange the cards of the two input commitments and the additional card as

$$\boxed{?}\;\boxed{?}\;\boxed{?}\;\boxed{?}\;\boxed{?}$$
$$\underbrace{}_{a^0}\;\underbrace{}_{\clubsuit}\;\underbrace{}_{a^1}\;\underbrace{}_{b^0}\;\underbrace{}_{b^1}$$

2. Apply $(2,3)$-division shuffle:

$$\left[\boxed{?}\boxed{?}\,\Big|\,\boxed{?}\boxed{?}\boxed{?}\right].$$

3. Reveal the card at position 1.
   (a) If the card is ♣, then the cards at positions 2 and 3 constitute a commitment to $a \wedge b$:

   $$\boxed{\clubsuit}\boxed{?}\,\boxed{?}\,\boxed{?}\,\boxed{?}.$$
   $$\underbrace{\qquad}_{a \wedge b}$$

   (b) If the card is ♡, then Alice and Bob create input commitments again to restart the protocol.

   This is Cheung's AND protocol. As seen from step 3, it fails with a probability of $1/2$ (in this case, we have to start from scratch). We verify the correctness of the protocol in the next section.

3   Improved Cheung's AND Protocol

In this section, we discuss Cheung's AND protocol and change its last step to develop an improved protocol.

Here, we confirm the correctness of Cheung's AND protocol. As discussed in Sect. 2.3, the input to Cheung's AND protocol consists of commitments to $a, b \in \{0, 1\}$ along with an additional card ♣. There are two possibilities due to the outcome of $(2,3)$-division shuffle:

$$\boxed{?}\;\boxed{?}\;\boxed{?}\;\boxed{?}\;\boxed{?} \quad \text{and} \quad \boxed{?}\;\boxed{?}\;\boxed{?}\;\boxed{?}\;\boxed{?}.$$
$$\underbrace{}_{a^0}\;\underbrace{}_{\clubsuit}\;\underbrace{}_{a^1}\;\underbrace{}_{b^0}\;\underbrace{}_{b^1} \qquad\qquad \underbrace{}_{a^1}\;\underbrace{}_{b^0}\;\underbrace{}_{b^1}\;\underbrace{}_{a^0}\;\underbrace{}_{\clubsuit}$$

We enumerate all possibilities of input and card sequences after step 2 of the protocol in Table 3 (recall encoding scheme (1)). Looking at the cards at positions 2 and 3 when the card at position 1 is ♣ in Table 3, we can easily confirm the correctness of the protocol, i.e., the cards at positions 2 and 3 surely constitute a commitment to $a \wedge b$.

In the remainder of this section, we analyze Cheung's AND protocol further to obtain an improved protocol.

Table 3. All possibilities of input and card sequences after step 2

Input	Card sequences									
(a,b)	a^0	♣	a^1	b^0	b^1	a^1	b^0	b^1	a^0	♣
$(0,0)$	♣	♣	♥	♣	♥	♥	♣	♥	♣	♣
$(0,1)$	♣	♣	♥	♥	♣	♥	♥	♣	♣	♣
$(1,0)$	♥	♣	♣	♣	♥	♣	♣	♥	♥	♣
$(1,1)$	♥	♣	♣	♥	♣	♣	♥	♣	♥	♣

3.1 Bonus Commitment to OR

When we succeed in obtaining a commitment to $a \wedge b$, i.e., when the card at position 1 is ♣ in the last step of Cheung's AND protocol, we are also able to simultaneously obtain a commitment to the OR value $a \vee b$. Thus, as indicated in Table 3, if the card at position 1 is ♣, then the cards at positions 4 and 5 constitute a commitment to $a \vee b$.

3.2 In Case of Failure

Suppose that the card at position 1 is ♥ in the last step of Cheung's AND protocol. This means that the AND computation failed and we have to start from scratch, i.e., Alice and Bob need to create their private input commitments again. However, we show that they need not do so: they can evaluate the AND value even when Cheung's AND protocol fails, as follows.

From Table 3, if the card at position 1 is ♥, the sequence of five cards

$$♥\ ?\ ?\ ?\ ? \tag{3}$$

is one of the four possibilities shown in Table 4, depending on the value of (a,b).

Table 4. Possible sequences when Cheung's AND protocol fails

Input (a,b)	Sequence of five cards				
$(0,0)$	♥	♣	♥	♣	♣
$(0,1)$	♥	♥	♣	♣	♣
$(1,0)$	♥	♣	♣	♣	♥
$(1,1)$	♥	♣	♣	♥	♣

Therefore, the card at position 4 indicates the value of $a \wedge b$, i.e., if the card at position 4 is ♣, then $a \wedge b = 0$, and if the card is ♥, then $a \wedge b = 1$. Note that opening the card does not reveal any information about the inputs a and b

besides the value of $a \wedge b$. Thus, Cheung's AND protocol does not fail to compute the AND value.

Actually, we can compute any Boolean function $f(a, b)$ in a non-committed format, given the sequence (3) above, as follows. Note that, as seen in Table 4, the position of the face-down card $\boxed{\heartsuit}$ (which is between 2 and 5) uniquely determines the value of the input (a, b). We shuffle all cards at positions corresponding to $f(a, b) = 1$ (possibly one card as in the case of $f(a, b) = a \wedge b$) and reveal all these cards. If $\boxed{\heartsuit}$ appears anywhere, then $f(a, b) = 1$; otherwise, $f(a, b) = 0$. Thus, we can evaluate the desired function (in a non-committed format).

3.3 Improved Protocol

From the discussion above, we have the following improved protocol.

1. Arrange the five cards as follows:

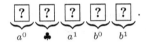

$$\underbrace{\boxed{?}}_{a^0}\ \underbrace{\boxed{?}}_{\clubsuit}\ \underbrace{\boxed{?}}_{a^1}\ \underbrace{\boxed{?}}_{b^0}\ \underbrace{\boxed{?}}_{b^1}\ .$$

2. Apply $(2, 3)$-division shuffle:

$$\left[\boxed{?}\boxed{?}\Big|\boxed{?}\boxed{?}\boxed{?}\right].$$

3. Reveal the card at position 1.

    (a) If the card is $\boxed{\clubsuit}$, then the cards at positions 2 and 3 constitute a commitment to $a \wedge b$; moreover, the cards at positions 4 and 5 constitute a commitment to $a \vee b$:

$$\boxed{\clubsuit}\ \underbrace{\boxed{?}\ \boxed{?}}_{a \wedge b}\ \underbrace{\boxed{?}\ \boxed{?}}_{a \vee b}\ .$$

    (b) If the card is $\boxed{\heartsuit}$, then we can evaluate any desired Boolean function $f(a, b)$. Shuffle all cards at positions corresponding to $f(a, b) = 1$ and reveal them. If $\boxed{\heartsuit}$ appears, then $f(a, b) = 1$; otherwise, $f(a, b) = 0$.

4   Five-Card Copy Protocols

In this section, we focus on protocols for copying a commitment.

From Table 2, using the six-card copy protocol [6], a commitment to bit $a \in \{0, 1\}$ can be copied with four additional cards:

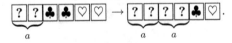

$$\underbrace{\boxed{?}\ \boxed{?}}_{a}\ \boxed{\clubsuit}\boxed{\clubsuit}\boxed{\heartsuit}\boxed{\heartsuit} \rightarrow \boxed{?}\ \underbrace{\boxed{?}\ \boxed{?}}_{a}\ \underbrace{\boxed{?}\ \boxed{?}}_{a}\ \boxed{\clubsuit}\boxed{\heartsuit}.$$

This is the most efficient protocol currently known for copying. In contrast, we prove that three additional cards (two $\boxed{\clubsuit}$s and one $\boxed{\heartsuit}$) are sufficient by proposing a five-card copy protocol using unequal division shuffle. We also propose another copy protocol that has fewer steps by considering a different shuffle.

4.1 Copy Protocol Using Unequal Division Shuffle

Given a commitment

$$\boxed{?}\boxed{?}$$
$$\underbrace{\qquad}_{a}$$

together with additional cards $\clubsuit\clubsuit\heartsuit$, our protocol makes two copied commitments, as follows.

1. Arrange the five cards as

$$\boxed{?}\ \boxed{?}\ \boxed{?}\ \boxed{?}\ \boxed{?}\ .$$
$$\underbrace{\ }_{\clubsuit}\ \underbrace{\ }_{a^0}\ \underbrace{\ }_{\heartsuit}\ \underbrace{\ }_{a^1}\ \underbrace{\ }_{\clubsuit}$$

2. Apply $(2,3)$-division shuffle:

$$\left[\,\boxed{?}\boxed{?}\,\middle|\,\boxed{?}\boxed{?}\boxed{?}\,\right].$$

3. Rearrange the sequence of five cards as

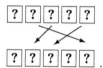

4. Reveal the card at position 5.

   (a) If the card is $\clubsuit$, then we have two commitments to a as follows:

$$\boxed{?}\boxed{?}\boxed{?}\boxed{?}\boxed{\clubsuit}.$$
$$\underbrace{\qquad}_{a}\ \underbrace{\qquad}_{a}$$

   (b) If the card is $\heartsuit$, then we have

   Swap the cards at positions 1 and 2 to obtain a commitment to a. After revealing the cards at positions 3 and 4 (which must be $\clubsuit\clubsuit$), return to step 1.

After step 3, there are two possibilities due to the shuffle outcome: the sequence of five cards is either $\clubsuit\heartsuit\clubsuit a^1 a^0$ or $\heartsuit\clubsuit a^0 \clubsuit a^1$. Table 5 enumerates all possibilities of input and card sequences after step 3 of the protocol. As can be easily seen in the table, we surely have two copied commitments in step 4(a). Note that opening the card at position 5 does not reveal any information about the input a. Thus, we have designed a five-card copy protocol that improves upon the previous results in terms of the number of required cards. It should be noted that the protocol is a Las Vegas algorithm with an average of two trials.

Table 5. Possible sequences after step 3 of our first copy protocol

Input	Card sequences	
a	♣ ♡ ♣ a^1 a^0	♡ ♣ a^0 ♣ a^1
0	♣ ♡ ♣ ♡ ♣	♡ ♣ ♣ ♣ ♡
1	♣ ♡ ♣ ♣ ♡	♡ ♣ ♡ ♣ ♣

4.2 Copy Protocol Using Double Unequal Division Shuffle

In this subsection, we reduce the number of steps for achieving copy computation by modifying the unequal division shuffle approach.

Remember that (2,3)-division shuffle changes the order of the two portions:

$$\overset{1\ \ 2}{\boxed{?}\boxed{?}} : \overset{3\ \ 4\ \ 5}{\boxed{?}\boxed{?}\boxed{?}} \rightarrow \overset{3\ \ 4\ \ 5}{\boxed{?}\boxed{?}\boxed{?}} : \overset{1\ \ 2}{\boxed{?}\boxed{?}} .$$

Here, we consider a further division of the three-card portion:

$$\overset{3\ \ 4}{\boxed{?}\boxed{?}} : \overset{5}{\boxed{?}}\ \overset{1\ \ 2}{\boxed{?}\boxed{?}} \rightarrow \overset{5}{\boxed{?}} : \overset{3\ \ 4}{\boxed{?}\boxed{?}}\ \overset{1\ \ 2}{\boxed{?}\boxed{?}} .$$

Thus, given a sequence of five cards

$$\overset{1\ \ 2\ \ 3\ \ 4\ \ 5}{\boxed{?}\boxed{?}\boxed{?}\boxed{?}\boxed{?}} ,$$

a shuffle operation resulting in either

$$\overset{1\ \ 2\ \ 3\ \ 4\ \ 5}{\boxed{?}\boxed{?}\boxed{?}\boxed{?}\boxed{?}} \ \text{ or } \ \overset{5\ \ 3\ \ 4\ \ 1\ \ 2}{\boxed{?}\boxed{?}\boxed{?}\boxed{?}\boxed{?}}$$

is called *double unequal division shuffle*.

Using such a shuffle, we can avoid rearranging the cards in step 3 of the protocol presented in Sect. 4.1.

1. Arrange the five cards as

$$\underset{a^0\quad\ \clubsuit\quad\ \heartsuit\quad\ \clubsuit\quad\ a^1}{\boxed{?}\ \boxed{?}\ \boxed{?}\ \boxed{?}\ \boxed{?}} .$$

2. Apply double unequal division shuffle:

$$\left[\boxed{?}\boxed{?}\ \boxed{?} : \boxed{?}\boxed{?}\right] .$$

3. Reveal the card at position 1.
   (a) If the card is $\boxed{\clubsuit}$, then we have two commitments to a:

$$\underset{a\qquad\quad a}{\boxed{\clubsuit}\boxed{?}\boxed{?}\boxed{?}\boxed{?}} .$$

(b) If the card is $\boxed{\heartsuit}$, then we have

Swap the cards at positions 2 and 3 to obtain a commitment to a. After revealing the cards at positions 4 and 5, return to step 1.

This protocol has two possibilities after step 2: the sequence of five cards is either $a^0 \clubsuit \heartsuit \clubsuit a^1$ or $a^1 \heartsuit \clubsuit a^0 \clubsuit$. Table 6 confirms the correctness of the protocol.

Table 6. Possible sequences after step 2 of our second protocol

Input	Card sequences	
a	$a^0 \ \clubsuit \ \heartsuit \ \clubsuit \ a^1$	$a^1 \ \heartsuit \ \clubsuit \ a^0 \ \clubsuit$
0	$\clubsuit \ \clubsuit \ \heartsuit \ \clubsuit \ \heartsuit$	$\heartsuit \ \heartsuit \ \clubsuit \ \clubsuit \ \clubsuit$
1	$\heartsuit \ \clubsuit \ \heartsuit \ \clubsuit \ \clubsuit$	$\clubsuit \ \heartsuit \ \clubsuit \ \heartsuit \ \clubsuit$

Although this protocol requires fewer steps, we are not sure whether double unequal division shuffle can be easily implemented by humans.

5 Conclusion

In this paper, we discussed the properties of the AND protocol designed by Cheung et al. and proposed an improved protocol. Although their original protocol produces only a commitment to the AND value with a probability of $1/2$, our improved protocol either produces commitments to the AND and OR values or evaluates any Boolean function. Thus, the improved protocol does not fail at all.

Furthermore, we proposed two five-card copy protocols that can securely copy an input commitment using three additional cards. Each of our protocols uses unequal division shuffle. Because the most efficient copy protocol currently known requires six cards, our new protocols improve upon the existing results in terms of the number of required cards.

An open problem is whether unequal division shuffle enables us to compute any other function using fewer cards than the existing protocols.

Acknowledgments. This work was supported by JSPS KAKENHI Grant Numbers 25289068 and 26330001.

A   How to Perform Unequal Division Shuffle

Here, we discuss how to implement unequal division shuffle. We consider the card cases shown in Fig. 1. Each case can store a deck of cards and has two sliding covers, an upper cover and a lower cover. We assume that the weight of a deck of cards is negligible compared to the case. To apply unequal division shuffle, we stow each portion in such a case and shuffle these two cases. Then, the cases are stacked one on top of the other. Removing the two middle sliding covers results in the desired sequence.

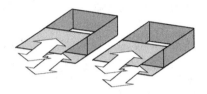

Fig. 1. Card cases suited for unequal division shuffle

References

1. den Boer, B.: More efficient match-making and satisfiability. In: Quisquater, J.-J., Vandewalle, J. (eds.) EUROCRYPT 1989. LNCS, vol. 434, pp. 208–217. Springer, Heidelberg (1990)
2. Cheung, E., Hawthorne, C., Lee, P.: CS 758 project: secure computation with playing cards (2013). http://csclub.uwaterloo.ca/~cdchawth/static/secure_playing_cards.pdf, Accessed 22–June–2015
3. Crépeau, C., Kilian, J.: Discreet solitary games. In: Stinson, D.R. (ed.) CRYPTO 1993. LNCS, vol. 773, pp. 319–330. Springer, Heidelberg (1994)
4. Mizuki, T., Asiedu, I.K., Sone, H.: Voting with a logarithmic number of cards. In: Mauri, G., Dennunzio, A., Manzoni, L., Porreca, A.E. (eds.) UCNC 2013. LNCS, vol. 7956, pp. 162–173. Springer, Heidelberg (2013)
5. Mizuki, T., Kumamoto, M., Sone, H.: The five-card trick can be done with four cards. In: Wang, X., Sako, K. (eds.) ASIACRYPT 2012. LNCS, vol. 7658, pp. 598–606. Springer, Heidelberg (2012)
6. Mizuki, T., Sone, H.: Six-card secure AND and four-card secure XOR. In: Deng, X., Hopcroft, J.E., Xue, J. (eds.) FAW 2009. LNCS, vol. 5598, pp. 358–369. Springer, Heidelberg (2009)
7. Mizuki, T., Uchiike, F., Sone, H.: Securely computing XOR with 10 cards. Australas. J. Comb. **36**, 279–293 (2006)
8. Niemi, V., Renvall, A.: Secure multiparty computations without computers. Theoret. Comput. Sci. **191**(1–2), 173–183 (1998)
9. Nishida, T., Mizuki, T., Sone, H.: Securely computing the three-input majority function with eight cards. In: Dediu, A.-H., Martín-Vide, C., Truthe, B., Vega-Rodríguez, M.A. (eds.) TPNC 2013. LNCS, vol. 8273, pp. 193–204. Springer, Heidelberg (2013)
10. Stiglic, A.: Computations with a deck of cards. Theoret. Comput. Sci. **259**(1–2), 671–678 (2001)

Straight Construction of Non-Interactive Quantum Bit Commitment Schemes from Indistinguishable Quantum State Ensembles

Tomoyuki Yamakami[✉]

Department of Information Science, University of Fukui,
3-9-1 Bunkyo, Fukui 910-8507, Japan
TomoyukiYamakami@gmail.com

Abstract. We propose two efficient quantum schemes performing quantum bit commitment, which is a simple cryptographic primitive involved with two parties, called a committer and a verifier. Our schemes are non-interactive with no supplemental shared information and they are built directly from two efficiently generated ensembles of reduced quantum states. The security conditions of our schemes come from an indistinguishability assumption of those ensembles. The first scheme achieves perfect hiding and computational binding, whereas the second scheme does computational hiding and statistical binding. It is known that the computational hardness of distinguishing between those two ensembles implies the existence of quantum one-way functions and that the existence of such functions leads to quantum bit commitment. Nonetheless, our schemes merit the simple and direct construction of quantum bit commitment schemes from those ensembles without bypassing the construction of quantum one-way functions but explicitly by exploiting specific features of the ensembles, which are interesting in their own right.

1 Introduction

Bit commitment is a fundamental cryptographic primitive between two parties and its schemes (or protocols) have been applied to build other useful cryptographic protocols, including secure coin flipping, zero-knowledge proofs, secure multiparty computation, signature schemes, and secret sharing. A scheme for bit commitment consists of two specific phases, in which two security conditions are ensured by the both parties. In a committing phase, Alice (committer) commits to a single bit and sends to Bob (verifier) its encrypted information, from which Bob cannot decipher her committed bit. In an opening phase, she reveals her bit; however, Bob must detect her wrongdoing if she presents the bit different from what she had committed to in the earlier phase. Those security conditions are known as *hiding* and *binding*, which may be met computationally, statistically, or even perfectly. Their detailed explanation will be given in Sect. 2.

Whereas the unconditional security of a *quantum key distribution scheme* [1] is well-known, no quantum bit commitment scheme has been proven to be

© Springer International Publishing Switzerland 2015
A.-H. Dediu et al. (Eds.): TPNC 2015, LNCS 9477, pp. 121–133, 2015.
DOI: 10.1007/978-3-319-26841-5_10

unconditionally secure [7,12] (namely, both statistically hiding and statistically binding). Nevertheless, this fact does not prevent us from constructing *practical* quantum bit commitment schemes with weak hiding and weak binding. Spekkens and Rudolph [13], for example, studied bounds on the degrees of hidingness and bindingness of any quantum bit commitment scheme. More recently, Chailloux and Kerenidis [2] argued that no scheme for quantum bit commitment achieves a cheating probability of less than 0.739. These results immediately prompt us to seek a reasonable means to build practically durable schemes for quantum bit commitment. In this direction, technological limitations of the existing quantum device, on one hand, have been used to design feasible protocols in, e.g., [4,5]. Dumais, Mayers, and Salvail [6], on the other hand, used a computationally difficult problem to construct a (non-interactive) scheme for perfectly-hiding quantum bit commitment. Their scheme requires the total communication cost of $O(n)$ qubits, where n is a *security parameter* agreed on by both parties, and the security of the scheme solely relies on an unproven assumption of the existence of *quantum one-way permutation* (namely, a function that permutes a given set of strings with the one-way property that the function is easy to compute but hard to invert). Koshiba and Odaira [11] later reduced this assumption to the existence of *quantum one-way functions* for statistically-hiding quantum bit commitment.

Lately, Kawachi, Koshiba, Nishimura, and Yamakami [9,10] studied a computational problem of distinguishing between two efficiently-generated ensembles of (reduced) quantum states and demonstrated how to construct from this distinction problem a quantum trapdoor one-way function as well as a secure public-key quantum cryptosystem. As a result, the existence of a secure quantum bit commitment scheme naturally follows. The purpose of this paper is, nonetheless, to describe explicitly how to build two efficient and natural schemes for quantum bit commitment from those two ensembles of quantum states *without bypassing the construction of quantum one-way functions* but by exploiting directly the ensembles's useful properties (Sect. 3.1), which are interesting in their own right. In short, our paper merits (1) a direct, simple construction of the schemes and (2) a clear exhibition of the use of the ensembles for the schemes.

As described in details in Sect. 3.2, our schemes are non-interactive with no use of auxiliary information to share by two parties. The first scheme achieves *perfect hiding* and *computational binding* at communication cost of $O(n \log n)$ qubits. The computational security of this scheme follows directly from our basic assumption on the computational difficulty of distinguishing between the aforementioned two ensembles of quantum states. From the same ensembles, we also construct another scheme whose security conditions are, in contrast, *computational hiding* and *statistical binding*. An advantage of our scheme is its concrete, explicit descriptions, independent of the correctness of the assumption.

Omitted or abridged proofs in this extended abstract are found in its complete version [14].

2   Two Main Theorems

We wish to describe two main theorems (Theorems 3 and 4), in which we claim the existence of two schemes for quantum bit commitment whose security conditions are guaranteed by the assumption on the computational hardness of distinguishing between two efficiently generated ensembles of quantum states. Let $\mathbb{N}^+$ denote the set of all positive integers and set $\mathbb{N} = \{0\} \cup \mathbb{N}^+$. Given $k \in \mathbb{N}^+$, we denote by $\mathcal{H}_k$ a k-dimensional Hilbert space; e.g., $\mathcal{H}_2 = \mathrm{span}\{|0\rangle, |1\rangle\}$. The security against a verifier requires the following notion of *hiding*. In a *committing phase*, Alice (committer) starts with $|0\rangle$ and commits to a certain bit a ($a \in \{0, 1\}$). She applies a quantum transformation, say, U_1 in order to encrypt a and then she sends Bob (verifier) a subsystem, say, $\mathcal{H}_{com}$. Let χ_a be the (reduced) quantum state that Bob receives from Alice. We use the next definition for the computationally/perectly hiding condition given in [6].

Definition 1 *(hiding condition)* [6]. *A non-interactive quantum bit commitment scheme $\mathcal{A}$ is* computationally hiding *if, for any positive polynomial p, there is no polynomial-time quantum algorithm that outputs a from instance χ_a with success probability at least $1/2 + 1/p(n)$ for any length $n \in \mathbb{N}^+$. On the contrary, the scheme $\mathcal{A}$ is called* perfectly hiding *if $\chi_0 = \chi_1$.*

In an *opening phase* (or a *revealing phase*), Bob asks Alice to reveal her committed bit. Suppose that Alice changes her mind and plans to deceive him by revealing a willfully chosen bit, say, b. For this purpose, she must apply a certain unitary operator, say, $U_2^{(b)}$ secretly at the beginning of the opening phase. Therefore, we can model Alice's *cheating strategy* $\mathcal{U}$ by a triplet $(U_1, U_2^{(0)}, U_2^{(1)})$. Let $T_b^{(\mathcal{U})}(n)$ denote the probability that Bob convinces himself that b is her committed bit after she applies $U_2^{(b)}$, provided that Bob faithfully follows the scheme. Note that $0 \leq \frac{1}{2}(T_0^{(\mathcal{U})}(n) + T_1^{(\mathcal{U})}(n)) \leq 1$. For the security against Alice, this paper takes the following definition of binding. Other definitions are also possible and found in, e.g., [3].

Definition 2 *(binding condition)* [6]. *A non-interactive quantum bit commitment scheme is* computationally *(resp., statistically)* binding *if there exists a negligible[1] function $\varepsilon(n)$ such that, for any polynomial-time computable (resp., time-unbounded) cheating strategy $\mathcal{U} = (U_1, U_2^{(0)}, U_2^{(1)})$ of Alice, the average success probability $\frac{1}{2}(T_0^{(\mathcal{U})}(n) + T_1^{(\mathcal{U})}(n))$ is at most $\frac{1}{2} + \varepsilon(n)$ for every $n \in \mathbb{N}^+$.*

Our main theorems concern the notion of indistinguishable ensembles of (reduced) quantum states, which are generated efficiently in a simple, explicit manner. Let us first recall special quantum states defined in [10]. Let n be any number in $\mathbb{N}^+$, which is used as a *security parameter*; for our purpose, we implicitly demand that *n is even and $n/2$ is odd*. Let S_n denote the set of all

---

[1] A function $\mu : \mathbb{N} \to [0, 1]$ is called *negligible* if, for any positive polynomial p, $\mu(n) \leq 1/p(n)$ holds for all but finitely many numbers $n \in \mathbb{N}$.

permutations $\sigma : [n] \to [n]$, where $[n] = \{1, 2, 3, \ldots, n\}$. Since $|S_n| = n!$, every element in S_n can be expressed using $O(n \log n)$ qubits. The special set K_n is composed only of all permutations $\pi \in S_n$ satisfying $\pi\pi = \mathrm{id}$ and $\pi(i) \neq i$ for each element $i \in [n]$.

Given three elements $s \in \{0, 1\}$, $\sigma \in S_n$, and $\pi \in K_n$, we define a useful quantum state $|\phi_{\sigma,s}^{(\pi)}(n)\rangle = (1/\sqrt{2})(|\sigma\rangle + (-1)^s|\sigma\pi\rangle)$. For each fixed permutation $\pi \in K_n$, we partition S_n into two arbitrarily fixed subsets $\hat{S}_0$ and $\hat{S}_1$, which must satisfy the following condition: for each index $a \in \{0, 1\}$ and for all elements $\sigma \in S_n$, $\sigma \in \hat{S}_a$ implies $\sigma\pi \in \hat{S}_{1-a}$. Let $S_n^{(\pi)}$ denote either $\hat{S}_0$ or $\hat{S}_1$ that contains the identity id. Notice that $\pi \notin S_n^{(\pi)}$. the choice of such $S_n^{(\pi)}$ is not important; however, for practicality, we assume that there is an efficient method of deciding whether σ belongs to $S_n^{(\pi)}$ or not. The set $\mathcal{B}^{(\pi)} = \{|\phi_{\sigma,s}^{(\pi)}(n)\rangle \mid \sigma \in S_n^{(\pi)}, s \in \{0, 1\}\}$ forms a computational basis for the Hilbert space $\mathcal{H}_{S_n} = \mathrm{span}\{|\sigma\rangle \mid \sigma \in S_n\}$. Any quantum state $|\gamma\rangle$ in $\mathcal{H}_{S_n}$ can be expressed as $\sum_{a \in \{0,1\}} \sum_{\sigma \in S_n^{(\pi)}} \alpha_{a,\sigma,\pi} |\phi_{\sigma,a}^{(\pi)}(n)\rangle$ for each fixed $\pi \in K_n$, where $\alpha_{a,\sigma,\pi}$'s are appropriate amplitudes. Two notable properties of $|\phi_{\sigma,a}^{(\pi)}\rangle$'s are: $|\phi_{\sigma,0}^{(\pi)}\rangle = \frac{1}{2}[|\phi_{\sigma,0}^{(\kappa)}\rangle + |\phi_{\sigma,1}^{(\kappa)}\rangle + |\phi_{\sigma\pi,0}^{(\kappa)}\rangle + |\phi_{\sigma\pi,1}^{(\kappa)}\rangle]$ and $|\phi_{\sigma,1}^{(\pi)}\rangle = (1/(|K_n| - 1)) \sum_{\kappa \in K_n} (|\phi_{\sigma,0}^{(\kappa)}\rangle - |\phi_{\sigma\pi,0}^{(\kappa)}\rangle)$.

Hereafter, we fix $n \in \mathbb{N}^+$ and $\pi \in K_n$, and we omit the parameter "n" whenever "n" is clear from the context. For each bit $s \in \{0, 1\}$, define $\rho_s^{(\pi)} = (1/|S_n|) \sum_{\sigma \in S_n} |\phi_{\sigma,s}^{(\pi)}\rangle\langle\phi_{\sigma,s}^{(\pi)}|$. Note that $\rho_0^{(\pi)}$ and $\rho_1^{(\pi)}$ are respectively denoted by ρ_π^+ and ρ_π^- in [10]. Let $|\Phi_s^{(\pi)}\rangle$ indicate $|S_n|^{-1/2} \sum_{\sigma \in S_n} |\sigma\rangle|\phi_{\sigma,s}^{(\pi)}\rangle$, which is a *purification* of $\rho_s^{(\pi)}$ because $\rho_s^{(\pi)} = \mathrm{tr}_1(|\Phi_s^{(\pi)}\rangle\langle\Phi_s^{(\pi)}|)$.

Let us recall the computational distinction problem QSCD$_{\mathrm{ff}}$ introduced in [10]. Since we need only a restricted form of this problem, we re-formulate the problem in the following fashion. Let k be any fixed constant in $\mathbb{N}^+$.

k-QUANTUM STATE COMPUTATIONAL DISTINCTION PROBLEM k-QSCD:

○ INSTANCE: 1^n and $\rho^{\otimes k}$ with $\rho \in \{\rho_0^{(\pi)}(n), \rho_1^{(\pi)}(n)\}$ for a certain fixed (but hidden) permutation $\pi \in K_n$, depending only on $n \in \mathbb{N}^+$.

○ OUTPUT: YES, if $\rho = \rho_0^{(\pi)}(n)$; NO, otherwise.

Given a function $p : \mathbb{N} \to [0, 1]$, we say that a quantum algorithm $\mathcal{A}$ *solves* k-QSCD *with advantage* $p(n)$ if $\mathcal{A}$ distinguishes[2] between $\{\rho_0^{(\pi)}(n)^{\otimes k}\}_{n \in \mathbb{N}^+}$ and $\{\rho_1^{(\pi)}(n)^{\otimes k}\}_{n \in \mathbb{N}^+}$ with advantage $p(n)$. For each constant $\gamma \in [0, 1]$, we also say that $\mathcal{A}$ solves k-QSCD*with average advantage* γ *for length* n if γ equals the expectation, over all $\pi \in K_n$ chosen uniformly at random, of the advantage with which $\mathcal{A}$ distinguishes between $\{\rho_0^{(\pi)}(n)^{\otimes k}\}_{n \in \mathbb{N}^+}$ and $\{\rho_1^{(\pi)}(n)^{\otimes k}\}_{n \in \mathbb{N}^+}$. It is known in [10] that efficiently distinguishing between $\rho_0^{(\pi)}$ and $\rho_1^{(\pi)}$ on average is as hard as efficiently distinguishing between them in the worst case.

Our first main theorem is now stated formally as follows.

---

[2] An algorithm $\mathcal{A}$ *distinguishes between two ensembles* $\{\rho(n)\}_{n \in \mathbb{N}^+}$ and $\{\chi(n)\}_{n \in \mathbb{N}^+}$ *with advantage* $p(n)$ if, for every $n \in \mathbb{N}^+$, $p(n)$ equals $|\mathrm{Prob}[\mathcal{A}(1^n, \rho(n)) = 1] - \mathrm{Prob}[\mathcal{A}(1^n, \chi(n)) = 1]|$, where $\mathcal{A}(1^n, \rho(n))$ is formally expressed as $\mathcal{A}(|1^n\rangle\langle 1^n| \otimes \rho(n))$.

Theorem 3 (first main theorem). *There exists a scheme for non-interactive quantum bit commitment for which the scheme is polynomial-time executable and has an explicit, direct construction from the ensembles $\{\rho_0^{(\pi)}(n), \rho_1^{(\pi)}(n)\}_{n \in \mathbb{N}, \pi \in K_n}$. Moreover, if no quantum algorithm solves k-QSCD in polynomial time with non-negligible average advantage for a certain $k \geq 2$, then the scheme achieves prefect hiding and computational binding.*

It is also possible to strengthen the above binding condition by way of weakening the hiding condition. More precisely, under the same assumption as in the first main theorem, we can construct another scheme that achieves computational hiding and statistical binding.

Theorem 4 (second main theorem). *As in Theorem 3, there is also another scheme for quantum bit commitment that achieves computational hiding and statistical binding.*

We stress that our schemes have concrete, explicit descriptions, independent of the correctness of the assumption, and potentially it might be applied to other fields of primary interest. The detailed construction of those schemes will be given in Sect. 3.

3   Quantum Bit Commitment

3.1   Three Key Procedures

Before giving the desired schemes, we shall quickly discuss three key quantum procedures, which are important ingredients of the construction of our quantum bit commitment schemes in Sect. 3.2.

The *Hadamard transform* H acts on the quantum system $\mathcal{H}_2$ as $H|s\rangle = (1/\sqrt{2})(|0\rangle + (-1)^s|1\rangle)$ for every index $s \in \{0,1\}$. Given $n \in \mathbb{N}^+$ and $\pi \in K_n$, the *controlled-π operator* C_π acts on $\mathcal{H}_2 \otimes \mathcal{H}_{S_n}$ as $C_\pi|a\rangle|\sigma\rangle = |a\rangle|\sigma\pi\rangle$ if $a = 1$, and $|a\rangle|\sigma\rangle$ otherwise.

[PROCEDURE 1] Let $\kappa \in K_n$. The procedure $P_{1,\kappa}$ generates the quantum state $|0\rangle|\sigma\rangle|\pi\rangle|\phi_{\kappa\sigma,0}^{(\pi)}\rangle$ in the system $\mathcal{H}_2 \otimes \mathcal{H}_{S_n} \otimes \mathcal{H}_{S_n} \otimes \mathcal{H}_{S_n}$ from $|0\rangle|\sigma\rangle|\pi\rangle|\text{id}\rangle$ if $\pi \neq \text{id}$. Whenever $\kappa = \text{id}$, we often drop "κ" from $P_{1,\kappa}$. Similarly, we can generate $|0\rangle|\pi\rangle|\Phi_0^{(\pi)}\rangle$ from $|0\rangle|\pi\rangle|\text{id}\rangle|\text{id}\rangle$. Call this procedure by $\tilde{P}_1$.

[PROCEDURE 2] The procedure P_2 transforms $|\sigma\rangle|\phi_{\sigma,s}^{(\pi)}\rangle$ to $|\sigma\rangle|\phi_{\sigma,1-s}^{(\pi)}\rangle$ *without knowing* (s, π). See [10] for details.

[PROCEDURE 3] The procedure P_{SPA} tries to "partition" a given quantum state χ in the system $\mathcal{H}_{S_n}$ into two orthogonal states χ_0 and χ_1 so that $\chi = \chi_0 + \chi_1$ holds, where χ_s is of the form $\sum_{\sigma \in S} p_{\sigma,s}|\phi_{\sigma,s}^{(\pi)}\rangle\langle\phi_{\sigma,s}^{(\pi)}|$ with certain amplitudes $p_{\sigma,s} \in \mathbb{R}$ for each index $s \in \{0,1\}$. This P_{SPA} is formally described as follows.

STATE PARTITION ALGORITHM: P_{SPA}

(S1) Take an instance of the form $\chi' = |\pi\rangle\langle\pi| \otimes \chi$ in the system $\mathcal{H}_{S_n} \otimes \mathcal{H}_{S_n}$. Prepare $|0\rangle\langle 0| \otimes \chi'$ in $\mathcal{H} = \mathcal{H}_2 \otimes \mathcal{H}_{S_n} \otimes \mathcal{H}_{S_n}$.

(S2) Apply $H \otimes I^{\otimes 2}$ in the system $\mathcal{H}$. Apply C_π to the third register conditioned on the first register. Finally, apply $H \otimes I^{\otimes 2}$ to $\mathcal{H}$.

(S3) The state $|0\rangle\langle 0| \otimes \chi'$ changes into $|0\rangle\langle 0| \otimes |\pi\rangle\langle\pi| \otimes \chi_0 + |1\rangle\langle 1| \otimes |\pi\rangle\langle\pi| \otimes \chi_1$.

3.2 Two New Schemes

Here, we shall describe in details two schemes for quantum bit commitment. For those schemes, we shall use the following quantum system. A quantum system $\mathcal{H}_{all}$ between Alice and Bob is $\mathcal{H}_{A,private} \otimes \mathcal{H}_{bit} \otimes \mathcal{H}_{open} \otimes \mathcal{H}_{com} \otimes \mathcal{H}_{B,private}$, where $\mathcal{H}_{A,private}$ is a system used only by Alice, $\mathcal{H}_{open} = \mathcal{H}_{open1} \otimes \mathcal{H}_{open2}$ holds a secret key produced by Alice, $\mathcal{H}_{bit}$ is a 1-qubit system for a committed bit by Alice, $\mathcal{H}_{com}$ is used to produce encrypted information regarding a committed bit, and $\mathcal{H}_{B,private}$ is a system used only by Bob.

In what follows, n denotes the security parameter on which Alice and Bob initially agree.

[**First Scheme**] For the first scheme, we need to make a crucial modification of $\Phi_s^{(\pi)}$'s and $\rho_s^{(\pi)}$'s defined in Sect. 2. Let $\kappa_0 = \mathrm{id}$ and let $\kappa_1 \in K_n$ be a properly selected element with $\kappa_0 \neq \kappa_1$. For each index $s \in \{0,1\}$, we define a new quantum state $\tilde{\Phi}_s^{(\pi)} = (1/\sqrt{|S_n|}) \sum_{\sigma \in S_n} |\sigma\rangle |\phi_{\kappa_s\sigma,1}^{(\pi)}\rangle$ and also a new reduced state $\tilde{\rho}_s^{(\pi)} = |S_n|^{-1} \sum_{\sigma \in S_n} |\phi_{\kappa_s\sigma,1}^{(\pi)}\rangle\langle\phi_{\kappa_s\sigma,1}^{(\pi)}|$. To help simplify its analysis in Sect. 4, the following description contains a detailed account of the scheme. In a committing phase, Alice commits to a certain bit and sends its encrypted (reduced) quantum state to Bob.

COMMITTING PHASE PROTOCOL $\mathcal{A}_{com}$:

(C1) Initially, Alice owns the system $\mathcal{H}_A^{(C1)} = \mathcal{H}_{A,private} \otimes \mathcal{H}_{bit} \otimes \mathcal{H}_{open} \otimes \mathcal{H}_{com}$ and Bob owns $\mathcal{H}_B^{(C1)} = \mathcal{H}_{B,private}$. Let a be a bit to which Alice commits. Let $\mathcal{H}_{open} = \mathcal{H}_{open1} \otimes \mathcal{H}_{open2}$. Starting with $|0\rangle$ in $\mathcal{H}_{all}$, she randomly chooses her secret key $\pi \in K_n$ in $\mathcal{H}_{open2}$.

(C2) She prepares $|\mathrm{id}\rangle|\mathrm{id}\rangle$ in $\mathcal{H}_{open1} \otimes \mathcal{H}_{com}$, generates $(1/\sqrt{|S_n|}) \sum_{\sigma \in S_n} |\sigma\rangle$ from $|\mathrm{id}\rangle$, and then creates $|\tilde{\Phi}_0^{(\pi)}\rangle$ in $\mathcal{H}_{open1} \otimes \mathcal{H}_{com}$ by applying P_{1,κ_0}.

(C3) She places $|a\rangle$ into $\mathcal{H}_{bit}$. She then transforms $|a\rangle|\tilde{\Phi}_0^{(\pi)}\rangle$ in $\mathcal{H}_{open1} \otimes \mathcal{H}_{com}$ into $|a\rangle|\tilde{\Phi}_a^{(\pi)}\rangle$ by applying P_{1,κ_1} and P_2 only when $a = 1$.

(C4) She sends the system $\mathcal{H}_{com}$ to Bob. Bob then receives the reduced state $\tilde{\rho}_a^{(\pi)}$, which is called a *commitment state*. Bob should protect it from decoherence until an opening phase. In the end, Alice's system becomes $\mathcal{H}_A^{(C4)} = \mathcal{H}_{A,private} \otimes \mathcal{H}_{bit} \otimes \mathcal{H}_{open}$ and Bob's becomes $\mathcal{H}_B^{(C4)} = \mathcal{H}_{com} \otimes \mathcal{H}_{B,private}$.

In an opening phase, Alice reveals her secret bit a together with additional information. Bob then tests whether a is actually the bit committed to by her in the committing phase.

OPENING PHASE $\mathcal{A}_{open}$:

(R1) Alice's current system is $\mathcal{H}_A^{(R1)} = \mathcal{H}_{A,private} \otimes \mathcal{H}_{bit} \otimes \mathcal{H}_{open}$ and Bob's system is $\mathcal{H}_B^{(R1)} = \mathcal{H}_{com} \otimes \mathcal{H}_{B,private}$. Alice sends the system $\mathcal{H}_{bit} \otimes \mathcal{H}_{open}$ to Bob.

(R2) Alice now owns the system $\mathcal{H}_A^{(R2)} = \mathcal{H}_{A,private}$ and Bob owns $\mathcal{H}_B^{(R2)} = \mathcal{H}_{open} \otimes \mathcal{H}_{bit} \otimes \mathcal{H}_{com} \otimes \mathcal{H}_{B,private}$. Note that the registers $\mathcal{H}_{bit} \otimes \mathcal{H}_{open2}$ contain (a, π) in superposition. If $\pi \notin K_n$, then Bob declares that Alice has deceived him. In what follows, we assume that $\pi \in K_n$.

(R3) Assume that, in the committing phase, Bob had received a reduced state χ in $\mathcal{H}_{com}$ from Alice. Bob runs P_{SPA} on input $|0\rangle\langle0| \otimes \chi$ in $\mathcal{H}_{B,private} \otimes \mathcal{H}_{com}$, provided that $\mathcal{H}_{B,private}$ is a 2-dimensional system.

(R4) Measure the system $\mathcal{H}_{B,private}$. If the bit in $\mathcal{H}_{B,private}$ does not match a in $\mathcal{H}_{bit}$, then Bob declares that Alice has deceived him. Now, assume otherwise.

(R5) Whenever $a = 1$, first apply P_{1,κ_1} and P_2 to change $|\tilde{\Phi}_1^{(\pi)}\rangle$ to $|\tilde{\Phi}_0^{(\pi)}\rangle$. Apply $\tilde{P}_1^{-1}$ to $\mathcal{H}_2 \otimes \mathcal{H}_{open} \otimes \mathcal{H}_{com}$. Observe $\mathcal{H}_{bit}$ and obtain a. Moreover, measure the system $\mathcal{H}_{open1} \otimes \mathcal{H}_{com}$ in state $|0\rangle|id\rangle$. If $(0, id)$ is observed, then Bob accepts a as Alice's committed bit. Otherwise, Bob declares that Alice has deceived him.

[**Second Scheme**] Unlike the first scheme, Alice generates $\{\Phi_0^{(\pi)}, \Phi_1^{(\pi)}\}$ and sends Bob an element in $\{\rho_0^{(\pi)}, \rho_1^{(\pi)}\}$. The committing phase and opening phase work as below. Since this protocol looks similar to the first scheme, we omit the detailed account of qubit transformations.

COMMITTING PHASE PROTOCOL $\mathcal{A}'_{com}$:

(C1') Let $\pi \in K_n$ be a random element and let a be a bit to which Alice commits.

(C2') Similarly to the first scheme, transform $|id\rangle|id\rangle$ to $|\Phi_0^{(\pi)}\rangle$ by P_1.

(C3') Transform $|a\rangle|\Phi_0^{(\pi)}\rangle$ into $|a\rangle|\Phi_a^{(\pi)}\rangle$ by applying P_2 if $a = 1$.

(C4') Alice sends the system $\mathcal{H}_{com}$ to Bob and he then receives $\rho_a^{(\pi)}$.

OPENING PHASE PROTOCOL $\mathcal{A}'_{open}$:

(R1') Alice sends the system $\mathcal{H}_{bit} \otimes \mathcal{H}_{open}$ to Bob.

(R2′)–(R4′) Let χ be a reduced state that Bob had received in the committing phase. Follow Steps (R2)–(R4) in the first scheme on his system $\mathcal{H}_B^{(R2')} = \mathcal{H}_{open} \otimes \mathcal{H}_{bit} \otimes \mathcal{H}_{com} \otimes \mathcal{H}_{B,private}$.

(R5′) Follow Step (R5) except that, when $a = 1$, he changes $|\Phi_1^{(\pi)}\rangle$ to $|\Phi_0^{(\pi)}\rangle$ by applying P_2.

---

4 Proof of the Main Theorems

To prove our main theorems, let us examine the schemes presented in Sect. 3.2 and prove their security conditions under the computational hardness assumption of k-QSCD for any number $k \geq 2$.

We first wish to prove that the second scheme indeed achieves the desired conditions of computational hiding and statistical binding. Because of page constraint, we omit this proof. See [14] for the detailed proof.

Next, we shall show that the first scheme achieves perfect hiding (Sect. 4.1) and computational binding (Sect. 4.2).

4.1 Perfect Hiding

Let $\pi \in K_n$. Recall that, in Step (C4), Alice faithfully sends Bob a reduced state $\tilde{\rho}_a^{(\pi)}$ associated with her committed bit a. Since $S_n = \{\kappa_0\sigma \mid \sigma \in S_n\} = \{\kappa_1\sigma \mid \sigma \in S_n\}$, we can conclude that $\sum_{\sigma \in S_n} |\phi_{\kappa_0\sigma,1}^{(\pi)}\rangle\langle\phi_{\kappa_0\sigma,1}^{(\pi)}| = \sum_{\sigma \in S_n} |\phi_{\kappa_1\sigma,1}^{(\pi)}\rangle\langle\phi_{\kappa_1\sigma,1}^{(\pi)}|$. This yields $\tilde{\rho}_0^{(\pi)} = \tilde{\rho}_1^{(\pi)}$, which leads to the perfectly hiding condition. This hiding condition holds without any assumption on $\{\rho_0^{(\pi)}(n), \rho_1^{(\pi)}(n)\}_{n\in\mathbb{N}^+, \pi\in K_n}$.

4.2 Computational Binding

We want to assert that our first scheme achieves the computationally binding condition, assuming the computational hardness of k-QSCD. For later convenience, we state this assertion as a proposition.

Proposition 5. *Let $k \geq 2$. If no polynomial-time quantum algorithm solves k-QSCD with non-negligible average advantage, then our first quantum bit commitment scheme is computationally binding.*

To prove Proposition 5, we consider a new problem, called the *hidden permutation search problem* (HPSP), in which we search for π from input $(1^n, \rho_0^{(\pi)}(n))$.

HIDDEN PERMUTATION SEARCH PROBLEM (HPSP):

o INSTANCE: 1^n ($n \in \mathbb{N}^+$) and $\rho_0^{(\pi)}(n)$ with hidden permutation $\pi \in K_n$.
o OUTPUT: π.

In Lemma 6, we connect the violation of computationally binding condition to the efficient solvability of HPSP. We say that a quantum algorithm $\mathcal{A}$ *solves* HPSP *with average probability* γ *for length* n if, over all permutations $\pi \in K_n$ chosen uniformly at random, $\mathcal{A}$ takes instance $(1^n, \rho_0^{(\pi)}(n))$ and outputs π with probability exactly γ.

Lemma 6. *Assume that there exist a positive polynomial p and a polynomial-time cheating strategy $\mathcal{U}$ of Alice satisfying $\frac{1}{2}(T_0^{(\mathcal{U})}(n) + T_1^{(\mathcal{U})}(n)) \geq 1/2 + 1/p(n)$ for infinitely many lengths n. Then, there exists a polynomial-time quantum algorithm that solves HPSP with average probability at least $1/2p(n)^2$ for infinitely many lengths n.*

Since the proof of Lemma 6 is quite involved, it will be given in Sect. 5. Lemma 7 further makes a bridge between HPSP and 2-QSCD.

Lemma 7. *If there are a positive polynomial p and a polynomial-time quantum algorithm that solves HPSP with average probability at least $1/p(n)$ for infinitely many lengths n, then there are a positive polynomial q and a polynomial-time quantum algorithm that solves 2-QSCD with average advantage at least $1/q(n)$ for infinitely many lengths n.*

As shown in [6], it suffices to consider only the case of $U_2^{(1)} = I$ for Alice's cheating strategy $\mathcal{U} = (U_1, U_2^{(0)}, U_2^{(1)})$. In the rest of this paper, we always set $\mathcal{U} = (U_1, U_2^{(0)}, I)$.

Proof of Proposition 5. Proposition 5 We shall show the contrapositive of the theorem. First, assume that there exist a positive polynomial p and Alice's polynomial-time cheating strategy $\mathcal{U} = (U_1, U_2^{(0)}, I)$ satisfying $\frac{1}{2}(T_0^{(\mathcal{U})}(n) + T_1^{(\mathcal{U})}(n)) \geq 1/2 + 1/p(n)$ for infinitely many lengths n. By Lemmas 6 and 7, we conclude that 2-QSCD can be solved by a certain polynomial-time quantum algorithm with average advantage at least $1/2p(n)^2$ for infinitely many n. Therefore, we have completed the proof.

5   Proof of Lemma 6

Let us provide the missing proof of Lemma 6 by constructing in Sect. 5.2 an appropriate quantum algorithm $\mathcal{A}_{HPSP}$ that efficiently solves HPSP with non-negligible probability, provided that the computationally binding condition does not hold. This algorithm $\mathcal{A}_{HPSP}$ tries to output π from input instance $(1^n, \rho_0^{(\pi)})$ with average probability at least $1/2p(n)^2$.

Hereafter, let $\mathcal{U} = (U_1, U_2^{(0)}, I)$ be Alice's polynomial-time cheating strategy and assume the existence of a positive polynomial p for which $\frac{1}{2}(T_0^{(\mathcal{U})} + T_1^{(\mathcal{U})}) \geq 1/2 + 1/p(n)$ for all but finitely many numbers n. Throughout the subsequent subsections, for readability, we tend to drop scripts "n" and "$\mathcal{U}$"; for example, we write T_1 for $T_1^{(\mathcal{U})}(n)$.

5.1 Distillation Algorithm

Firstly, we shall present an important subroutine that makes up of the desired quantum algorithm $\mathcal{A}_{HPSP}$ for HPSP. Conventionally, we say that Alice *unveils* a (with probability p) if, in the opening phase, when Bob conducts a measurement and observes a and convinces himself that this is her committed bit (with probability p).

At the beginning of the committing phase, *adversarial Alice* starts with $|0\rangle$ in the quantum system $\mathcal{H}_A^{(C1)} = \mathcal{H}_{A,private} \otimes \mathcal{H}_{bit} \otimes \mathcal{H}_{open} \otimes \mathcal{H}_{com}$. Instead of taking Steps (C1)–(C3), she applies the unitary operator U_1 to $|0\rangle$ in $\mathcal{H}_A^{(C1)}$ and generates a quantum state

$$|\eta^{(C1)}\rangle = U_1|0\rangle = \sum_{a\in\{0,1\}} \sum_{\sigma\in S_n} \sum_{\pi\in K_n} |\xi_{a,\pi,\sigma}\rangle|a\rangle|\pi\rangle|\sigma\rangle|\gamma_{a,\pi,\sigma}\rangle$$

satisfying $\sum_{a,\sigma,\pi} \||\xi_{a,\pi,\sigma}\rangle\|^2 = 1$. Since $|\gamma_{a,\pi,\sigma}\rangle \in \mathcal{H}_{S_n} = \mathrm{span}\{|\phi_{\tau,s}^{(\pi)}\rangle \mid \tau \in S_n^{(\pi)}, s \in \{0,1\}\}$, it holds that $|\gamma_{a,\pi,\sigma}\rangle = \sum_{\tau,s} \alpha_{\tau,s}^{(a,\pi,\sigma)}|\phi_{\tau,s}^{(\pi)}\rangle$ for appropriate amplitudes $\alpha_{\tau,s}^{(a,\pi,\sigma)}$'s. Hence, we obtain

$$|\eta^{(C1)}\rangle = \sum_{\pi\in K_n} \sum_{\sigma\in S_n} \sum_{\tau\in S_n^{(\pi)}} \sum_{a,s\in\{0,1\}} |\xi_{a,\pi,\sigma}^{(\tau,s)}\rangle|a\rangle|\pi\rangle|\sigma\rangle|\phi_{\tau,s}^{(\pi)}\rangle,$$

where $|\xi_{a,\pi,\sigma}^{(\tau,s)}\rangle = \alpha_{\tau,s}^{(a,\pi,\sigma)}|\xi_{a,\pi,\sigma}\rangle$.

We define $N_a \equiv \sum_{\pi\in K_n} M_{bit}^{(a)} \otimes M_{open1}^{(\pi)} \otimes N_{mix}^{(a,\pi)}$, where $N_{mix}^{(a,\pi)}$ projects $\mathcal{H}_{open1} \otimes \mathcal{H}_{com}$ onto $\mathrm{span}\{|\phi_{\kappa_a\sigma,0}^{(\pi)}\rangle \mid \sigma \in S_n\}$. Note that T_1 equals $\|(I \otimes N_1)|\eta^{(C1)}\rangle\|^2$. We want to define $|\eta_{ideal}^{(C1)}\rangle$ to be an *ideal* quantum state for adversarial Alice so that, from this quantum state, Alice can unveil 1 with certainty. This is done by taking the normalized state of $(I \otimes N_1)|\eta^{(C1)}\rangle$; that is, $|\eta_{ideal}^{(C1)}\rangle = (1/\sqrt{T_1})(I \otimes N_1)|\eta^{(C1)}\rangle$. We can assume that $|\eta_{ideal}^{(C1)}\rangle$ has the form $\sum_{\pi\in K_n} |\xi_{1,\pi}\rangle|1\rangle|\pi\rangle|\tilde{\Phi}_1^{(\pi)}\rangle$ for an appropriate set $\{|\xi_{1,\pi}\rangle\}_{\pi\in K_n}$ satisfying $\sum_{\pi\in K_n} \||\xi_{1,\pi}\rangle\|^2 = 1$.

Next, we shall demonstrate how to implement $I \otimes N_1$ algorithmically and to distill $|\eta_{ideal}^{(C1)}\rangle$ from $|\eta^{(C1)}\rangle$ with probability T_1 by a projective measurement.

DISTILLATION ALGORITHM $\mathcal{A}_{dis}$:

(D1) Prepare an additional register in state $|0\rangle$ in $\mathcal{H}_2$. Given $|0\rangle|\eta^{(C1)}\rangle$ in $\mathcal{H}_2 \otimes \mathcal{H}_A^{(C1)}$, where $|\eta^{(C1)}\rangle = |\xi_{a,\pi,\sigma}^{(\tau,s)}\rangle|a\rangle|\pi\rangle|\sigma\rangle|\phi_{\tau,s}^{(\pi)}\rangle$, measure the second register in state $|1\rangle$. The state $|\eta^{(C1)}\rangle$ collapses to $|\xi_{1,\pi,\sigma}^{(\tau,s)}\rangle|1\rangle|\pi\rangle|\sigma\rangle|\phi_{\tau,s}^{(\pi)}\rangle$.

(D2) Transform $|0\rangle|\pi\rangle|\phi_{\tau,s}^{(\pi)}\rangle$ in $\mathcal{H}_2 \otimes \mathcal{H}_{open2} \otimes \mathcal{H}_{com}$ to $|s\rangle|\pi\rangle|\phi_{\tau,s}^{(\pi)}\rangle$ by applying P_{SPA}. Measure the first register in state $|1\rangle$ and then obtain $|\xi_{1,\pi,\sigma}^{(\tau,1)}\rangle|1\rangle|\pi\rangle|\phi_{\tau,1}^{(\pi)}\rangle$.

(D3) Change $|\phi_{\tau,1}^{(\pi)}\rangle$ to $|\phi_{\tau,0}^{(\pi)}\rangle$ by applying P_2. Prepare $|\mathrm{id}\rangle$ and transform $|\pi\rangle|\mathrm{id}\rangle|\phi_{\tau,0}^{(\pi)}\rangle$ in $\mathcal{H}_{open1}\otimes\mathcal{H}_{S_n}\otimes\mathcal{H}_{com}$ to $|\pi\rangle|\tau\rangle|\mathrm{id}\rangle$ by applying P_1^{-1}. This yields

$$|\xi_{1,\pi,\sigma}^{(\tau,1)}\rangle|\pi\rangle|\tau\rangle|\mathrm{id}\rangle.$$

Measure the fourth register in state $|\sigma\rangle$ and obtain $|\xi_{1,\pi,\sigma}^{(\sigma,1)}\rangle|\pi\rangle|\sigma\rangle|\mathrm{id}\rangle.$

(D4) Apply P_{1,κ_1} to $|\pi\rangle|\sigma\rangle|\mathrm{id}\rangle$ in $\mathcal{H}_{open}\otimes\mathcal{H}_{com}$ to obtain $|\pi\rangle|\sigma\rangle|\phi_{\kappa_1\sigma,0}^{(\pi)}\rangle$ and then change $|\phi_{\kappa_1\sigma,0}^{(\pi)}\rangle$ to $|\phi_{\kappa_1\sigma,1}^{(\pi)}\rangle$ by applying P_2.

The above algorithm $\mathcal{A}_{dis}$ transforms $|\eta^{(C1)}\rangle$ into $\sqrt{T_1}|\eta_{ideal}^{(C1)}\rangle$, which equals $\sqrt{T_1/|S_n|}\sum_{\sigma,\pi}|\xi_{1,\pi}\rangle|1\rangle|\pi\rangle|\sigma\rangle|\phi_{\kappa_1\sigma,1}^{(\pi)}\rangle$. Let $\pi'\in K_n$ be a (hidden) permutation of an input instance $\rho_0^{(\pi')}$ given to HPSP. Note that $span\{|\phi_{\sigma,0}^{(\pi')}\rangle \mid \sigma\in S_n\}$ is completely specified by a basis $\mathcal{B}_0^{(\pi')}=\{|\phi_{\sigma,0}^{(\pi')}\rangle \mid \sigma\in S_n^{(\pi')}\}$. Let $N_{com}^{(a,\sigma,\pi)}$ be an operator projecting this space onto $|\phi_{\kappa_a\sigma,0}^{(\pi)}\rangle$. First, we measure $\mathcal{H}_{com}$ in states $|\phi_{\kappa_0\sigma,0}^{(\pi')}\rangle$ for an arbitrary permutation $\sigma\in S_n^{(\pi')}$ by applying $\tilde{N}_{\pi'}\equiv\sum_{\sigma\in S_n^{(\pi')}}N_{com}^{(0,\sigma,\pi')}$, which projects $\mathcal{H}_{com}$ onto $span\{|\phi_{\kappa_0\sigma,0}^{(\pi')}\rangle \mid \sigma\in S_n\}$. Let $|\eta^{(\pi')}\rangle=(I\otimes\tilde{N}_{\pi'})|\eta_{ideal}^{(C1)}\rangle$. Denote by $|\eta_{norm}^{(\pi')}\rangle$ the normalized state of $|\eta^{(\pi')}\rangle$.

Lemma 8. *Given any permutation π' in K_n, the quantum state $|\eta_{norm}^{(\pi')}\rangle$ coincides with $\omega_n'\sum_{\sigma\in S_n}\sum_{\pi\in K_n}|\xi_{1,\pi}\rangle|1\rangle|\pi\rangle|\phi_{\kappa_1\sigma,1}^{(\pi)}\rangle|\phi_{\kappa_0\sigma,0}^{(\pi')}\rangle$, where*

$$\omega_n'=(\sqrt{|S_n|(1-\||\xi_{1,\pi'}\rangle\|^2)})^{-1}.$$

This lemma comes from the fact that, for each fixed permutation π' in K_n, the quantum state $|\eta^{(\pi')}\rangle$ equals $\omega_n\sum_{\sigma\in S_n}\sum_{\pi\in K_n}|\xi_{1,\pi}\rangle|1\rangle|\pi\rangle|\phi_{\kappa_1\sigma,1}^{(\pi)}\rangle|\phi_{\kappa_0\sigma,0}^{(\pi')}\rangle$, where $\omega_n=\dfrac{|K_n|+1}{\sqrt{2|S_n|(|K_n|-1)}}$.

5.2   HPSP Algorithm

Finally, using the distillation algorithm $\mathcal{A}_{dis}$ as a subroutine, we describe the desired quantum algorithm $\mathcal{A}_{HPSP}$, which efficiently solves HPSP with average advantage at least $1/2p(n)^2$ for infinitely many n.

HPSP Algorithm $\mathcal{A}_{HPSP}$:

(M1) Let $\rho=\rho_0^{(\pi')}$ be an input with unknown permutation $\pi'\in K_n$. Starting with $|0\rangle$, we apply $U_1\otimes I$ and then run $\mathcal{A}_{dis}$. We then obtain

$$\sqrt{T_1/|S_n|}\sum_{\sigma,\pi}|\xi_{1,\pi}\rangle|1\rangle|\pi\rangle|\sigma\rangle|\phi_{\kappa_1\sigma,1}^{(\pi)}\rangle\otimes(1/\sqrt{|S_n|})\sum_\tau|\tau\in K_n\rangle|\phi_{\kappa_0\tau,0}^{(\pi')}\rangle$$

since $\kappa_0=\mathrm{id}$.

(M2) Transform $|\pi\rangle|\sigma\rangle|\phi^{(\pi)}_{\kappa_1\sigma,1}\rangle$ into $|\pi\rangle|\sigma\rangle|\mathrm{id}\rangle$ by running P_2 and P^{-1}_{1,κ_1}. We obtain $\sqrt{T_1/|S_n|}\sum_{\sigma,\pi}|\xi_{1,\pi}\rangle|1\rangle|\pi\rangle|\sigma\rangle|\mathrm{id}\rangle \otimes (1/\sqrt{|S_n|})\sum_\tau |\tau\rangle|\phi^{(\pi')}_{\kappa_0\tau,0}\rangle$.

(M3) Swap two registers containing $|\sigma\rangle|\mathrm{id}\rangle$ and $|\tau\rangle|\phi^{(\pi')}_{\kappa_0\tau,0}\rangle$ to obtain

$$\sqrt{T_1/|S_n|}\sum_{\tau,\pi}|\xi_{1,\pi}\rangle|1\rangle|\pi\rangle|\tau\rangle|\phi^{(\pi')}_{\kappa_0\tau,0}\rangle \otimes (1/\sqrt{|S_n|})\sum_\sigma |\sigma\rangle|\mathrm{id}\rangle.$$

(M4) Transform $|\pi\rangle|\tau\rangle$ into $|\pi\rangle|\phi^{(\pi)}_{\kappa_1\tau,1}\rangle$ by applying P_{1,κ_1} as well as P_2. Moreover, transform $(1/\sqrt{|S_n|})\sum_\sigma |\sigma\rangle|\mathrm{id}\rangle$ into $|\mathrm{id}\rangle|\mathrm{id}\rangle$. The current state must be of the from $\sqrt{T_1/|S_n|}\sum_{\tau,\pi}|\xi_{1,\pi}\rangle|1\rangle|\pi\rangle|\phi^{(\pi)}_{\kappa_1\tau,1}\rangle|\phi^{(\pi')}_{\kappa_0\tau,0}\rangle \otimes |\mathrm{id}\rangle|\mathrm{id}\rangle$, which equals $\sqrt{T_1(1-\||\xi_{1,\pi'}\rangle\|^2)}|\eta^{(\pi')}_{norm}\rangle \otimes |\mathrm{id}\rangle|\mathrm{id}\rangle$ by Lemma 8.

(M5) Apply $U^{(0)}_2 \otimes I$ to the subsystem $\mathcal{H}^{(R1)}_A \otimes \mathcal{H}^{(R1)}_B$, simulating Alice's strategy.

(M6) Observe the subsystem $\mathcal{H}_{bit} \otimes \mathcal{H}_{open1}$. If we obtain (a,π) with $a \neq 0$, then reject. Otherwise, output π.

To complete the proof of Lemma 6, it suffices to show that the success probability $p_{\pi'}$ of obtaining π' from $\rho^{(\pi')}_0$ by running $\mathcal{A}_{HPSP}$, over all $\pi \in K_n$ chosen uniformly at random, is at least $2(1 - \frac{2}{|K_n|+1})^2 \cdot \frac{1}{p(n)^2} \geq 2 \cdot (\frac{1}{2})^2 \cdot \frac{1}{p(n)^2} \geq \frac{1}{2(n)^2}$. This is immediate from the following claim.

Claim. 1. For any fixed permutation $\pi' \in K_n$, the success probability $p_{\pi'}$ of obtaining π' from input $\rho^{(\pi')}_0$ by running the quantum algorithm $\mathcal{A}_{HPSP}$ is at least $2(1 - \frac{2}{|K_n|+1})^2\|(I \otimes N_0)(U^{(0)}_2 \otimes I)(I \otimes N_1)|\eta^{(C1)}\rangle\|^2$.

2. $\|(I \otimes N_0)(U^{(0)}_2 \otimes I)(I \otimes N_1)|\eta^{(C1)}\rangle\|^2 \geq 1/p(n)^2$.

In the end, we have completed the proof of Lemma 6, as requested.

Acknowledgements. The author is grateful to Paulo Mateus for inviting him to Departamento de Matemática do Instituto Superior Técnico da Universidade de Lisboa during March 12–21, 2013, where a discussion with André Souto, Paulo Mateus, and Pedro Adão inspired this work.

References

1. Bennett, C. H., Brassard, G.: Quantum cryptography: public key distribution and coin flipping. In: Proc. of the IEEE International Conference on Computers, Systems, and Signal Processing, pp. 175–179, 1984

2. Chailloux, A., Kerenidis, I.: Optimal bounds for quantum bit commitment. In: Proceedings of the FOCS 2011, pp. 354–362 (2011)

3. Damgård, I.B., Fehr, S., Renner, R.S., Salvail, L., Schaffner, C.: A Tight High-Order Entropic Quantum Uncertainty Relation with Applications. In: Menezes, A. (ed.) CRYPTO 2007. LNCS, vol. 4622, pp. 360–378. Springer, Heidelberg (2007)

4. Damgård, I., Fehr, S., Salvail, L., Schaffner, C.: Cryptography in the bounded quantum-storage model. In: Proceedings of the FOCS 2005, pp. 449–458 (2005)
5. Danan, A.: Vaidman., L.: Practical quantum bit commitment protocol. Quantum Inf. Process. **11**, 769–775 (2011)
6. Dumais, P., Mayers, D., Salvail, L.: Perfectly concealing quantum bit commitment from any quantum one-way permutation. In: Preneel, B. (ed.) EUROCRYPT 2000. LNCS, vol. 1807, p. 300. Springer, Heidelberg (2000)
7. Lo, H.K., Chau, H.F.: Is quantum bit commitment really possible? Phys. Rev. Lett. **78**, 3410–3413 (1997)
8. M. Kada, H. Nishimura, and T. Yamakami. The efficiency of quantum identity testing of multiple states. J. Phys. A: Math. Theor. 41 (2008) article no. 395309
9. Kawachi, A., Koshiba, T., Nishimura, H., Yamakami, T.: A quantum trapdoor one-way function that relies on the hardness of the graph automorphism problem. Poster Presentation, ERATO Conference on Quantum Information Science (EQIS 2003), Kyoto (2003). See http://qci.is.s.u-tokyo.ac.jp/qci/eqis03/program/index. html#ListOfPosters
10. Kawachi, A., Koshiba, T., Nishimura, H., Yamakami, T.: Computational indistinguishability between quantum states and its cryptographic application. J. Crypt. **25**, 528–555 (2012)
11. Koshiba, T., Odaira, T.: Non-interactive statistically-hiding quantum bit commitment from any quantum one-way function. Available at arXiv:1102.3441v1, 2011
12. Mayers, D.: Unconditionally secure quantum bit commitment is impossible. Phys. Rev. Lett. **78**, 3414–3417 (1997)
13. Spekkens, R. W., Rudolph, T.: Degrees of concealment and bindingness in quantum bit commitment protocols. Phys. Rev. A, 65 (2001) article no. 012310
14. Yamakami, T.: A complete version of this current paper. arXiv:1309.0436

Formal Models

Discrete Geodesics and Cellular Automata

Pablo Arrighi[1]([✉]) and Gilles Dowek[2]

[1] LIF, Aix-Marseille University, 13288 Marseille Cedex 9, France
pablo.arrighi@univ-amu.fr
[2] Inria, CS 81321, 23 Avenue d'Italie, 75214 Paris Cedex 13, France
gilles.dowek@inria.fr

Abstract. This paper proposes a dynamical notion of discrete geodesics, understood as straightest trajectories in discretized curved spacetime. The proposed notion is generic, as it is formulated in terms of a general deviation function, but readily specializes to metric spaces such as discretized pseudo-riemannian manifolds. It is effective: an algorithm for computing these geodesics naturally follows, which allows numerical validation—as shown by computing the perihelion shift of a Mercury-like planet. It is consistent, in the continuum limit, with the standard notion of timelike geodesics in a pseudo-riemannian manifold. Whether the algorithm fits within the framework of cellular automata is discussed at length.

Keywords: Discrete connection · Parallel transport · General relativity · Regge calculus

1 Introduction

Three reasonable hypotheses—bounded velocity of propagation of information, homogeneity in time and space, and bounded density of information—lead to the thesis that natural phenomena can be described and simulated by cellular automata. This implication has in fact been formalized into a theorem both in the classical [9] and the quantum case [1], albeit in flat space. Further evaluating this thesis leads to the project of selecting specific physical phenomena, such as gravitation, and attempting to describe them as cellular automata. A first step in this direction is to build discrete models of the phenomena. In the case of gravitation, this leads to the main question we address in this paper: what is a discrete geodesics?

Geodesics generalize the flat space notion of line, to curved spaces. A line is both the shortest, and the straightest path between two points, but in curved space the two criteria do not coincide [12]. In computer graphics and discrete geometry, discrete geodesics as shortest path between two given point have been studied extensively [13,14]. This is not the case of geodesics as straightest path given an initial point and velocity—with the noticeable exception of [15], in the framework of simplicial complexes. Yet, it is this criterion that one must adopt in order to describe and simulate the timelike geodesics trajectories of particles.

© Springer International Publishing Switzerland 2015
A.-H. Dediu et al. (Eds.): TPNC 2015, LNCS 9477, pp. 137–149, 2015.
DOI: 10.1007/978-3-319-26841-5_11

In this paper we adopt the dynamical, spacetime view on geodesics which is typical of numerical relativity [16], but with one key difference. Instead of discretizing geodesics as defined by partial differential equations in a continuous spacetime, we define discrete geodesics as a native notion on discretized spacetimes—for instance on a grid endowed with a metric.

More precisely, the paper proposes both a notion of discrete-spacetime geodesics and a notion of discrete-time continuous-space geodesics (Sect. 2). Both are generic, that is formulated in terms of a general deviation function, but readily specialize for metric spaces (Sect. 4). They are effective: an algorithm for computing timelike geodesics naturally follows (Sect. 3), which allows us to validate the notions numerically: as an example we compute the perihelion shift of a Mercury-like planet (Sect. 5). They are consistent with one another: the former is clearly a discretization the latter. Moreover, the latter is proven to have the standard notion of continuous-spacetime geodesics in a Riemanian space as its limit, which validates both notions as legitimate discrete counterparts (Sect. 9). Whether the algorithm fits within the framework of cellular automata is discussed at length, as well as how this impacts on precision (Sects. 6, 7 and 8).

The proposed notion naturally applies to natively discrete formulations of General Relativity such as Regge calculus [4,17]. For instance, this discrete geodesics definition yields perihelion shift computations of the right order, an issue in [17] pointed out in [4]. We discuss how our approach differs from [15] and why it fixes this issue. More generally we believe that this approach can be applied in any inherently discrete geometrical setting, as may arise in computer vision and graphics [14] including computer anatomy [10].

Finally, an often underestimated contribution is the pedagogical: the simple discrete model summarized in Fig. 1 has continuum limit the complicated, well-known Eqs. (9) and (10).

2   Discrete Geodesics

Consider a discrete-time continuous-space spacetime $\mathbb{Z} \times \mathbb{R}^n$ where $\mathbb{Z}$ is the discrete timeline and $\mathbb{R}^n$ a continuous space. We consider a *deviation* function w from $(\mathbb{Z} \times \mathbb{R}^n)^3$ to $\mathbb{R}^+$, the number $w(E, F, G)$ measuring how the path E, F, G deviates from "going straight ahead". In this setting, we define a *geodesic* to be a sequence of points in $\mathbb{Z} \times \mathbb{R}^n$ $(E_i)_i$ such that for any i, $w(E_{i-1}, E_i, E_{i+1}) = 0$. Such a property can be read as a condition on E_{i+1}: if the points E_{i-1} and E_i are given, the geodesics must continue with a point E_{i+1} such that $w(E_{i-1}, E_i, E_{i+1}) = 0$.

Consider now a discrete spacetime $M = \mathbb{Z} \times \mathbb{Z}^n$ where $\mathbb{Z}$ is the discrete timeline and $\mathbb{Z}^n$ a discrete space and a deviation function w from M^3 to $\mathbb{R}^+$ which, as above, measures how the path E, F, G deviates from going straight ahead. In this setting we cannot demand $w(E_{i-1}, E_i, E_{i+1})$ to be exactly zero, and so we demand that it be a minimum with respect to *spatial local variations* of E_{i+1}. In this sense we depart from [11].

Spatial local variations can be defined as follows. Let us write $\langle x_0, x_1, ..., x_n \rangle$, the coordinates of a point E in M, where x_0 is the time coordinate and $x_1, ..., x_n$

the space coordinates. Two points of M, $\langle x_0, x_1, ..., x_n \rangle$ and $\langle x'_0, x'_1, ..., x'_n \rangle$ are said to be *spatial neighbors* if $x_0 = x'_0$ and for all $i \geq 1$, $|x'_i - x_i| \leq 1$.

Thus, we define a *discrete geodesics* in M to be as a sequence of points in M, $(E_i)_i$ such that for any i, the deviation $w(E_{i-1}, E_i, E_{i+1})$ is a local minimum with respect to spatial local variations of E_{i+1}, that is for any spatial neighbor G of E_{i+1}, we have

$$w(E_{i-1}, E_i, G) \geq w(E_{i-1}, E_i, E_{i+1}) \tag{1}$$

Notice how this condition may be understood as a discrete counterpart of the Euler-Lagrange equation, in the spirit of [11].

3   An Algorithm to Compute a Geodesic

We now give a gradient descent-like algorithm to compute such a discrete geodesic, $\langle t_0, A_0 \rangle, \langle t_1, A_1 \rangle, \langle t_2, A_2 \rangle$ given a deviation function w, a timeline $t_0, t_1, t_2, ...$, and two starting points A_0 and A_1.

Assume, A_{i-1} and A_i are computed. To compute A_{i+1} start with a point $\langle t_{i+1}, C \rangle$. Compute $w(\langle t_{i-1}, A_{i-1} \rangle, \langle t_i, A_i \rangle, \langle t_{i+1}, C' \rangle)$ for all 3^n spatial neighbour C' of C. If they are all larger than $w(\langle t_{i-1}, A_{i-1} \rangle, \langle t_i, A_i \rangle, \langle t_{i+1}, C \rangle)$ take C for A_{i+1}. Otherwise chose a C' which minimizes $w(\langle t_{i-1}, A_{i-1} \rangle, \langle t_i, A_i \rangle, \langle t_{i+1}, C' \rangle)$ and iterate, starting from this C'.

Whether this iteration will eventually end depends, in general, on $w(., ., .)$. For instance, say that $w(\langle t_{i-1}, A_{i-1} \rangle, \langle t_i, A_i \rangle, \langle t_{i+1}, C' \rangle)$ increases as soon as $A_i C' > t_{i+1} - t_i$. Then A_{i+1} will have to lie within distance $t_{i+1} - t_i$ of A_i, thereby imposing a bounded velocity $c = 1$, as well as enforcing termination.

4   Distance Induced Deviation Function

Most of the times, the idea of deviating from going straight is induced from a notion of distance. Here is how. Suppose a distance function d, and define the three point distance function

$$l(E, F, G) = d(E, F) + d(F, G).$$

Intuitively, **FG** is understood to deviate from **EF** if it "leans" in some spatial direction **FF'**, as witnessed by the fact that

$$l(E, F', G) < l(E, F, G)$$

for F' some neighbour of F.

In a continuous-space discrete-time setting this would be formalized by letting $w(E, \langle x_0, ..., x_n \rangle, G)$ be

$$\partial_0 l(E, \langle x_0, ..., x_n \rangle, G))^2 + ... + (\partial_n l(E, \langle x_0, ..., x_n \rangle, G))^2. \tag{2}$$

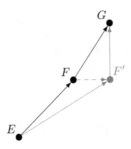

Fig. 1. Discrete geodesics seek to find G such that **FG** minimizes its deviation relative to **EF**. In the case of metric spaces, **FG** is understood to "deviate towards **FF′** relative to **EF**", whenever $l(E, F', G) < l(E, F, G)$—such deviations must be minimized.

Thus, for continuous-space discrete-time geodesics $(E_i)_i$ each point E_i is a local extremum for $l(E_{i-1}, E_i, E_{i+1})$.

In the discrete spacetime case, $w(E, \langle x_0, \ldots, x_n \rangle, G)$ is simply obtained by replacing partial derivatives with finite differences in Eq. (2): $\partial_\mu l(E, \langle x_0, \ldots, x_n \rangle, G)$ becomes

$$(l(E, \langle x_0, \ldots, x_\mu - 1, \ldots, x_n \rangle, G) - l(E, \langle x_0, \ldots, x_\mu + 1, \ldots x_n \rangle, G))/2. \qquad (3)$$

And, for discrete spacetime geodesics $(E_i)_i$ each point E_i minimizes the possibly non-zero $w(E_{i-1}, E_i, E_{i+1})$.

5   Discrete Schwarzschild Spacetime

In this section, we give an example of discrete spacetime, which is a discretization of the Schwarzschild spacetime of General Relativity.

Discretize spacetime down to $\Delta = 1$ cm. Consider a star of mass $M = 2.10^{30}$ kg—alike the Sun. Its Schwarzschild radius is $m = 2\mathcal{G}M/c^2 = 3$ km $= 3.10^5$ cm. In order to evaluate distances, consider the metric tensor

$$g(\langle t, x, y \rangle) = \begin{pmatrix} 1 - \frac{m}{r} & 0 & 0 \\ 0 & -\frac{x^2}{r(r-m)} - \frac{y^2}{r^2} & -\frac{mxy}{r^2(r-m)} \\ 0 & -\frac{mxy}{r^2(r-m)} & -\frac{x^2}{r^2} - \frac{y^2}{r(r-m)} \end{pmatrix}$$

where $r = \sqrt{x^2 + y^2}$, and let the distance function d be defined by

$$d(E, F) = \sqrt{\mathbf{EF}^\dagger g(E) \mathbf{EF}}.$$

We study the geodesics trajectory of a planet, with respect to a timeline 0, $r\Delta$, $2r\Delta$, $3r\Delta$, ... with $r = 10^7$. Thus $r\Delta = 10^7$ cm $= 3.33.10^{-4}$ s. The fake planet has parameters chosen so as to maximize relativistic effects: its first point

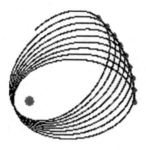

Fig. 2. The computed trajectory of a planet.

is $E = \langle x_0 = 0, x_1 = 10^8 \, \mathrm{cm} = 1000 \, \mathrm{km}, x_2 = 0 \rangle$, and its initial velocity is $vx = 0, vy = 2.10^{-2}c = 6000 \, \mathrm{km.s^{-1}}$.

We compute the geodesics with respect to the $w(.,.,.)$ induced by $d(.,.)$ as in Sect. 4, and following the algorithm of Sect. 3. Recall that in this algorithm at iteration i the point A_{i+1} is found by gradient descent starting from some point C. In the context of planetary movement, a good guess for C is obtained as follows. Define velocity $S_i = A_i - A_{i-1}$ and acceleration $R_i = S_i - S_{i-1}$, and make the guess that acceleration will remain constant, that is $R_{i+1} = R_i$. This would entail that $A_{i+1} = A_i + S_i + R_i$, thus take $C = A_i + S_i + R_i$ as the first guess and start exploring for the real A_{i+1}. Within reasonable ranges other heuristics—for instance, $C = A_i + S_i$—lead to the same trajectories, but may require longer computation times.

A run of the simulation is shown in Figs. 2 and 3. Computation time is a few seconds. The code is available in [2]. The code is easily augmented to detect aphelion, typically $a = 1000 \, \mathrm{km}$, and perihelion, typically $p = 150 \, \mathrm{km}$.

The perihelion shift is visible on Fig. 2. A well-known formula [8] states that perihelion shift in radians per revolution should roughly be

$$\sigma = \frac{24\pi^3 L^2}{T^2 c^2 (1 - e^2)} = \frac{6\pi \mathcal{G} M}{c^2 L (1 - e^2)} = \frac{3\pi m}{P}$$

where T is the revolution period of the planet, L is the semi-major axis of the trajectory of the planet, e its eccentricity, and $P = L(1 - e^2)$ its parameter— recall that, by Kepler's third law, $T^2 = 4\pi^2 L^3/(\mathcal{G} M)$, and $m = 2\mathcal{G} M/c^2$. Then an easy geometrical relation is

$$P = \frac{2}{1/a + 1/p}$$

hence

$$\sigma = (3/2)\pi m(1/a + 1/p)$$

which typically is 6.17 deg. The observed shift is indeed around 6.2 deg, based on a few hundreds of rounds, without observed divergence, see Fig. 3.

```
Perihelion
t = 3580000000 cm x = -15031004 cm y = -1398397 cm
angle = -174.6849818385271 deg
distance = 1.5095913202506995E7 cm
velocity = 0.13034045668302685 c
-------------------------------------------------
Aphelion
t = 7150000000 cm x = 99552205 cm y = 11035292 cm
angle = 6.325378791430483 deg
distance = 1.0016196478647615E8 cm
velocity = 0.019968511905497616 c
theoretical shift = 6.174380835177214 deg
observed shift = 6.210787288401395 deg
-------------------------------------------------
Perihelion
t = 10730000000 cm x = -14847048 cm y = -2698767 cm
angle = -169.69789787187233 deg
distance = 1.5090333913952766E7 cm
velocity = 0.13035029101632262 c
-------------------------------------------------
Aphelion
t = 14310000000 cm x = 97909925 cm y = 21872062 cm
angle = 12.592542500595265 deg
distance = 1.0032318032058926E8 cm
velocity = 0.019937902185786747 c
theoretical shift = 6.175065136027821 deg
observed shift = 6.267163709164782 deg
```

Fig. 3. Numerics of the computed trajectory of a planet.

6   Cellular Automata in Mechanics

As suggested in the Introduction, one motivation for discretizing General Relativity is to describe the motion of a planet in a cellular automaton.

Recall that, in the cellular automata vocabulary, a configuration σ is a function which associates, to each cell C of the grid $\mathbb{Z}^n$, some internal state $\sigma(C)$ taken in the set Σ. A cellular automaton is a function F from configurations to configurations, which has the following physics-inspired symmetries:

– bounded velocity of propagation of information;
– homogeneity time and space;
– bounded density of information, that is Σ is finite.

The state of a cell can be used to express the presence or the absence of a particle in this region of space. This way cellular automata can describe particle motions. For instance the simplest n-dimensional cellular automata—2 states, radius 1—can describe one particle motion among 3^n, as in each dimension, it could have velocity -1, 0, or 1.

To describe more complex motions, we must increase the number of states. For instance in a 1-dimensional automaton with radius 1, we can describe the motion of a particle that goes to the right at velocity $1/2$, by alternating states s_1—stay still—and s_2—step—, but also the motion of a particle that goes to the right at velocity 1, staying in the state s_3.

Another option is to increase the radius of the automaton. For instance, in a 1-dimensional automaton, with radius 2 we can describe the motion of a particle that goes on the right at velocity 1 staying in a state s_1 or at velocity 2 staying in a state s_2. Notice that modulo changing the units, the former behaviour can be obtained from the latter just by cell grouping.

We want to address the following question: to what extent is the algorithm of Sect. 3 just a cellular automaton?

7 Geodesics as Cellular Automata

Whether the algorithm of Sect. 3 enforces a bounded velocity of propagation of information $c = 1$ depends, in general, on the properties of $w(.,.,.)$. If such a velocity bound is enforced, then the motion of the body can be described in a cellular automaton of radius r. It is well-known that the velocity of a particle in a continuous Schwarzschild spacetime is bounded by $c = 1$. We conjecture that this is also the case for the discretized Schwarztchild spacetime.

If $w(.,.,.)$ does not depend on space and time, then the algorithm clearly acts the same everywhere and everywhen, so that homogeneity is also enforced. In the important case where it depends upon a space-dependent metric, then this metric field has to be carried by the internal state of the cells, even if it does not contain a particle, so that homogeneity is still enforced.

Let us evaluate whether bounded density of information holds. Even when $w(.,.,.)$ does not depend on space and time, it is still the case that if a particle is at E_i, we need its velocity $\mathbf{E_{i-1}}\mathbf{E_i}$ to compute its next position E_{i+1}. But thanks to bounded velocity of propagation, and the fact that positions are discrete, the number of possible velocities is bounded above by $b = (2r+1)^n$, so that bounded density of information is preserved. In the important case of a space-dependent metric carried by the internal state of the cells, whether bounded density holds depends upon whether we can assume that the metric field can be given with bounded precision. Even if this is not the case, notice that for a given cell, all that matters is to distinguish, for each input velocity of the particle, between b output candidate target cells. This map is a discrete counterpart to the connection associated to the metric. It contains just the finite amount of information that needs to be attached to the cell in order to compute geodesics. It could in fact be pre-compiled into each cell, thereby yielding a cellular automaton with $b + 1$ internal states to code for presence and velocity, times b^b to code for the discrete connection.

8   Time Versus Space, Precision

Geodesics have been popularized by General Relativity. General Relativity likes to put space and time on an equal footing. Numerical schemes for General Relativity ought to pursue that path, in particular it would be nice if the timeline of the computed geodesic were just 0, Δ, 2Δ, 3Δ, ... that is if r was equal to 1. In the scheme of Sect. 3, this choice leads to a cellular automaton of radius 1, which is appealing, but it also restricts to $b = 3^n$ the number of possible velocities. As we discussed in Sect. 6, this severely limits the number of motions that can be described. In the quantum setting, superpositions of basic velocities may compensate for this [3,6,7]. Classically, this is dramatic loss in precision. This is why, in Sect. 5, we took $r = 10^7$.

However, we also saw that a radius of $r' = 1$ can be obtained from a cellular automaton of arbitrary radius r simply by grouping each r^n hypercube of cells into one supercell. Each supercell now has an internal state in $\Sigma' = \Sigma^{r^n}$. Notice that keeping the position of the single particle within the hypercube is crucial. Otherwise, all the velocities of norm less than one supercell are rounded up to the center of the supercell—and so the increased precision in the velocities is not much use. Hence, Σ' is really just coding for a velocity amongst b possibilities, which is appealing... but also for the position of the single particle within the hypercube, which perhaps is not so satisfactory. After all, what this space grouping has done is really just to hide the discrepancy between the discretization step Δ and the computed geodesics timeline step $r\Delta$, by hiding some of spatial precision within the internal space of the supercells.

Hence, $r \gg 1$ appears to be fundamental requirement for precision. Notice that large values for r are better obtained by diminishing the discretization step Δ rather than augmenting the timeline step $r\Delta$, as we cannot hope to achieve a pseudo-elliptic trajectory with just a handful of velocity changes per revolution. Running the simulations, it was indeed observed that r large, for instance $r = 10^7$, yields increased stability. But only to some extent: after a while the number of possible velocities $b = (2r + 1)^n$ exceeds those which can be stored as a vector of machine-sized integers.

It also helps to fine-grain the discretization step Δ, keeping r constant. Running the simulations, it was indeed observed that this yields increased stability and convergence—at the expense of (reasonably) longer computation times. At some point, however, the finite-differences of (3) can become unstable, due to very small differences between $l(E, F, G)$ and $l(E, F', G)$ when $FF' = 1$, again hitting bounded machine floating point-arithmetic precision—but this can easily be fixed by evaluating these derivatives with FF' a fraction of $l(E, F, G)$ independent of Δ.

9   Recovering Continuous Spacetime Geodesics

The algorithm of Sect. 3 is successful in computing geodesics in discrete time and space $\mathbb{Z} \times \mathbb{Z}^n$, in a way which is consistent with continuous-space discrete-time geodesics. We now explain how continuous-space discrete-time geodesics are themselves consistent with the standard geodesics of the fully continuous setting. For this question to make sense, we place ourselves in the case of Sect. 4: a distance-induced deviation function.

As in Fig. 4, consider three points E, F, G. Say that the distance EF is measured according to $g(E)$, and that the distance FG is measured according to $g(F)$. We said that trajectory EFG is a continuous-space discrete-time geodesics if and only if it minimizes the distance $EF + FG$, with respect to infinitesimal changes of F into F'. Let us take $\mathbf{EF} = \varepsilon v$ with v normalized with respect to $g(E)$, and $\mathbf{FG} = \varepsilon v'$ with v' normalized with respect to $g(F)$. Let us take $FF' = \delta d$ with d normalized with respect to $g(F)$.

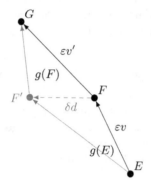

Fig. 4. The continuum limit is obtained for ε and δ tending to zero.

The distance $EF' + F'G$ is given by:

$$\sqrt{(\varepsilon v + \delta d)^\dagger g(E)(\varepsilon v + \delta d)} + \sqrt{(\varepsilon v' - \delta d)^\dagger g(F')(\varepsilon v' - \delta d)}$$

Consider the first term. Its derivative with respect to δ is

$$\frac{d^\dagger g(E)(\varepsilon v + \delta d) + (\varepsilon v + \delta d)^\dagger g(E)d}{2\sqrt{(\varepsilon v + \delta d)^\dagger g(E)(\varepsilon v + \delta d)}}$$

Taken at $\delta = 0$ and using the symmetry of $g(E)$ we get:

$$\frac{d^\dagger g(E)(\varepsilon v)}{\sqrt{(\varepsilon v)^\dagger g(E)(\varepsilon v)}} = d^\dagger g(E)v$$

Consider the second term. If $g(F')$ was just $g(F)$, the same process would yield $-d^\dagger g(F)v'$. We would then just have $d^\dagger g(E)v - d^\dagger g(F)v' = 0$, yielding $v' = g(F)^{-1}g(E)v$. This is the equation derived in [17], and is in the same spirit as that obtained [15] in the framework of simplicial complexes. Unfortunately it does not yield accurate predictions for perihelion shift, as pointed out in [4,17] and confirmed by our simulations. This is because one has to take into account that the variations of $g(F)$ around F yield a third term:

$$\frac{(\varepsilon v')^\dagger(\partial g(F).d)(\varepsilon v')}{2\sqrt{(\varepsilon v')^\dagger g(F)(\varepsilon v')}} = \frac{\varepsilon}{2}v'^\dagger(\partial g(F).d)v'$$

Let us emphasize that straightest geodesics on simplicial complexes [15] do not see this term either: quite simply because a path EFG between two adjacent simplices sees the geometry of the first simplex—that is the term $g(E)$—and the geometry of the second simplex—that is the term $g(F)$—, but ignores the variations of the geometry in some arbitrary direction FF'. In other words, simplices are usually thought of as polyhedrons of constant metric—but in order to be consistent with the continuum they must be interpreted as surfaces of constant metric derivatives. Altogether, we get that trajectory EFG is a geodesics if and only if

$$d^\dagger\left(g(F)v' - g(E)v\right) = \frac{\varepsilon}{2}v'^\dagger(\partial g(F).d)v' \tag{4}$$

in every directions d. Unfortunately, this is still inconvenient to solve for v'. At this stage the traditional, continuous approach to geodesics follows two simplifying steps, which in the discrete setting translate into two approximations. The first step is to evaluate the condition for d only along the coordinate directions:

$$\left(g(F)_\lambda.v' - g(E)_\lambda.v\right) = \frac{\varepsilon}{2}v'^\dagger(g(F),_\lambda)v' \tag{5}$$

for all λ. The second step is to neglect the difference between v and v' on the right-hand side, as it yields only second order terms. We get:

$$g(F)_\lambda.v' = g(E)_\lambda.v + \frac{\varepsilon}{2}v^\dagger(g(F),_\lambda)v \tag{6}$$

$$v' = g(F)_{.\lambda}^{-1}\left(g(E)_\lambda.v + \frac{\varepsilon}{2}v^\dagger g(F),_\lambda v\right) \tag{7}$$

Notice that this provides another explicit discrete scheme for geodesics: it suffices to evaluate each $g,_\lambda$ as $(g(F(\lambda)) - g(F))/\varepsilon$, where $F(\lambda)$ is point F moved by ε along coordinate λ.

Another useful form is obtained letting $g = g(F)$ and using $g(E) = g - \varepsilon\partial g.v$. We get:

$$g_\lambda.\,v' = g_\lambda.\,v - \varepsilon g_{\lambda.,\mu}v^\mu v + \frac{\varepsilon}{2}v^\dagger g,_\lambda v$$

$$g_\lambda.\,(v' - v) = \frac{\varepsilon}{2}\left(v^\dagger g,_\lambda v - 2g_{\lambda\nu,\mu}v^\mu v^\nu\right)$$

$$g_\lambda.\,(v' - v) = \frac{\varepsilon}{2}\left(g_{\mu\nu,\lambda}v^\mu v^\nu - g_{\lambda\nu,\mu}v^\mu v^\nu - g_{\lambda\mu,\nu}v^\mu v^\nu\right)$$

$$(v' - v) = -\varepsilon\Gamma_{\mu\nu}v^\mu v^\nu \tag{8}$$

where

$$\Gamma_{\mu\nu} = g_{.\lambda}^{-1} \left(g_{\lambda\nu,\mu} + g_{\lambda\mu,\nu} - g_{\mu\nu,\lambda} \right)/2 \tag{9}$$

Let us study the continuum limit $\varepsilon \to 0$. We have $\ddot{x} = \lim_{\varepsilon \to 0}(v' - v)/\varepsilon$, $\dot{x} = \lim_{\varepsilon \to 0} v$, and hence

$$\ddot{x} = -\Gamma_{\mu\nu} \dot{x}^{\mu} \dot{x}^{\nu} \tag{10}$$

which is your traditional geodesics equation.

10 Conclusion

Summarizing, we have introduced a generic notion of discrete geodesics as straightest trajectories in discretized spacetime, which are such that any three successive points E, F, G must minimize the deviation function $w(E, F, G)$. Given E and F, G is implicitly determined: this can be viewed as a dynamical system and computed via a gradient descent algorithm. For a metric space, the canonical choice for $w(., ., .)$ measures how the length $EF+FG$ varies with small variation of F. This was validated numerically, by computing the trajectory of a planet in discretized Schwarzschild spacetime, and recovering a perihelion shift of the right order. This was also validated by taking the continuum limit and recovering the standard geodesics equations on pseudo-riemannian manifolds.

Part of our motivations were to evaluate the strength and limits of cellular automata. Recall that three well-accepted postulates about physics—bounded velocity of propagation of information, homogeneity in time and space, and bounded density of information—necessarily imply that physics may be cast in the framework of cellular automata—both in the classical and quantum settings [1,9]. Both theorems, however, rely on the implicit hypothesis of a flat spacetime. To which extent can cellular automata account for relativistic trajectories, that is geodesics? This paper shows that discrete geodesics can be cast in the framework of cellular automata, provided that a few extra assumptions are met: that the metric can be given with bounded precision, and that it has the property of fixing a velocity limit. These extra assumptions do not contradict the three postulates: they are but instances of them.

Yet, this paper shows that a large discrepancy between the time discretization step the space discretization step is necessary in order to maintain a good precision on the velocity of particles. Namely, the number of particle velocities varies in $(2r + 1)^n$, with n the dimension of space and the radius r of the cellular automaton, which is therefore inherently large. Thus, computing discrete geodesics—and straight lines in euclidean space, for that matter—is local...but not that local. This may come as a surprise, and suggest that geodesics equations are better-behaved in the continuum. An alternative is to live with imprecise velocities. A planet is a collection of particles, and so it may be the average of their imprecise velocities which grants it a precise averaged velocity. In fact, a single particle is itself quantum, and may thus be in a superposition of these imprecise velocities, yielding a precise averaged velocity—as is made formal in the eikonal approximation [5]. This is in fact precisely what happens in quantum cellular automata models of quantum particles in curved spacetime, as shown in [3,6,7]. All of these considerations suggest that nature's way of working out timelike geodesics trajectories may in fact be emergent, from the simpler and more local behaviour of spinning particles.

Hence, for future work, it may be interesting to look for discrete models based on spinning particles, oscillating along a few, cardinal, light-like directions. These may in fact be closer to mimicking the real behaviour of fermions in curved spacetime, with the hope to recover the Mathisson-Papapetrou-Dixon equation—a generalization of the geodesics equation to spatially extended massive spinning bodies—as emergent, in analogy with the continuum [5]. Such discrete models may be more local. Another approach is to work directly in terms of a discrete connection [10]. In the continuum, the Levi-Civita connection is axiomatized as being the unique metric-compatible and torsion-free connection. That given in Eq. (9) is exactly torsion-free, but interpreted as a discrete connection, as in Eq. (8), it is metric-compatible only to first order. One can ask for both properties to be met exactly even in the discrete setting, this specifies the intersection of two ellipses. In 2-dimensions the number of solutions is finite, but this is not even the case in higher-dimensions: the axiomatization suggested by the continuum breaks down and demands fixing.

Acknowledgements. This work has been funded by the ANR-12-BS02-007-01 TAR-MAC grant, the ANR-10-JCJC-0208 CausaQ grant, and the John Templeton Foundation, grant ID 15619. Pablo Arrighi benefited from a visitor status at the IXXI institute of Lyon.

References

1. Arrighi, P., Dowek, G.: The physical Church-Turing thesis and the principles of quantum theory. Int. J. Found. of Comput. Sci. **23**, 1131 (2012)
2. Arrighi, P., Dowek, G.: Discrete geodesics. arXiv Pre-print, with program available when downloading source (2015)
3. Arrighi, P., Facchini, S., Forets, M.: Quantum walks in curved spacetime (2015). Pre-print arXiv:1505.07023
4. Brewin, L.: Particle paths in a schwarzschild spacetime via the regge calculus. Class. Quantum Gravity **10**(9), 1803 (1993)
5. Cianfrani, F., Montani, G.: Dirac equations in curved space-time vs. papapetrou spinning particles. EPL (Europhysics Letters) **84**(3), 30008 (2008)
6. Di Molfetta, G., Brachet, M., Debbasch, F.: Quantum walks as massless dirac fermions in curved space-time. Phys. Rev. A **88**(4), 042301 (2013)
7. Di Molfetta, G., Brachet, M., Debbasch, F.: Quantum walks in artificial electric and gravitational fields. Phys. A: Stat. Mech. Appl. **397**, 157–168 (2014)
8. d'Inverno, R.: Introducing Einstein's Relatvity. Oxford University Press, USA (1899)
9. Gandy, R.: Church's thesis and principles for mechanisms. In: Barwise, J., Keisler, H.J., Kunen, K. (eds.) The Kleene Symposium. North-Holland Publishing Company, Amsterdam (1980)

10. Lorenzi, M., Ayache, N., Pennec, X.: Schilds ladder for the parallel transport of deformations in time series of images. In: Székely, G., Hahn, H.K. (eds.) Information Processing in Medical Imaging, pp. 463–474. Springer, Heidelberg (2011)

11. Marsden, J.E., West, M.: Discrete mechanics and variational integrators. Acta Numer. 2001 **10**, 357–514 (2001)

12. Martínez, D., Velho, L., Carvalho, P.C.: Computing geodesics on triangular meshes. Comput. Graph. **29**(5), 667–675 (2005)

13. Mitchell, J.S.B., Mount, D.M., Papadimitriou, C.H.: The discrete geodesic problem. SIAM J. Comput. **16**(4), 647–668 (1987)

14. Peyré, G., Péchaud, M., Keriven, R., Cohen, L.D.: Geodesic methods in computer vision and graphics. Found. Trends Comput. Graph. Vis. **5**(3–4), 197–397 (2010)

15. Polthier, K., Schmies, M.: Straightest geodesics on polyhedral surfaces. In: Discrete Differential Geometry: An Applied Introduction, SIGGRAPH 2006, p. 30 (2006)

16. Vincent, F.H., Gourgoulhon, E., Novak, J.: 3+1 geodesic equation and images in numerical spacetimes. Class. Quant. Gravity **29**(24), 245005 (2012)

17. Williams, R.M., Ellis, G.F.R.: Regge calculus and observations. i. formalism and applications to radial motion and circular orbits. Gen. Relativ. Gravit. **13**(4), 361–395 (1981)

A Quantitative Approach for Detecting Symmetries and Complexity in 2D Plane

Mohammad Ali Javaheri Javid[1]([⊠]), Robert Zimmer[1],
Anna Ursyn[2], and Mohammad Majid al-Rifaie[1]

[1] Department of Computing, Goldsmiths, University of London,
London SE14 6NW, UK
{m.javaheri,r.zimmer,m.majid}@gold.ac.uk
[2] School of Art & Design, University of Northern Colorado,
Greeley, CO 80639, USA
ursyn@unco.edu

Abstract. Aesthetic evaluation of computer generated patterns is a growing filed with several challenges. This paper focuses on the quantitative evaluation of order and complexity in multi-state two-dimensional (2D) cellular automata (CA). CA are known for their ability to generate highly complex patterns through simple and well defined local interaction of rules. It is suggested that the order and complexity of 2D patterns can be quantified by using mean information gain. This measure, also known as conditional entropy, takes into account conditional and joint probabilities of the elements of a configuration in a 2D plane. A series of experiments is designed to demonstrate the effectiveness of the mean information gain in quantifying the structural order and complexity, including the orientation of symmetries of multi-state 2D CA configurations.

Keywords: Symmetry · Complexity · Entropy · Information gain · Cellular automata · 2D patterns

1 Introduction

The quantitative evaluation of *order* and *complexity* of patterns in two dimensional (2D) plane which conforms with human intuitive perception of visual structures is of a great importance in computational aesthetics. Various models have been suggested based on Shannon's information theory to address this problem, however, it is shown that entropic measures fails to discriminate accurately structurally different patterns in 2D plane [9,10,12].

In this paper, following our previous studies [9,10,12], we examine *information gain* model, in detecting symmetries, as a measure of order, and randomness of 2D patterns. We use a multi-state 2D cellular automaton as our test-bed since they are capable of generating a diverse number of structurally and perceptually distinct 2D patterns from the iteration of simple rules. Although classical one-dimensional cellular automata (CA) with binary states can exhibit complex

© Springer International Publishing Switzerland 2015
A.-H. Dediu et al. (Eds.): TPNC 2015, LNCS 9477, pp. 150–160, 2015.
DOI: 10.1007/978-3-319-26841-5_12

behaviours, experiments with multi-state 2D CA reveal a very rich spectrum of symmetric and asymmetric patterns [11,13]. The main aim of this paper is to demonstrate the effectiveness of information gain as a measure of order and complexity in a 2D plane.

This paper is organised as follows. Section 2 provides formal definition of CA. Section 3 demonstrates that Shannon entropy is not an adequate measure for evaluating order and complexity in a 2D plane. Considering human intuitive perception of visual structures, a spatial complexity spectrum is formulated and the potential of information gain as a structural complexity measure is discussed. Section 4 gives details of experiments that examine the effectiveness of information gain. The paper closes with a discussion and results.

2   Cellular Automata

CA are one of the early bio-inspired systems invented by von Neumann and Ulam in the late 1940s to study the logic of self-reproduction in a material-independent framework. CA are known to exhibit complex behaviour from the iterative application of simple rules. The popularity of Conway's Game of Life [8] drew the attention of a wider community of researchers and digital artists to the unexplored potential of CA applications and especially in their capacity to generate complex behaviour [5], often with aesthetic qualities [20].

Definition 1. A cellular automaton is a regular tiling of a lattice with uniform deterministic finite state automata.

A cellular automaton $\mathcal{A}$ is specified by a quadruple $\langle L, S, N, f \rangle$ where:

1. L is a finite square lattice of cells (i, j).
2. $S = \{1, 2, \ldots, k\}$ is set of states. Each cell (i, j) in L has a state $s \in S$.
3. N is neighbourhood, as specified by a set of lattice vectors $\{e_a\}$, $a = 1, 2, \ldots, N$. The neighbourhood of cell $r = (i, j)$ is $\{r + e_1, r + e_2, \ldots, r + e_N\}$. A a cell is considered to be in its own neighbourhood so that one of $\{e_a\}$ is the zero vector $(0, 0)$. With an economy of notation, the cells in the neighbourhood of (i, j) can be numbered from 1 to N; the neighbourhood states of (i, j) can therefore be denoted $(s_1, s_2, \ldots, s_N)$. Periodic boundary conditions are applied at the edges of the lattice so that complete neighbourhoods exist for every cell in L.
4. f is the update rule. f computes the state $s_1(t + 1)$ of a given cell from the states $(s_1, s_2, \ldots, s_N)$ of cells in its neighbourhood: $s_1(t + 1) = f(s_1, s_2, \ldots, s_N)$. A quiescent state s_q satisfies $f(s_q, s_q, \ldots, s_q) = s_q$.

There are two common neighbourhoods; (1) a five-cell *von Neumann* neighbourhood $\{(0,0), (\pm 1, 0), (0, \pm 1)\}$ and (2) a nine-cell *Moore neighbourhood* $\{(0,0), (\pm 1, 0), (0, \pm 1), (\pm 1, \pm 1)\}$. The collection of states for all cells in L is known as a configuration (C). The global rule F maps the whole automaton forward in time; it is the synchronous application of f to each cell. The behaviour of a particular $\mathcal{A}$ is the sequence $c^0, c^1, c^2, \ldots, c^{T-1}$, where c^0 is the initial configuration (IC) at $t = 0$.

CA behaviour are sensitive to the IC and to L, S, N and f. The behaviour is generally nonlinear and sometimes very complex; no single mathematical analysis can describe, or even estimate, the behaviour of an arbitrary cellular automaton. The vast size of the rule space, and the fact that this rule space is unstructured, mean that knowledge of the behaviour a particular cellular automaton, or even of a set of CA, gives no insight into the behaviour of any other CA. In the lack of any practical model to predict the behaviour of a cellular automaton, the only feasible method is to run simulations.

3   Measuring Order and Complexity in 2D

The introduction of *information theory* provided a quantitative model to measure the order and complexity of systems. Shannon's information theory was an attempt to address reliable communication over an unreliable channel [17]. Entropy is the core of this theory [6]. Let $\mathcal{X}$ be discrete alphabet, X a discrete random variable, $x \in \mathcal{X}$ a particular value of X and $P(x)$ the probability of x. Then the entropy, $H(X)$, is:

$$H(X) = - \sum_{x \in \mathcal{X}} P(x) \log_2 P(x). \tag{1}$$

The quantity H is the average uncertainty in bits, $\log_2(\frac{1}{p})$ associated with X. Entropy can also be interpreted as the average amount of information needed to describe X. The value of entropy is always non-negative and reaches its maximum for the uniform distribution, $\log_2(|\mathcal{X}|)$:

$$0 \leqslant H \leqslant \log_2(|\mathcal{X}|). \tag{2}$$

The lower bound of relation (2) corresponds to a deterministic variable (no uncertainty) and the upper bound corresponds to a maximum uncertainty associated with a random variable. Another interpretation of entropy is as a measure of *order* and *complexity*. A low entropy implies low uncertainty so the message is highly predictable, ordered and less complex. And high entropy implies a high uncertainty, less predictability, highly disordered and complex.

Moles [15], Bense [4] and Arnheim [2] were pioneers of the application of entropy to quantify order and complexity by adapting statistical measure of information in aesthetic objects. Since then entropy is commonly used to measure order and complexity in most of aesthetic evaluation functions [7,14,16,18], however entropy fails to discriminate accurately structurally different patterns in two-dimensions. The main reason for this drawback is that it only reflects on the distribution of the symbols, and not on their ordering [9,10,12].

This fact is illustrated in Fig. 1 where the entropy of 2D patterns with different structural characteristics is evaluated. Both of the patterns have a lattice

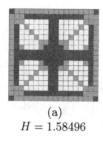 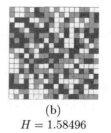

(a)

$H = 1.58496$

(b)

$H = 1.58496$

Fig. 1. Measurements of H for ordered and random 2D patterns with equally probable distribution of elements (Color figure online).

size of 18×18 consisting of three elements (*white, blue* and *orange*). The distribution of elements are equally probable ($\frac{1}{108}$). Figure 1(a) is a pattern with ordered structure, a complete symmetry and Fig. 1(b) is a fairly structureless (random) pattern.

As it is clear from the comparison of the above patterns with their corresponding entropy value, despite their structural differences, both of the patterns have the same entropy value. This is in contrast to our intuitive perception of the order and complexity of patterns in 2D plane.

If the human perception of visual structures are taken into account in perceiving order and complexity in a 2D plane, any potential measure of order and complexity must be bounded by two extreme points of complete order and disorder. It is reasonable to assume that *regular structures, irregular structures* and *structureless* patterns lie along between these extremes, as illustrated in Fig. 2.

A complete regular structure is a pattern of full symmetry, an irregular structure is a pattern with some local structural orders but not as regular as a fully symmetrical pattern and finally a structureless pattern is a random arrangement of elements.

A measure introduced in [1, 3, 19] and known as *information gain*, has been suggested as a means of characterising the complexity of dynamical systems and of patterns in 2D plane. It measures the amount of information gained in bits when specifying the value, x, of a random variable X given knowledge of the value, y, of another random variable Y,

$$G_{x,y} = -\log_2 P(x|y). \tag{3}$$

$P(x|y)$ is the conditional probability of a state x conditioned on the state y. Then the *mean information gain*, $\overline{G}_{X,Y}$, is the average amount of information gain from the description of the all possible states of Y:

$$order \longleftarrow \overline{\text{regular structure} \mid \text{irregular structure} \mid \text{structureless}} \longrightarrow disorder$$

Fig. 2. The spectrum of spatial complexity.

$$\overline{G}_{X,Y} = \sum_{x,y} P(x,y)G_{x,y} = -\sum_{x,y} P(x,y)\log_2 P(x|y) \tag{4}$$

where $P(x,y)$ is the joint probability, $\text{prob}(X = x, Y = y)$. $\overline{G}$ is also known as the conditional entropy, $H(X|Y)$ [6]. Conditional entropy is the reduction in uncertainty of the joint distribution of X and Y given knowledge of Y, $H(X|Y) = H(X,Y) - H(Y)$. The lower and upper bounds of $\overline{G}_{X,Y}$ are

$$0 \leqslant \overline{G}_{X,Y} \leqslant \log_2 |\mathcal{X}|. \tag{5}$$

Definition 2. A structural complexity measure G, of a cellular automaton configuration is the sum of the mean information gains of cells having homogeneous/heterogeneous neighbouring cells over 2D lattice.

For a cellular automaton configuration, $\overline{G}$ can be calculated by considering the distribution of cell states over pairs of cells r, s,

$$\overline{G}_{r,s} = -\sum_{s_r,s_s} P(s_r,s_s)\log_2 P(s_r,s_s) \tag{6}$$

where s_r, s_s are the states at r and s. Since $|\mathcal{S}| = N$, $\overline{G}_{r,s}$ is a value in $[0, N]$.

The vertical, horizontal, primary diagonal ($\diagdown$) and secondary diagonal ($\diagup$) neighbouring pairs provide eight $\overline{G}$s; $\overline{G}_{(i,j),(i-1,j+1)}$, $\overline{G}_{(i,j),(i,j+1)}$, $\overline{G}_{(i,j),(i+1,j+1)}$, $\overline{G}_{(i,j),(i-1,j)}$, $\overline{G}_{(i,j),(i+1,j)}$, $\overline{G}_{(i,j),(i-1,j-1)}$, $\overline{G}_{(i,j),(i,j-1)}$ and $\overline{G}_{(i,j),(i+1,j-1)}$.

The relative positions for non-edge cells are given by matrix M:

$$M = \begin{bmatrix} (i-1,j+1) & (i,j+1) & (i+1,j+1) \\ (i-1,j) & (i,j) & (i+1,j) \\ (i-1,j-1) & (i,j-1) & (i+1,j-1) \end{bmatrix}. \tag{7}$$

Correlations between cells on opposing lattice edges are not considered. The result of this edge condition is that $G_{i+1,j}$ is not necessarily equal to $\overline{G}_{i-1,j}$. In addition the differences between the horizontal (vertical) and two diagonal mean information rates reveal left/right (up/down), primary and secondary diagonals of 2D patterns. So the sequence of generated configurations by a multi-state 2D cellular automaton can be analysed by the differences between the vertical $(i, j \pm 1)$, horizontal $(i \pm 1, j)$, primary diagonal (P_d) and secondary diagonal (S_d) mean information gains by

$$\Delta\overline{G}_{i,j\pm1} = |\overline{G}_{i,j+1} - \overline{G}_{i,j-1}|, \tag{8a}$$

$$\Delta\overline{G}_{i\pm1,j} = |\overline{G}_{i-1,j} - \overline{G}_{i+1,j}|, \tag{8b}$$

$$\Delta\overline{G}_{P_d} = |\overline{G}_{i-1,j+1} - \overline{G}_{i+1,j-1}|, \tag{8c}$$

$$\Delta\overline{G}_{S_d} = |\overline{G}_{i+1,j+1} - \overline{G}_{i-1,j-1}|. \tag{8d}$$

The mean information gains of the sample patterns in Fig. 1 are presented in Fig. 3. The merits of $\Delta\overline{G}$s in discriminating structurally different patterns, the

(a)   (b)

$$H = 1.58496 \qquad\qquad H = 1.58496$$
$$\Delta\overline{G}_{i,j\pm1} = 0 \qquad\qquad \Delta\overline{G}_{i,j\pm1} = 0.00078$$
$$\Delta\overline{G}_{i\pm1,j} = 0 \qquad\qquad \Delta\overline{G}_{i\pm1,j} = 0.00009$$
$$\Delta\overline{G}_{P_d} = 0 \qquad\qquad \Delta\overline{G}_{P_d} = 0.00052$$
$$\Delta\overline{G}_{S_d} = 0 \qquad\qquad \Delta\overline{G}_{S_d} = 0.00109$$

Fig. 3. The comparison of H with $\Delta\overline{G}s$ for ordered and random 2D patterns with equally probable distribution of elements.

full symmetrical (Fig. 3a), the structureless and random (Fig. 3b), are clearly evident.

4 Experiments and Results

A series of experiments was designed to investigate the effectiveness of $\Delta\overline{G}s$ in quantifying order (i.e. symmetry) and complexity of patterns generated by a multi-state 2D cellular automaton. A cellular automaton considered for the purpose of experimentations is specified in Table 1. The update rule maps four states, represented by *red, blue, orange* and *white*; the quiescent state is *white*.

The experiments are conducted with three different ICs: (1) all white cells except for a single *blue* cell at the centre of 65×65 lattice (Fig. 4a), (2) a 6 cell configuration (Fig. 4b) and (3) a random configuration with 2957 *white* quiescent states, 417 *orange*, 403 *blue* and 448 *red* cells (Fig. 4c). The update rule has been

Table 1. The update rule of experimental cellular automaton.

$L = 65 \times 65$ (4225 cells).
$S = \{0, 1, 2, 3\} \equiv \{\,\square,\blacksquare,\blacksquare,\blacksquare\,\}$
N: Moore neighbourhood
$f : S^9 \mapsto S$

$$f(s_{i,j})(t) = s_{i,j}(t+1) = \begin{cases} 1 \text{ if } s_{(i,j)}(t) = 0 \text{ and } \sigma = 1, 3 \\ 2 \text{ if } s_{(i,j)}(t) = 1 \text{ and } \sigma = 1-8 \\ 3 \text{ if } s_{(i,j)}(t) = 2 \text{ and } \sigma = 0-8 \\ 0 \text{ otherwise} \end{cases}$$

where σ is the sum total of the neighbourhood states.

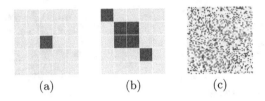

(a)   (b)   (c)

Fig. 4. The three different ICs (Color figure online).

iterated synchronously for 100 successive time steps. The sequence of generated configurations are analysed by Eqs. 8a, b, c and d. Figures 5, 7 and 9 illustrate the space-time diagrams for a sample of time steps starting from the three ICs.

The behaviour of cellular automaton starting from the single cell IC is a sequence of symmetrical patterns (Fig. 5). The measurements of $\Delta \overline{G}s$ are constant for the 100 time steps ($\Delta \overline{G}_{i,j\pm 1} = \Delta \overline{G}_{i,j\pm 1} = \Delta \overline{G}_{P_d} = \Delta \overline{G}_{S_d} = 0$) (Fig. 6). This indicates the development of full symmetrical patterns along the up/down, left/right, primary diagonal and secondary diagonal directions.

The behaviour of cellular automaton from the 6 cell IC is a sequence of symmetrical patterns with primary diagonal orientations (Fig. 7). The measurements of $\Delta \overline{G}s$, and especially $\Delta \overline{G}_{P_d}$ are reflecting the orientation of symmetries (Fig. 8) where $\Delta \overline{G}_{P_d} = 0$ for 100 time steps.

The behaviour of cellular automaton starting from the random IC is a sequence of irregular structures with local structures (Fig. 9). $\Delta \overline{G}s$ rates for random IC are plotted in Fig. 10. The measurements of $\Delta \overline{G}s$ are different for all

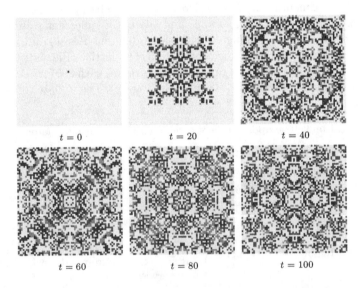

$t = 0$ $t = 20$ $t = 40$

$t = 60$ $t = 80$ $t = 100$

Fig. 5. Space-time diagram of the experimental cellular automaton for sample time steps starting from the single cell IC.

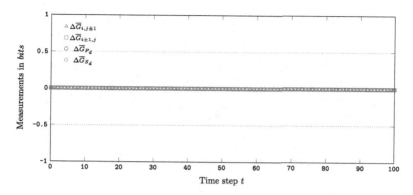

Fig. 6. Measurements of $\Delta\overline{G}s$ for 100 time steps starting from the single IC.

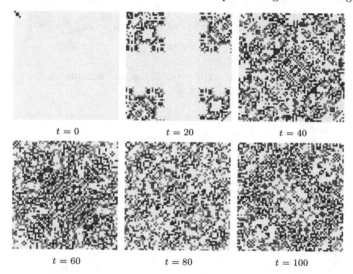

$t = 0$ $t = 20$ $t = 40$

$t = 60$ $t = 80$ $t = 100$

Fig. 7. Space-time diagram of the experimental cellular automaton for sample time steps starting from the 6 cell IC.

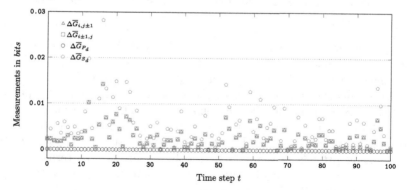

Fig. 8. Measurements of $\Delta\overline{G}s$ for 100 time steps starting from the 6 cell IC.

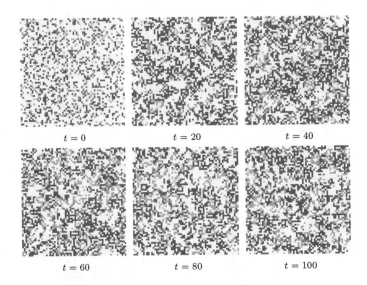

$t = 0$ $t = 20$ $t = 40$

$t = 60$ $t = 80$ $t = 100$

Fig. 9. Space-time diagram of the experimental cellular automaton for sample time steps starting from the random IC (Fig. 4c).

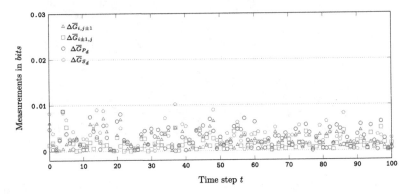

Fig. 10. Measurements of $\Delta\overline{G}s$ for 100 time steps starting from the random IC.

the directional measurements ($\Delta\overline{G}_{i,j\pm1} \neq \Delta\overline{G}_{i,j\pm1} \neq \Delta\overline{G}_{P_d} \neq \Delta\overline{G}_{S_d}$). This is an indicator of the development of irregular structures.

The measurements of H rates for three ICs are plotted in Fig. 11. It is clear that entropy fails to discriminate structural variations in the three set of patterns generated by experimental cellular automaton rule. These experiments demonstrate that a cellular automaton rule seeded with different ICs leads to the formation of patterns with structurally different characteristics. The gradient of the $\Delta\overline{G}s$ rate along lattice axes is able to detect the symmetrical patterns, including their orientation from the unstructured random configuration generated by this particular multi-state 2D cellular automaton.

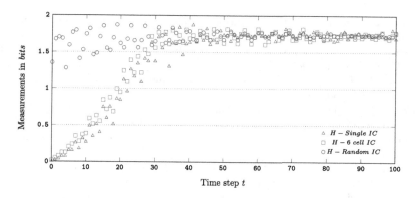

Fig. 11. Measurements of H for 100 time steps starting from the three ICs.

5   Conclusion

One of the earliest and most well-known bio-inspired models of self-replicating systems is cellular automata (CA). Multi-state two dimensional (2D) CA are capable of generating complex and often aesthetically pleasing configurations. The focus of this work, is an information-theoretic classification of order and complexity in these patterns.

Among the most used statistical measures in the field is entropy which fails to provide a comprehensive picture on the structure of a given input pattern. Mean information gain, on the other hand, is based on correlations between homogeneity and heterogeneity of elements which takes into account conditional and joint probabilities between pairs of elements in 2D plane. Using different initial conditions of a multi-state 2D cellular automaton, this paper presents a set experiments to investigate the behaviour of mean information gain and demonstrate its efficiency in distinguishing structurally different configurations. As shown in the paper, mean information gain presents a particularly competitive behaviour in distinguishing symmetries and their orientation.

Acknowledging that CA are one of the generative tools used in computer art, exploring techniques to evaluate the aesthetic qualities of CA generated patterns plays a significant role in enriching the automation of CA art. Furthermore, since information gain measure is based on correlations between homogeneity and heterogeneity of elements, it exhibits a promising application for pattern classification.

References

1. Andrienko, Y.A., Brilliantov, N.V., Kurths, J.: Complexity of two-dimensional patterns. Eur. Phys. J. B **15**(3), 539–546 (2000)
2. Arnheim, R.: Towards a psychology of art/entropy and art an essay on disorder and order. The Regents of the University of California (1966)

3. Bates, J.E., Shepard, H.K.: Measuring complexity using information fluctuation. Phys. Lett. A **172**(6), 416–425 (1993)
4. Bense, M.: Kleine abstrakte ästhetik [small abstract aesthetics], Rot edn., vol. 38. E. Walther, March 1969
5. Brown, P.: Emergent behaviours: towards computational aesthetics. Artlink **16** (2 & 3), 16–20 (1996)
6. Cover, T.M., Thomas, J.A.: Elements of Information Theory. Wiley Series in Telecommunications and Signal Processing. Wiley, Hoboken (2006)
7. Franke, H.W.: A cybernetic approach to aesthetics. Leonardo **10**(3), 203–206 (1977)
8. Gardner, M.: Mathematical games - the fantastic combinations of john conway's new solitaire game, life. Sci. Am. **223**(4), 120–123 (1970)
9. Javaheri Javid, M.A., Blackwell, T., al Rifaie, M.M., Zimmer, R.: Information gain measure for structural discrimination of cellular automata configurations. In: 2015 7th Computer Science and Electronic Engineering Conference (CEEC) (CEEC 2015). Colchester, Essex, United Kingdom, September 2015
10. Javaheri Javid, M.A., Blackwell, T., Zimmer, R., Al-Rifaie, M.M.: Spatial complexity measure for characterising cellular automata generated 2D patterns. In: Pereira, F., Machado, P., Costa, E., Cardoso, A. (eds.) EPIA 2015. LNCS, vol. 9273, pp. 201–212. Springer, Heidelberg (2015)
11. Javaheri Javid, M.A., al-Rifaie, M.M., Zimmer, R.: Detecting symmetry in cellular automata generated patterns using swarm intelligence. In: Dediu, A.-H., Lozano, M., Martín-Vide, C. (eds.) TPNC 2014. LNCS, vol. 8890, pp. 83–94. Springer, Heidelberg (2014)
12. Javaheri Javid, M.A., al Rifaie, M.M., Zimmer, R.: An informational model for cellular automata aesthetic measure. In: AISB 2015 Symposium on Computational Creativity. University of Kent, Canterbury, UK (2015)
13. Javid, M.A.J., te Boekhorst, R.: Cell dormancy in cellular automata. In: Alexandrov, V.N., van Albada, G.D., Sloot, P.M.A., Dongarra, J. (eds.) ICCS 2006. LNCS, vol. 3993, pp. 367–374. Springer, Heidelberg (2006)
14. Machado, P., Cardoso, A.: Computing aesthetics. In: de Oliveira, F.M. (ed.) SBIA 1998. LNCS (LNAI), vol. 1515, pp. 219–228. Springer, Heidelberg (1998)
15. Moles, A.: Information Theory and Esthetic Perception. University of Illinois Press, Urbana (1968). Trans. JE Cohen
16. Rigau, J., Feixas, M., Sbert, M.: Informational aesthetics measures. IEEE Comput. Graph. Appl. **28**(2), 24–34 (2008)
17. Shannon, C.: A mathematical theory of communication. Bell Syst. Tech. J. **27**, 379–423 & 623–656 (1948)
18. Staudek, T.: Exact aesthetics. object and scene to message. Ph.D. thesis, Faculty of Informatics, Masaryk University of Brno (2002)
19. Wackerbauer, R., Witt, A., Atmanspacher, H., Kurths, J., Scheingraber, H.: A comparative classification of complexity measures. Chaos, Solitons Fractals **4**(1), 133–173 (1994)
20. Wolfram, S.: A New Kind of Science. Wolfram Media Inc., Champaign (2002)

A Generalized Minimum-Time
Minimum-State-Change FSSP Algorithm

Hiroshi Umeo$^{(\boxtimes)}$, Keisuke Imai, and Akihiro Sousa

University of Osaka Electro-Communication,
Neyagawa-shi, Hatsu-cho, 18-8, Osaka 572-8530, Japan
umeo@cyt.osakac.ac.jp

Abstract. The firing squad synchronization problem (FSSP) on cellular automata has been studied extensively for more than fifty years, and
a rich variety of synchronization algorithms has been proposed. Here we
consider the FSSP from a view point of state-change-complexity that
models the energy consumption of SRAM-type storage with which cellular automata might be built. In the present paper, we construct an
$n - 2 + \max(k, n - k + 1)$ minimum-time, $\Theta(n \log n)$ minimum-state-
change generalized FSSP (GFSSP, for short) algorithm for synchronizing any one-dimensional (1D) cellular automaton of length n, where the
synchronization operations are started from any position k ($1 \leq k \leq n$)
in the array. The realized minimum-time GFSSP algorithm can be
implemented on a cellular automaton with 215 internal states and 4077
state-transition rules and has a minimum-state-change complexity. The
algorithm is optimum not only in time but also in state-change complexity. The implemented minimum-time GFSSP algorithm is the first
one having the minimum-state-change complexity. In addition, we also
present a six-state 145-rule non-minimum-time, minimum-state-change
GFSSP algorithm. The implemented GFSSP algorithm is a smallest one,
known at present, in number of states of the finite state automaton.

Keywords: Cellular automaton · Firing squad synchronization problem · FSSP · State-change complexity

1 Introduction

We study a synchronization problem that gives a finite-state protocol for
synchronizing large-scale cellular automata. The synchronization in cellular
automata has been known as a firing squad synchronization problem (FSSP)
since its development, in which it was originally proposed by J. Myhill in Moore
(1964) to synchronize some/all parts of self-reproducing cellular automata. The
problem has been studied extensively for more than fifty years, and a rich variety
of synchronization algorithms has been proposed.

Here we consider the FSSP from a view point of state-change-complexity
that models the energy consumption of SRAM-type storage with which cellular automata might be built. In the present paper, we construct an $n - 2 +$

© Springer International Publishing Switzerland 2015
A.-H. Dediu et al. (Eds.): TPNC 2015, LNCS 9477, pp. 161–173, 2015.
DOI: 10.1007/978-3-319-26841-5_13

$\max(k, n - k + 1)$ minimum-time, $\Theta(n \log n)$ minimum-state-change generalized FSSP (GFSSP, for short) algorithm for synchronizing any one-dimensional (1D) cellular automaton of length n, where the synchronization operations are started from any position k ($1 \leq k \leq n$) in the array. The realized minimum-time GFSSP algorithm can be implemented on a cellular automaton with 215 internal states and 4077 state-transition rules and has a minimum-state-change complexity. The algorithm is optimum not only in time but also in state-change complexity. The implemented minimum-time GFSSP algorithm is the first one having the minimum-state-change complexity. Some snapshots for the generalized synchronization processes are also given. In addition, we present a six-state 145-rule non-minimum-time, minimum-state-change GFSSP algorithm. The implemented GFSSP algorithm is a smallest one, known at present, in number of states of the finite state automaton.

In Sect. 2 we give a description of the 1D FSSP and review some basic results on FSSP algorithms. Sections 3 and 4 give new implementations and generalizations to the GFSSP algorithms having minimum-state-change complexities.

2 Firing Squad Synchronization Problem

2.1 Definition of Firing Squad Synchronization Problem

The firing squad synchronization problem (FSSP, for short) is formalized in terms of a model of cellular automata. Consider a 1D array of finite state automata. All cells (except the end cells) are identical finite state automata. The array operates in lock-step mode such that the next state of each cell (except the end cells) is determined by both its own present state and the present states of its right and left neighbors. All cells (*soldiers*), except one *general* cell, are initially in the *quiescent* state at time $t = 0$ and have the property whereby the next state of a quiescent cell having quiescent neighbors is the quiescent state. At time $t = 0$ the *general* cell is in the *fire-when-ready* state, which is an initiation signal to the array. The FSSP is stated as follows: given an array of n identical cellular automata, including a *general* on the left end which is activated at time $t = 0$, we want to give the description (state set and next-state transition function) of the automata so that, *at some future time*, all of the cells will *simultaneously* and, *for the first time*, enter a special *firing* state. The initial general is on the left end of the array in the original FSSP.

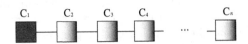

C_1 C_2 C_3 C_4 $\quad\quad$ C_n

Fig. 1. A one-dimensional (1D) cellular automaton.

Figure 1 shows a finite 1D cellular array consisting of n cells, denoted by C_i, where $1 \leq i \leq n$. The set of states and the next-state transition function must be independent of n. Without loss of generality, we assume $n \geq 2$. The tricky part of the problem is that the same kind of soldiers having a fixed number of states must be synchronized, regardless of the length n of the array.

A formal definition of the FSSP is as follows: A cellular automaton $\mathcal{M}$ is a pair $\mathcal{M} = (Q, \delta)$, where

1. Q is a finite set of states with three distinguished states G, Q, and F. G is an initial general state, Q is a quiescent state, and F is a firing state, respectively.
2. δ is a next state function such that $\delta : Q \cup \{*\} \times Q \times Q \cup \{*\} \to Q$. The state $* \notin Q$ is a pseudo state of the border of the array.
3. The quiescent state Q must satisfy the following conditions: $\delta(Q, Q, Q) = \delta(*, Q, Q) = \delta(Q, Q, *) = Q$.

A cellular automaton of length n, $\mathcal{M}_n$ consisting of n copies of $\mathcal{M}$ is a 1D array of $\mathcal{M}$, numbered from 1 to n. Each $\mathcal{M}$ is referred to as a cell and denoted by C_i, where $1 \leq i \leq n$. We denote a state of C_i at time (step) t by S_i^t, where $t \geq 0, 1 \leq i \leq n$. A *configuration* of $\mathcal{M}_n$ at time t is a function $\mathcal{C}^t : [1, n] \to Q$ and denoted as $S_1^t S_2^t \ldots S_n^t$. A *computation* of $\mathcal{M}_n$ is a sequence of configurations of $\mathcal{M}_n$, $\mathcal{C}^0, \mathcal{C}^1, \mathcal{C}^2, \ldots, \mathcal{C}^t, \ldots$, where $\mathcal{C}^0$ is a given initial configuration. The configuration at time $t + 1$, $\mathcal{C}^{t+1}$, is computed by synchronous applications of the next transition function δ to each cell of $\mathcal{M}_n$ in $\mathcal{C}^t$ such that:
$S_1^{t+1} = \delta(*, S_1^t, S_2^t)$, $S_i^{t+1} = \delta(S_{i-1}^t, S_i^t, S_{i+1}^t)$, and $S_n^{t+1} = \delta(S_{n-1}^t, S_n^t, *)$.
A *synchronized configuration* of $\mathcal{M}_n$ at time t is a configuration $\mathcal{C}^t$, $S_i^t = $ F, for any $1 \leq i \leq n$.

The FSSP is to obtain an $\mathcal{M}$ such that, for any $n \geq 2$,

1. A synchronized configuration at time $t = T(n)$, $\mathcal{C}^{T(n)} = \overbrace{\text{F}, \cdots, \text{F}}^{n}$ can be
   computed from an initial configuration $\mathcal{C}^0 = \text{G} \overbrace{\text{Q}, \cdots, \text{Q}}^{n-1}$.
2. For any t, i such that $1 \leq t \leq T(n) - 1$, $1 \leq i \leq n, S_i^t \neq $ F.

The generalized FSSP (GFSSP) is to obtain an $\mathcal{M}$ such that, for any $n \geq 2$ and for any k such that $1 \leq k \leq n$,

1. A synchronized configuration at time $t = T(n)$, $\mathcal{C}^{T(n)} = \overbrace{\text{F}, \cdots, \text{F}}^{n}$ can be
   computed from an initial configuration $\mathcal{C}^0 = \overbrace{\text{Q}, \cdots, \text{Q}}^{k-1} \text{G} \overbrace{\text{Q}, \cdots, \text{Q}}^{n-k}$.
2. For any t, i, such that $1 \leq t \leq T(n) - 1$, $1 \leq i \leq n, S_i^t \neq $ F.

No cells fire before time $t = T(n)$. We say that $\mathcal{M}_n$ is synchronized at time $t = T(n)$ and the function $T(n)$ is a time complexity for the synchronization.

2.2 Some Related Results

Here we summarize some basic results on FSSP algorithms. See Umeo (2009) for a survey on FSSP algorithms.

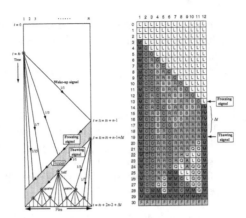

Fig. 2. Space-time diagram for delayed firing squad synchronization scheme based on the *freezing-thawing* technique (left) and delayed (for $\Delta t = 5$) configuration on $n = 12$ cells (right).

- ## Minimum-time FSSP algorithm with a general at one end

  The FSSP problem was first solved by J. McCarthy and M. Minsky who presented a $3n$-step algorithm for n cells. In 1962, the first minimum-time, i.e. $(2n - 2)$-step, synchronization algorithm was presented by Goto (1962), with each cell having several thousands of states. Waksman (1966) presented a 16-state minimum-time synchronization algorithm. Afterward, Balzer (1967) and Gerken (1987) developed an eight-state algorithm and a seven-state synchronization algorithm, respectively, thus decreasing the number of states required for the synchronization. In 1987, Mazoyer (1987) developed a six-state synchronization algorithm which, at present, is the algorithm having the fewest states. Yunès (2008c) gave a new Goto-type minimum-time FSSP algorithm using minimum-time 4-state partial solutions in Yunès (2008b).

  Theorem 1 Goto (1962), Waksman (1966). There exists a cellular automaton that can synchronize any 1D array of length n in minimum $2n-2$ steps, where the general is located at a left (or right) end.

- ## Generalized minimum-time FSSP algorithm

  The generalized FSSP (GFSSP, for short) has been also studied, where an initial general can be located at any position in the array. The same kind of soldiers having a fixed number of states must be synchronized, regardless of the position k of the general and the length n of the array. Moore and Langdon (1968) first considered the problem and presented a 17-state minimum-time GFSSP algorithm, i.e. operating in $n-2+\max(k, n-k+1)$ steps for n cells with the general on the kth cell from left end of the array. See Umeo, Kamikawa, Nishioka and Akiguchi (2010) for a survey on GFSSP algorithms and their implementations. Concerning the GFSSP, it has been shown impossible to synchronize any array of length n less than $n - 2 + \max(k, n - k + 1)$ steps, where the general is located on C_k, $1 \leq k \leq n$.

Theorem 2 Moore and Langdon (1968) (Lower Bounds). The minimum-time in which the generalized firing squad synchronization could occur is no earlier than $n - 2 + \max(k, n - k + 1)$ steps, where the general is located on the kth cell from left end.

Theorem 3 Umeo et al. (2010). There exists an 8-state cellular automaton that can synchronize any 1D array of length n in minimum $n - 2 + \max(k, n - k + 1)$ steps, where the general is located on the kth cell from left end.

- **Delaying synchronization steps**

  We introduce a *freezing-thawing technique* that yields a delayed synchronization for 1D arrays. The technique was developed by Umeo (2004) for designing several fault-tolerant FSSP algorithms for 1D arrays. The freezing-thawing technique will be employed efficiently in the next section for the design of a minimum-time minimum-state-change GFSSP algorithm.

  Theorem 4 Umeo (2004). Let t_0, t_1, t_2 and Δt be any integer such that $t_0 \geq 0$, $t_1 = t_0 + n - 1$, $t_1 \leq t_2$ and $\Delta t = t_2 - t_1$. We assume that a usual synchronization operation is started at time $t = t_0$ by generating a special signal which acts as a general at the left end of 1D array of length n. We also assume that the right end cell of the array receives another special signals from outside at time $t_1 = t_0 + n - 1$ and $t_2 = t_1 + \Delta t$, respectively. Then, there exists a 1D cellular automaton that can synchronize the array of length n at time $t = t_0 + 2n - 2 + \Delta t$. (Fig. 2)

  The array operates as follows:
  1. Start a minimum-time FSSP algorithm at time $t = t_0$ at the left end of the array. A 1/1 speed, i.e., 1 cell per 1 step, signal is propagated towards the right direction to wake-up cells in quiescent state. We refer the signal as *wake-up signal*. A *freezing signal* is given from outside at time $t_1 = t_0 + n - 1$ at the right end of the array. The signal is propagated in the left direction at its maximum speed, that is, 1 cell per 1 step, and freezes the configuration progressively. Any cell that receives the freezing signal from its right neighbor has to stop its state-change and transmit the freezing signal to its left neighbor. The frozen cell keeps its state as long as no thawing signal will arrive.
  2. A special signal supplied with outside at the right end at time $t_2 = t_1 + \Delta t$ is used as a *thawing signal* that thaws the frozen configuration progressively. The thawing signal forces the frozen cell to resume its state-change procedures immediately. See Fig. 3 (left). The signal is also transmitted toward the left end at speed 1/1.

  The readers can see how those three special signals work. We can freeze the entire configuration during Δt steps and delay the synchronization on the array for Δt steps. Figure 3 (right) shows some snapshots of delayed (for $\Delta t = 5$)

configurations for minimum-time synchronization algorithm on 12 cells. In this example, note that the wake-up signal is supplied with the array at time $t_0 = 3$. We refer the scheme as *freezing-thawing technique*.

- **State-change complexity**

Vollmar (1982) introduced a *state-change complexity* in order to measure the efficiency of cellular automata, motivated by energy consumption in certain SRAM-type memory systems. The state-change complexity is defined as the sum of *proper* state changes of the cellular space during the computations. A formal definition is as follows: Consider an FSSP (GFSSP) algorithm operating on n cells. Let $T(n)(T(k,n))$ be synchronization steps of the FSSP (GFSSP) algorithm. We define a matrix C of size $T(n) \times n$ ($T(n)$ rows, n columns) ($T(k,n) \times n$ ($T(k,n)$ rows, n columns)) over $\{0,1\}$, where each element $c_{i,j}$ on ith row, jth column of the matrix is defined:

$$c_{i,j} = \begin{cases} 1 & \mathsf{s}_i^j \neq \mathsf{s}_i^{j-1} \\ 0 & otherwise. \end{cases} \tag{1}$$

The state-change complexity $SC(n)(SC_g(n))$ of the FSSP (GFSSP) algorithm is the sum of 1's elements in C defined as:

$$SC(n) = \sum_{j=1}^{T(n)} \sum_{i=1}^{n} c_{i,j}. \tag{2}$$

$$SC_g(n) = 1/n \sum_{k=1}^{n} \sum_{j=1}^{T(k,n)} \sum_{i=1}^{n} c_{i,j}. \tag{3}$$

Vollmar (1982) showed that $\Omega(n \log n)$ state-changes are required for synchronizing n cells in $(2n - 2)$ steps.

Theorem 5 Vollmar (1982). $\Omega(n \log n)$ state-change is necessary for synchronizing n cells in minimum-steps.

Gerken (1987) presented a minimum-time, $\Theta(n \log n)$ minimum-state-change FSSP algorithm with a general at one end.

Theorem 6 Gerken (1987). $\Theta(n \log n)$ state-change is sufficient for synchronizing n cells in $2n - 2$ steps.

3   A Minimum-Time, Minimum-State-Change GFSSP Algorithm

3.1   A General Methodology for Designing Minimum-Time GFSSP Algorithms

In this section we develop a general methodology for designing a minimum-time GFSSP algorithm based on freezing-thawing technique. We can construct

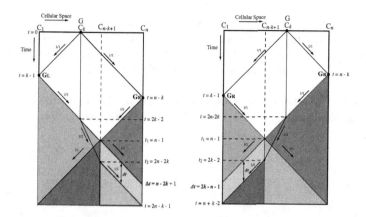

Fig. 3. Space-time diagram for the construction of generalized minimum-time FSSP algorithm.

a minimum-time GFSSP algorithm from any minimum-time FSSP algorithm with a general at one end.

Consider a cellular array C_1, C_2, ..., C_n of length n with an initial general on C_k, where $1 \leq k \leq n$. At time $t = 0$ the general sends a unit speed (1 cell/1 step) signal to both ends. The cell C_k keeps its state to indicate its position on the array. The signal reaches at the left and right ends at time $t = k - 1$ and $t = n - k$, respectively, and generates a new general, denoted as G_L and G_R at each end. In Fig. 3, we illustrate a space-time diagram for the GFSSP construction. Each general, G_L and G_R, starts minimum-time synchronization operation for the cellular space where the general is at its end by sending out a wake-up signal. At time $t = n - 1$ the two signals collide with each other on the cell C_{n-k+1} and the cellular space is divided into two parts by the collision. First, we consider the case where the initial general is in the left half of the given cellular space, i.e. $k \leq n - k + 1$. The wake-up signal generated by G_L reaches C_k at time $t = 2k - 2$, then collides with the wake-up signal generated by G_R. The larger part (left one in this case) is synchronized by a usual way, however, the small one is synchronized with time delay $\Delta t = n - 2k + 1$. The wake-up signal for the larger part splits into two signals on C_k, one is an original wake-up signal and the other is a new slow signal which follows the wake-up signal at 1/2-speed. Note that the wake-up signal for the smaller part (right one in this case) never reaches C_k. As for the synchronization for the smaller part, a freezing-signal is generated at time $t_1 = n - 1$ on C_{n-k+1} and the state configuration in the smaller part is frozen by the propagation of the 1/1-speed right-going freezing signal. At time $t_2 = 2n - 2k$, the split slow signal reaches C_{n-k+1} and there a thawing signal is generated. The thawing signal thaws the frozen configuration progressively. Theorem 4 shows that the smaller part of length k is synchronized at time $t = 2n - k - 1$. The larger part is also synchronized at time $t = 2n - k - 1$. Thus, the whole space can be synchronized at time

$t = 2n - k - 1 = n - 2 + \max(k, n - k + 1)$. Similar discussions can be made in the case where the initial general is in the right half of the cellular space. It is seen that any minimum-time FSSP algorithm with a general at one end can be embedded as a sub-algorithm for the synchronization of divided parts. Thus, we have:

Theorem 7. The schema given above can realize a minimum-time GFSSP algorithm by implementing two minimum-time FSSP algorithms with a general at one end.

Fig. 4. Snapshots of configurations for minimum-time, minimum-state-change GFSSP algorithm developed on $n = 32$ cells with a general on C_7 (left) and C_{20} (right), respectively.

3.2 A Minimum-Time, Minimum-State-Change GFSSP Algorithm

In order to get a minimum-time, minimum-state-change GFSSP algorithm, we embed Gerken's FSSP algorithms with a general at left/right end. The state-change complexity for the right and left parts are $O((n - k + 1) \log(n - k + 1))$ and $O(k \log k)$, thus the total state-change-complexity of the constructed GFSSP algorithm is $O((n - k + 1) \log(n - k + 1)) + O(k \log k) \leq O(n \log n)$.

Thus, we have:

Theorem 8. There exists a minimum-time, minimum-state-change GFSSP algorithm.

Figure 4 shows some snapshots for the constructed GFSSP algorithm on 32 cells. We also show a comparison of state-change complexities among several GFSSP algorithms in Fig. 5.

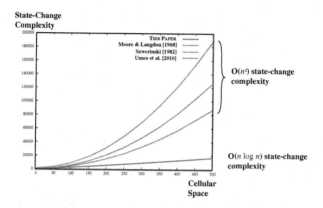

Fig. 5. A comparison of state-change complexities among several minimum-time GFSSP algorithms (Color figure online).

4   A 6-State Non-minimum-time, Minimum-State-Change GFSSP Algorithm

4.1   3n-Step FSSP Algorithms

A class of 3n-step algorithms is an interesting class of synchronization algorithms among many variants of FSSP algorithms due to its simplicity and straightforwardness and it is important in its own right in the design of cellular algorithms. Figure 6 (left) shows a space-time diagram for the well-known 3n-step firing squad synchronization algorithm with a general at left end. The synchronization process can be viewed as a typical *divide-and-conquer strategy* that operates in parallel in the cellular space. An initial *general* G, located at left end of the array of size n, generates two signals, referred to as *a-signal* and *b-signal*, which propagate in the right direction at a speed of 1/1 and 1/3, respectively. The a-signal arrives at the right end at time $t = n - 1$, reflects there immediately, and continues to move at the same speed in the left direction. The reflected signal is referred to as *r-signal*. The b- and the r-signals meet at one or two center cells of the arry, depending on the parity of n. In the case where n is odd, the cell $C_{\lceil n/2 \rceil}$ becomes a *general* at time $t = 3\lceil n/2 \rceil - 2$. The *general* is responsible

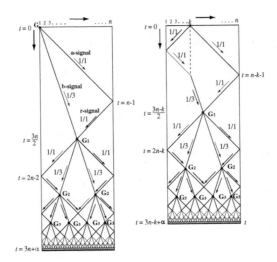

Fig. 6. A space-time diagram for thread-like $3n$-step firing squad synchronization algorithm.

for synchronizing both its left and right halves of the cellular space. Note that the *general* is shared by the two halves. In the case where n is even, two cells $C_{\lceil n/2 \rceil}$ and $C_{\lceil n/2 \rceil +1}$ become the next *general* at time $t = 3\lceil n/2 \rceil$. Each *general* is responsible for synchronizing its left and right halves of the cellular space, respectively.

Thus, at time $t = t_{center}$:

$$t_{center} = \begin{cases} 3\lceil n/2 \rceil - 2 & n: \text{odd} \\ 3\lceil n/2 \rceil & n: \text{even,} \end{cases} \qquad (4)$$

the array knows its center point and generates one or two new *general(s)* G_1. The new *general(s)* G_1 generates the same 1/1- and 1/3-speed signals in both left and right directions simultaneously and repeat the same procedures as above. Thus, the original synchronization problem of size n is divided into two subproblems of size $\lceil n/2 \rceil$. In this way, the original array is split into equal two, four, eight, ..., subspaces synchronously. Note that the first general G_1 itself generated at the center is synchronized at time $t = t_{center}$, and the second general G_2 are also synchronized, and the generals generated after that time on are also synchronized. In the last, the original problem of size n can be split into many small sub-problems of size 2. In this way, by increasing the synchronized generals step by step, most of the $3n$-step synchronization algorithms developed so far. It can be seen that, from the path of the b-signal with or without 1 step delay at the center points at each halving iteration, the time complexity $T(n)$ for synchronization scheme above is $T(n) = 3n \pm O(\log n)$. A survey on a class of $3n$-step FSSP algorithms can be seen in Umeo et al. (2015).

Figure 6 (right) illustrates a space-time diagram for a generalized $3n$-step FSSP algorithm that can synchronize the array from any position in the array.

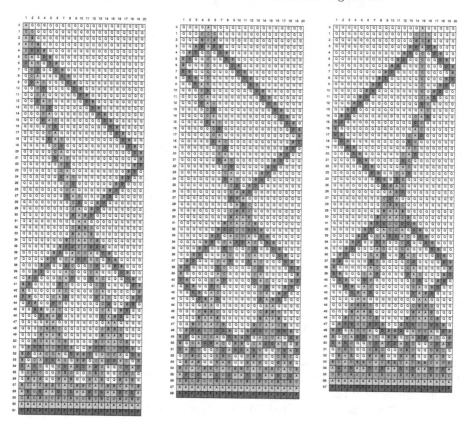

Fig. 7. A 6-state transition table of the new algorithm.

Fig. 8. Snapshots of the synchronization process of the 6-state algorithm for 20 cells with a general on the 1st, 5th, and 15th cells, respectively.

The initial general generates two unit-speed signals, each propagating to the left and right ends. Each signal reflects at each end and continues to move towards the center of the array. Depending on the position of the initial general in the array, the right or left reflected signal arrives at the cell where the initial general was. Then, the reflected signal reduces its propagating speed to $1/3$ and continues to move in the same direction at $1/3$ speed. The $1/3$-speed signal meets the other reflected signal at a center point of the array at time $t = t_{center}$:

$$t_{center} = \begin{cases} 3\lceil n/2 \rceil - \min(k, n - k + 1) - 1 & n: \text{odd} \\ 3\lceil n/2 \rceil - \min(k, n - k + 1) + 1 & n: \text{even,} \end{cases} \quad (5)$$

A new general G_1 is generated at time $t = t_{center}$. The synchronization operations afterwards are the same as in the case of the initial general at left end. The time complexity $T(k, n)$ for the generalized synchronization scheme above is $T(k, n) = 3n - \min(k, n - k + 1) \pm O(\log n)$.

4.2 A 6-State Non-minimum-time, Minimum-State-Change GFSSP Algorithm

Yunès (2008a) presented a 6-state implementation for the $3n$-step FSSP algorithm with a general at one end. Our 6-state GFSSP implementation is based on Yunès (2008a). The set Q of the internal states for the constructed GFSSP algorithm is $Q=\{\text{A}, \text{Q}, \text{B}, \text{C}, \text{D}, \text{E}\}$, where the state A is the initial *general* state, Q is the *quiescent* state, and E is the *firing* state, respectively.

The following Fig. 7, consisting of 145 rules, is the transition table. The time complexity for synchronizing any array of length n is $2n+\max(k, n-k)+O(\log n)$. Figure 8 shows some snapshots of the synchronization process of the algorithm on 20 cells with a general on 1st, 5th and 15th cells, respectively.

Thus, we have:

Theorem 9. There exists a 6-state, non-minimum-time, minimum-state-change GFSSP algorithm.

5 Summary

We have constructed two $\Theta(n \log n)$ minimum-state-change GFSSP algorithms on a cellular automaton. One is a minimum-time GFSSP algorithm that can be implemented on a cellular automaton with 215 internal states and 4077 state-transition rules. The algorithm is minimum not only in time but also in state-change complexity. The other is the 6-state 145-rule non-minimum-step GFSSP algorithm. Both the implemented GFSSP algorithms are the first ones having minimum-state-change complexity.

References

Balzer, R.: An 8-state minimal time solution to the firing squad synchronization problem. Inf. Control **10**, 22–42 (1967)

Gerken, H.D.: Über Synchronisationsprobleme bei Zellularautomaten, p. 50. Diplomarbeit, Institut für Theoretische Informatik, Technische Universität Braunschweig (1987)

Goto, E.: A minimal time solution of the firing squad problem. Dittoed course notes for Applied Mathematics, vol. 298, pp. 52–59. Harvard University (1962)

Mazoyer, J.: A six-state minimal time solution to the firing squad synchronization problem. Theor. Comput. Sci. **50**, 183–238 (1987)

Moore, E.F.: The firing squad synchronization problem. In: Moore, E.F. (ed.) Sequential Machines, Selected Papers, pp. 213–214. Addison-Wesley, Reading (1964)

Moore, F.R., Langdon, G.G.: A generalized firing squad problem. Inf. Control **12**, 212–220 (1968)

Umeo, H.: A simple design of time-efficient firing squad synchronization algorithms with fault-tolerance. IEICE Trans. Inf. Syst. **E87–D**(3), 733–739 (2004)

Umeo, H.: Firing squad synchronization problem in cellular automata. In: Meyers, R.A. (ed.) Encyclopedia of Complexity and System Science, vol. 4, pp. 3537–3574. Springer, New York (2009)

Umeo, H., Kamikawa, N., Nishioka, K., Akiguchi, S.: Generalized firing squad synchronization protocols for one-dimensional cellular automata - a survey. Acta Phys. Pol. B Proc. Suppl. **3**, 267–289 (2010)

Umeo, H., Maeda, M., Sousa, A., Taguchi, K.: A class of non-optimum-time 3n-step FSSP algorithms - a survey. In: Malyshkin, V. (ed.) PaCT 2015. LNCS, vol. 9251, pp. 231–245. Springer, Heidelberg (2015)

Vollmar, R.: Some remarks about the efficiency of polyautomata. Int. J. Theor. Phys. **21**(12), 1007–1015 (1982)

Waksman, A.: An optimum solution to the firing squad synchronization problem. Inf. Control **9**, 66–78 (1966)

Yunès, J.-B.: An intrinsically non minimal-time Minsky-like 6-states solution to the firing squad synchronization problem. Theor. Inf. Appl. **42**(1), 55–68 (2008a)

Yunès, J.B.: A 4-states algebraic solution to linear cellular automata synchronization. Inf. Process. Lett. **19**(2), 71–75 (2008b)

Yunès, J.-B.: Goto'sconstruction and Pascal's triangle: new insights into cellular automata synchronization. In: Proceedings of the 1st Symposium on Cellular Automata, JAC 2008, pp. 195–203 (2008c). ISBN 978-5-54057-337-3

Author Index

Printed in the United States
By Bookmasters